PAY EQUITY

The Labour–Feminist Challenge

Carl J. Cuneo

TORONTO
OXFORD UNIVERSITY PRESS
1990

Oxford University Press, 70 Wynford Drive, Don Mills, Ontario, M3C 1J9

Toronto Oxford New York Delhi Bombay Calcutta Madras Karachi
Petaling Jaya Singapore Hong Kong Tokyo Nairobi Dar es Salaam
Cape Town Melbourne Auckland

and associated companies in
Berlin Ibadan

Dedicated to
Tony, Jean Marie, and Helen Ann

CANADIAN CATALOGUING IN PUBLICATION DATA

Cuneo, Carl J.
Pay equity: the labour/feminist challenge

(Studies in Canadian sociology)
Includes bibliographic references.
ISBN 0-19-540782-2

1. Pay equity – Canada – Political aspects.
2. Pay equity – United States – Political aspects.
3. Trade-unions – Canada – Political activity.
4. Trade-unions – United States – Political activity.
5. Feminists – Canada – Political activity.
6. Feminists – United States – Political activity.
7. Wages – Women – Canada. 8. Wages – Women –
United States. I. Title. II. Series.

HD6061.2.C3C86 1990   331.2′153′0971   C90-093227-9

68764

Copyright © Oxford University Press 1990

OXFORD is a trademark of Oxford University Press

1 2 3 4 - 3 2 1 0

Printed in Canada

Contents

Acknowledgements

For assistance in tracking down countless documents and bibliographic items, I would like to thank the staff at Mills Memorial Library, McMaster University, Hamilton. Special thanks are due to David Cook, Merike Koger, Carol Mazur, Linda Michtics, Valerie Parke, and Anne Pottier. Kate Humpage at the Women's Bureau of Labour Canada provided me with statistics on collective agreements containing pay-equity clauses. Catherine Walker at the Ontario Pay Equity Commission provided me with briefs of various organizations. Individuals too numerous to mention in government agencies, women's organizations, trade unions, and business associations supplied me with documents and briefs. I am especially grateful to Pat McDermott for her incisive reading of the manuscript, which weeded out a number of errors and misinterpretations. Helpful comments and suggestions were also offered by Hugh Armstrong, Charlene Gannagé, Tom Langford, Jerry White and Julie White, to whom I am grateful. Any mistakes and weaknesses are, of course, entirely my own responsibility. At Oxford University Press, I owe a special debt to Richard Teleky for his patience in waiting for a manuscript that kept being eaten up by other projects; to Sally Livingston, who devoted considerable time and effort to making the text readable and understandable; and to Anna Macina, who put it all into the computer. Most importantly, I owe a great debt to Hanna Schayer for showing the way through action, and to Sara Helen Schayer Cuneo for her never-ending questions, 'but why?'. For financial aid, I am grateful to the Social Sciences and Humanities Research Council of Canada for a leave fellowship during 1986-87, and to McMaster University.

1

Introduction

In 1984 Shirley Ittas, a faculty secretary in the film department at York University in Toronto, worked a 35-hour week for $15,745 per year. Shirley's job requirements were many and complex:

> she uses her judgement as well as her clerical skills. There are many hectic days when students need quick responses. In fielding inquiries, providing information about the department's regulations and courses, sorting out hundreds of portfolios and grades for evaluation, she believes she affects student's lives.

Shirley was paid $8.65 per hour. The groundskeepers at York were getting $9.19 per hour. Was Shirley being paid fairly in comparison with the groundskeepers? She certainly didn't think so:

> 'I didn't feel angry that they [the groundskeepers] were earning a certain amount of money. I felt angry I was paid less. I do have a lot of responsibility and I think my contribution is as valuable as their contribution, and my salary should be at least equal . . . . My job is important.'[1]

PURPOSE

Investigation into the income differences between women and men has been dominated by three types of studies: quantitative estimations by economists and sociologists of the components of the gendered wage gap;[2] estimations of the actual or expected economic and employment effects of equal-pay legislation;[3] and legal analyses of the grounds for litigation ever unequal pay.[4] There have been virtually no analyses of the dynamic political struggles along class and gender lines over the formulation of legislation on equal pay for equal work, or equal pay for work of equal value.

The purpose of this book is to examine the three basic areas in which the political struggles over pay equity have been waged. These are the *paid capitalist workplace* (offices and factories), the capital and labour *marketplace* (where jobs are obtained in exchange for wages), and the *household workplace* (where the work involved in bearing and raising children is performed). Most of the examples in this book are drawn from the federal levels in Canada and the United States, the provinces of Manitoba and Ontario, and, to a lesser extent, Quebec, Nova Scotia, and Prince Edward Island.

The first thesis of this book is that in both countries a coalition of business and neo-conservative anti-feminist organizations has opposed equal pay for work of equal value by seeking to restrict questions of gender-based income to non-discriminatory factors in the household and marketplace, and to prevent state intervention in the capitalist workplace and marketplace. At the same time, a feminist-labour alliance of women's organizations and trade unions has supported state intervention in the form of equal pay for work of equal value by struggling to place responsibility for unequal pay on the shoulders of employers in the workplace, who by their discriminatory hiring and promotion practices have, in effect, taken advantage of women's double day of labour in the household and the paid labour force. The polar-opposite participants in these struggles have been activist trade-union and new middle-class women on the one side and senior corporate executive men on the other. Corporate women have leaned towards gender rather than class in supporting pay equity, though not without some compromise with their privileged class position. After decades of socialization into patriarchal ideologies, trade-union men have leaned towards gender and class interests to support equal-pay legislation, though not without a painful struggle with their sister unionists. In danger of being left out of the struggle over pay equity altogether, men in the new middle class of professionals, managers, and intelligentsia in both the public and private sectors have been pulled towards both sides. This split has been especially evident among male economists, corporate consultants, lawyers, media writers, and state bureaucrats, although their centre of gravity, especially in the United States, appears to have shifted somewhat to an ideological defence of the male business-class position.[5]

Anti-feminists and neo-conservatives have feared that the hidden agenda in the campaign for equal pay for work of equal value is the destruction of the patriarchal nuclear family. Giving women pay equivalent to men's would make them less dependent on men, loosen their ties to the home, and provide them with greater

incentive to pursue careers outside. It has therefore been important for anti-feminist neo-conservatives to maintain the traditional
separation between the public sphere of the state, the capitalist
workplace, and the marketplace, and the private sphere of the
household, since they see the labour and women's movements as
attempting to link them in assessing the causes of, and recommending the solutions to, unequal pay. The irony is that feminist
and labour organizations have not forcefully made such links
between the private and public spheres, even though they have
often been made by both socialist and radical feminists.

In each of the three areas of struggle (paid workplace,
marketplace, and household workplace), the focal points are class
and gender. A third issue, race/ethnicity, has often been pushed
into the background,[6] and in response, women-of-colour organizations have fought to bring this issue to the centre of pay-
equity struggles.[7] A dialectical relation exists between the
structures and struggles of class, gender, and race/ethnicity: even
though the structuring of class, gender, and race/ethnicity im-
poses limits on the kinds of struggles that can emerge, class,
feminist, and anti-racist struggles may set the agenda as to the
content of structural changes that will occur through equal-pay
legislation. For example, the structural differences in wealth between white businessmen and visible-minority working-class
women has meant that the former could use high-priced lawyers
and consultants in lobbying governments over pay equity while
the latter could not. Structure thus places limits on struggles. At
the same time, the struggle by trade unions and working-class
women's organizations to ensure that pay equity is not achieved
simply by lowering the wages of men has put so much pressure
on governments that they have inserted clauses in pay-equity acts
forbidding employers to lower men's wages to equalize the pay
between women and men. Thus struggles affect the content of
structural changes in women's and men's wages. As noted in
Appendix A, in the 1980s the women's movement has become
much more conscious of racism both in the broader society and
within itself. But business and neo-conservative elements within
the new middle class have sought to exploit racial and ethnic (as
well as gender) divisions in both the women's movement and the
labour movement in order to divide the solidarity of the campaign
for a political solution to gender-based unequal pay. Trade unions
and visible-minority women's organizations have fought back by

minimizing their internal racial, gender, and class differences.

Using Gramsci's concept of 'passive revolution', a second thesis will be suggested in Chapter 5: that (a) racist and anti-feminist neo-conservative elements, reacting to a perceived threat to the patriarchal nuclear household from the labour-feminist alliance, have tried to fracture the solidarity of the labour and women's movements along the lines of classism, racism, and sexism; and (b) patriarchal capitalist states have tried to co-opt these movements by framing weak pay-equity legislation containing numerous loopholes and defects that make it difficult for women to win pay-equity adjustments. The legislation of equal pay for work of equal value, although a victory for feminists and trade unionists, also represents an attempt on the part of the state to co-opt the labour and women's movements not only on behalf of business, anti-feminist, and neo-conservative interests, but at their behest.

CAVEATS

Six caveats are in order here. First, this book deals almost exclusively with those jurisdictions where equal-pay-for-work-of-equal-value legislation is now in place. It does not examine the *lack* of such legislation in Alberta, British Columbia, New Brunswick, Newfoundland, and Saskatchewan. And it pays only cursory attention to developments in Prince Edward Island and Nova Scotia, both of which legislated equal pay for work of equal value in the public sector in 1988, and in Quebec, which legislated equal value in its human-rights law of 1975.

Second, although it is possible to analytically separate the components of the gendered wage gap in terms of workplace, marketplace, and household, those three areas overlap considerably: together they form a triangle, with each merely an extension of the other two.

Third, the intricacies of the strategies negotiated between women's groups and labour organizations, and the gender tensions between them, are not dealt with in detail in this book. That is a separate research project requiring intensive in-depth interviewing of participants in both kinds of organizations as they develop their respective tactics in the fight for pay equity.

Fourth, the intricate process of collective bargaining over the setting up of job-evaluation and pay-equity plans—in other words, the implementation of legislation, once it is on the statute books—is not discussed. This is another subject that requires a separate project, based, again, on in-depth interviewing of participants in the process.

The fifth caveat concerns 'class'. Although working-class trade-union organizations have clashed with business-class associations over the shape of pay-equity legislation, there is a sense in which class has not been a consideration. Framers of pay-equity legislation have tended to ignore the question not only of ethnic and racial differences, but also of class differences, in favour of an exclusive emphasis on gender differences in rates of pay. There has been little discussion of the value of working-class labour compared to that of the work performed by managers and employers, the class superiors of workers. In a retrospective critical examination of equal pay for work of equal value, George Ehring, legislative assistant in the NDP caucus of the Ontario legislature, observed: 'What we really need is a mechanism that compares the relative value of the work performed by secretaries, childcare workers and hair-dressers with that of their bosses.'[8]

The sixth caveat is the most difficult to discuss. There is considerable ambiguity in the literature as to the precise meanings of 'equal pay', 'equal work', 'equal value', 'equivalent value,' 'comparable worth', and 'pay equity'. 'Equal work' is based on comparisons between jobs that are identical. 'Similar work' depends on comparisons between jobs that are similar or substantially similar. 'Equal value' or, to use the American term, 'comparable worth', is based on comparisons between jobs that may be quite dissimilar but that can be equated in terms of a composite of effort, skill, responsibility, and working conditions (some subdimensions of these four factors are listed in Appendix B). The ambiguity in the use of these terms reflects in part the nature of class and feminist struggles as business and anti-feminists attempt to restrict the meaning of pay equity to equal pay for identical or similar work, while labourites and feminists attempt to broaden the term to include equal pay for work of equal or comparable value.

The Vancouver Women's Resource Centre has raised the question of whether the state has used the term 'pay equity'—rather than the more potent 'equal pay for work of equal value'—to co-opt or defeat the feminist drive for truly equivalent wages between women and men.[9] One example might be the use of 'pay equity' in the 1987 Ontario Pay Equity Act, which went into effect on 1 Jan. 1988.[10] As this Act was being debated and amended between 1985 and 1987, lobby groups on both sides of the issue widely interpreted it to mean equal pay for work of equal value. Although the term 'equal value' appears in the Act, the complete phrase 'equal pay for work of equal value' does not, despite the efforts of the Ontario Equal Pay Coalition to have it inserted.[11] In 1989, after the dust in the debate had settled, the Ontario Pay Equity Commission stated that *equal pay for work of equal value* means that 'male and female employees must be equally compensated where work undertaken within an establishment is of equal value. Jobs are deemed to be comparable where the same skill, effort, responsibility and working conditions apply.' *Pay equity*, on the other hand, is 'a policy or legislated provision requiring that work performed by women which is comparable in value to that performed by men in the same establishment should be paid the same. Jobs are evaluated according to the composite of skill, effort, responsibility and working conditions.' These two definitions look the same. What is the difference, apart from that between the *abstract principle* of equal pay for work of equal value and the *concrete legislation* of pay equity? The Pay Equity Commission has pointed out a significant difference: equal pay for work of equal value is 'often interpreted more broadly than the concept of pay equity in that it is not necessarily restricted to systemic discrimination in compensation based on gender'.[12] Although the commission does not say so, an example of such discrimination might be that directed against 'visible minority groups'. Yet the equal-value language occurs throughout the Ontario Act, and lobby groups and the public should be forgiven if they confuse the Act with equal pay for work of equal value.[13] Why would the state, after passing a pay-equity act incorporating the equal-value principle, now point to a difference between pay equity and equal pay for work of equal value? Why would it now raise the issue of non-gender grounds of discrimination when it always resisted extending pay equity to these areas? Is the reason to reassure business and neo-conservatives that the provincial state has not, in fact, implemented equal pay for work of equal value? Or is the state now agreeing with women-of-colour organizations that equal pay for work of equal value should be implemented on non-gender cultural grounds as well? Or is this a case of one branch of the state, the Pay Equity Commission, being more advanced in its thinking than another branch, the provincial Cabinet?

It will be argued in this book that the more powerful concept of equal pay for work of equal value, as advocated by the women's movement, has been incorporated in the Ontario and other acts, but that in the process it has become distorted and weakened, since its legislative form contains numerous loopholes and defects that deny many women equal pay for work of equal or comparable value while granting it to others. This has the potential effect of dividing women against women, and co-opting the women's movement through a legalistic state agenda. This view is somewhat different from that of the Ontario Equal Pay Coalition, which insists that the Ontario Pay Equity Act does not mean 'equal pay for work of equal value' because its coverage is not universal: it excludes many women workers, as well as all male workers, from seeking pay-equity adjustments. In this sense it violates (a) Canada's international treaty commitments under the International Labour Organization Convention 100, signed in 1972, which provides for universal coverage of equal pay for work of equal value, and (b) the Canadian Charter of Human Rights and Freedoms.[14] The extent of the confusion over terms is suggested in the 1986 brief to the Ontario government by the Ontario Mining Association, which stated that it fully supported equal pay for work of equal value, yet went on to state the typical business position by listing a number of restrictions it favoured that would exclude a sizeable number of women from any pay-equity act.[15] In the view of the Ontario Equal Pay Coalition, this is not equal pay for work of equal value; in the argument of this book, it is a distortion and co-optation of that principle.

For the sake of clarity, and because many authors are not clear on the distinction, I will use 'pay equity' or 'equal pay' as generic terms that do not differentiate between 'equal work', 'similar work', or 'equal value'; 'equal work' will be used to refer to legislation restricted to comparisons between jobs that are identical; 'similar work' will refer to comparisons between jobs that are substantially the same, or similar; and 'equal value', 'equal pay for work of equal value', and 'comparable worth' will refer to principles and laws based on comparisons either between jobs that are similar or between jobs that are substantially different but that can be equated in terms of a composite of skill, effort, responsibility, and working conditions.

FEMINIST-LABOUR COALITION POLITICS

Frequent reference will be made throughout this book to the labour-feminist alliance, as if the positions on pay equity of feminist organizations and trade unions were identical. But some caution is advised. Historically, there have been considerable differences between women's organizations and trade unions generally on women's issues and specifically on equal pay. Since the 1970s, however, the two groups have been converging on the organizational strategy and ideological principles surrounding pay equity. In the words of the Congress of Canadian Women: 'It is our experience that, in the struggle for women's equality, women have no better ally than the trade unions.'[16] The process of making alliances is best illustrated by such groups as the National Committee on Pay Equity in the United States and the Equal Pay Coalitions of both Manitoba and Ontario, all of which include as members both women's organizations and trade unions. In 1985 the National Committee on Pay Equity in the US claimed to have over 280 organizations and individuals including women's groups, labour organizations, civil-rights groups, legal associations, and educational and 'grass-roots' groups. Among the women's groups were the Coalition of Labor Union Women, the Mexican-American Women's National Association, the National Council of Jewish Women, the National Organization of Women, and the Organization of Pan Asian American Women; among the labour affiliates, the Communications Workers of America, the American Federation of State, County and Municipal Employees, the Service Employees International Union, the United Auto Workers, and the United Electrical Workers.[17] In 1987 the Ontario Equal Pay Coalition claimed to have 35 constituent groups in Ontario representing over one million women and men. Through one of its groups, the National Action Committee on the Status of Women (NAC), it claimed to represent nationally 'over three million people and four hundred and fifteen groups'. Some of the Coalition's women's groups, besides the NAC, were Organized Working Women, the Business and Professional Women's Clubs of Ontario, the Sudbury Women's Centre, the Coalition of Visible Minority Women, the Canadian Women's Educational Press, and the International Women's Day Committee. Some of its labour constituents were the Ontario Public Service Employees Union, the Ontario Federation of Labour, the

Canadian Union of Public Employees, the Communications Workers of Canada, and the Labour Council of Metropolitan Toronto.[18] Such coalitions are the basis for the concept of 'labour-feminist alliance' used throughout the book. However, an organization does not have to be structurally part of one of these coalitions to be considered part of that alliance; it may be ideologically in tune with the alliance's views without having formal membership in it. For example, in Canada the Amalgamated Clothing and Textile Workers Union and the United Food and Commercial Workers International Union did not belong to the Ontario Equal Pay Coalition, yet many of their views on pay equity were consistent with those of the Coalition.[19]

Not all trade unions or women's organizations are part of such alliances, either in membership or in ideology, partly because they disagree with either their goals or their tactics. This is most clearly evident among those women's organizations and pseudo trade unions that have moved closer, either organizationally or ideologically, to the business class, such as the Canadian Association of Women Executives and the Christian Labour Association of Canada.

The existence of equal-pay coalitions does not necessarily mean that their members are unanimous on the principles, strategies, and tactics in the battle for equal pay for work of equal value. As Pat McDermott has argued, alliances, such as the Ontario Equal Pay Coalition, consist of 'a broad political spectrum from the YWCA and the Business and Professional Women's Group, through to the mainstream labour movement, and a minority of "left-of-the-NDP" groups (such as the International Women's Day Committee, Women Working With Immigrant Women, and so on)'.[20] Negotiations and compromises among these groups have to take place 'in the back rooms' before going public. One of the purposes of any coalition is to minimize public differences of opinion. In the case of the Ontario Equal Pay Coalition, two points of tension arose. First, one member of the coalition, the Ontario Public Service Employees Union (OPSEU), had reservations about a pay-equity act that threatened to drastically change the nature of collective bargaining in the public sector. James Clancy, President of OPSEU, called the public-sector pay-equity bill that Ontario initially proposed 'an attack on our democratic right to free collective bargaining. It will irreparably damage our strength at the negotiating table.'[21] OPSEU wanted to do more research and analysis, rather than concentrate all the Coalition's resources on holding press conferences and lobbying the provincial government. It was also more critical of job-evaluation methodology than some other members of the Coalition. It was interested in an alternative 'policy-capturing' methodology (see pp. 105-8 below), pioneered in New York state, that was more sensitive to the actual work performed by female and male employees. Some members of the Coalition, viewing OPSEU as 'nitpicking', worried that it might weaken the solidarity necessary for giving the final push to the equal-value legislation under consideration by the Ontario legislature in 1986 and 1987.[22] The second point of tension concerned two criticisms of Coalition tactics offered by some members of the women's movement. First, in the rush to support equal-value legislation, there was not enough time for feminists to examine critically the process of state reform in this area or to draw upon the experiences of 'femocrats' or feminists in state bureaucracies.[23] Some feminists felt that critical debate had been cut off and they had been lulled into silence in the rush of the moment to fit a timetable established by the state.[24]

There may be four possible reasons for this. (1) The diverse groups in the Coalition necessarily had disagreements among themselves; these had to be kept quiet or private, away from the public eye, while solidarity in public was required so that the campaign for pay equity would not be undermined. Although each group was free to submit its independent and critical briefs to the provincial government, Pat McDermott, an Organized Working Women member of the Coalition, said: 'I personally felt bound . . . to avoid openly criticizing the Equal Pay Coalition's position.'[25] (2) Because the business lobby against pay equity was so strong, it was essential that groups in the Coalition provide a solid public front in support of pay equity. (3) When Ontario's final bill on pay equity was made public, there was 'excitement, exhaustion and fear'.[26] Excitement emerged from its application to both the public and private sectors—a considerable improvement over the government's previous public-sector bill; this led to quick support from several Coalition members. Exhaustion resulted from all the work Coalition members had put into studying the ills. As McDermott noted in 1987:

There have been many periods in the past two years when the Equal Pay Coalition met two and three times a week for long, tedious meetings about legislative amendments. Given the complexity of the two Bills we were dealing with, these meetings left people, all of whom work at full-time jobs, drained and often frustrated. It is easy to lose one's perspective when involved in such a process.[27]

Fear arose from the possibility that, if debate about the bills continued to drag on, the Liberal government of David Peterson, released after two years from its agreement with the NDP to introduce a comprehensive pay-equity package, might renege or backtrack. It was important that the Coalition not 'mess up' a unique political opportunity through public wrangling over the specific sections in the proposed act. In McDermott's words, 'there was pressure not to be too expansive in one's criticism, for fear of extending the [Administration of Justice] committee hearing for too long.'[28] (4) The operations of the state and media impose severe constraints. McDermott graphically illustrates how this affected the tactics of the Coalition:

Immediately after the lock-up that follows the tabling of a draft bill, the media are ready to receive the responses of lobby groups. The response must be made then, or you lose the critically important media needed to make your point on the issue. There is no doubt it would have been a serious political blunder not to have had a clear message about the Coalition's position on Bill 154 after the lock-up. The problem with this, however, is that we basically had to decide how we would respond *before* the legislation was released. This was done by setting basic parameters about what would be acceptable and what would make the Coalition oppose the bill. This decision is critical since once a group comes out in favour of or against a particular legislative initiative, it is difficult to say later that it has changed its mind.[29]

Second, some feminists pointed out that in the push for state reforms, single-issue personnel and organizations, such as equal-pay coalitions, have developed within the labour and women's movements. While these are essential to put pressure on the state, they have also had the effect of creating two 'classes' of feminists, the experts and the non-experts. The fact that the latter have deferred to the former and been hesitant to criticize them has also functioned to block critical scrutiny of the principles, strategies, and tactics used in the attempt to find legislative solutions to the problem of unequal pay.[30] McDermott, who holds advanced degrees in both law and sociology, readily admits the problem:

> Most people do not have legal training, and without it, it can be difficult to understand the ins and outs of how the [pay equity] legislation is supposed to work. . . . Pay equity in North America is a very legal and technical enterprise, and this fact creates serious barriers to communication. I'm not sure what can be done about this.[31]

TWO THEORETICAL QUESTIONS

In Appendix A, I raise the question of whether a patriarchal capitalist state can produce policies and laws opposed to patriarchal and capitalist interests. This question takes several forms throughout the book. Can a patriarchal capitalist state, split and dominated by gender and class contradictions, produce a pay-equity law that overcomes the gender and class contradictions within itself and in society at large? Assuming that unequal pay is one of the supports of patriarchal capitalism, is it possible for a patriarchal capitalist state to produce a law that undermines this support? Is it possible for the patriarchal capitalist state to create a pay-equity law that, in the longer term, favours the working class over the capitalist class, and women over men? Submissions by trade unions and women's organizations to state commissions on pay equity in both Canada and the US have assumed that this could be the case, while submissions by business organizations have assumed that it should not.

The second theoretical problem has to do with understanding the nature of Canadian-American similarities and differences in class and feminist struggles over pay equity. Why do business associations and anti-feminist neo-conservatives on both sides of the border take a remarkably similar position on pay equity? What accounts for the similarity in the positions taken by the women's movements in Canada and the US? Why have trade unions on both sides of the border taken almost identical positions on equal pay? There are two possible explanations: either class and gender override national differences on pay equity, or else direct cross-border organizational lines exist, so that there is some common marshalling of positions separately within the business class, the labour movement, and the women's movement. Both explanations have some merit. At least in the North American context, national differences may indeed have receded in the face of the class and patriarchal structures that are so deeply rooted in both countries. The second explanation seems most plausible in the case of the business class: in their briefs, Canadian business associations have constantly cited either American business associations or other US sources of opposition to 'comparable worth'.[32] Perhaps this is understandable given the subsidiary-parent relationship between the Canadian and American economies; it is interesting to note that business associations in the US have hardly ever cited Canadian business opposition to equal-value legislation. The cross-border linkage explanation seems much less plausible in the case of the women's movement: women's groups in Canada have hardly ever cited feminist support for comparable worth in the US. Finally, the linkage explanation is somewhat plausible for the trade-union movement, although Canadian unions have not cited US unions as often as Canadian business associations have followed their American counterparts.

There has been one interesting Canadian-American difference in the pay-equity debates. As will be evident from this book, the marketplace has seemed to be a more important area of discussion and debate in the US than in Canada, while the capitalist workplace has appeared to be more important in Canada. Since the marketplace was the favoured topic of business and the neo-conservative forces, it would seem that the opponents of pay equity have been more successful in the US than in Canada in defining the ideological territory on which the struggle over pay equity would proceed.

THE GENDERED WAGE GAP

1. Size

One of the most graphic illustrations of the wage gap was provided by the Ontario Coalition for Better Daycare when it pointed out that zookeepers and farmhands, predominantly male, were making $21,200 to $22,400 per year in 1983, compared to day-care workers, predominantly female, who were making only $13,000.[33] Do employers value animals more than children? Do employers value zookeepers more than child-care workers? Social scientists have calculated different estimates of the size of the gendered wage gap; the only feature they have in common is that, in all cases, women earn lower incomes than men. Mincer shows that, in a list of twelve developed countries, the wage gap in 1980 varied from a low of 10 per cent in Sweden to a high of 46 per cent in Japan (Canada was not included).[34] In other words, women in

Sweden earned 10 per cent less than men; women in Japan, 46 per cent less. However, this range is probably overstated because of national variations in definitions of wages (hourly, weekly, monthly, or annually) and coverage of workers (all workers, full-time workers, or workers in either the public or the private sector). The narrower the definition of wages (e.g., hourly) and coverage (e.g., an economic sub-sector, such as manufacturing), the smaller the wage gap. In Canada the range in the size of the wage gap between studies is smaller because factors affecting international differences are controlled, but the size of the gap still depends on the definition of wages, coverage, year, and sampling procedures. Following are some Canadian estimates of the wage gap: 54 per cent among those 30 to 44 years of age reporting an annual income in the 1973 Canadian Mobility Study;[35] 45 per cent among those full- and part-time gainfully employed in a 1973 Monthly Labour Force survey of Canada;[36] from 39 to 41 per cent among full-year workers with annual earnings in the years 1982 to 1985;[37] 40 per cent among those with jobs with annual earnings in the 1981 Quality of Life Survey;[38] and 35 per cent as the average for the entire period between 1946 and 1979 in Ontario.[39] It is safe to say that in Canada women make from 35 to 54 per cent less than men (this is the size of the wage gap); expressed in other terms, women earn anywhere from 46 to 65 per cent of what men earn (these are women's earnings in relation to men's).

The wage gap usually has a small range *between national juris-dictions within* population sub-groups. Among manual industrial workers in the six founder countries of the European Economic Community (France, Luxembourg, Italy, Germany, the Nether-lands, and Belgium), the wage gap based on hourly earnings varied from a low of 19 per cent in Italy to a high of 41 per cent in Luxembourg.[40]

Within the same national jurisdiction, however, the size of the wage gap between population sub-groups can be quite marked. This is especially the case for women of colour. In the US, as shown in Table 1.1, black and Hispanic women have consistently suffered larger wage gaps than white women. In 1983, the percentages in median incomes that women earned in relation to men were the following: white women, 65.2 per cent; black women, 57.8 per cent; Hispanic women, 52.8 per cent. In the private sector—i.e., when public-sector workers are excluded—the earning differen-tials are even greater: white women, 56.8 per cent; black women,

50.2 per cent; Hispanic women, 47.9 per cent. Such wage gaps are reflected in the kind of poverty suffered by single mothers, especially among women of colour: 36 per cent of all female-headed households live in poverty; this figure rises to 53 per cent among Hispanic women and 54 per cent among black women.[42] Two other wage gaps are evident in Table 1.1. First, a racial wage gap exists not only among women, but also among men; black and Hispanic men have lower incomes than white men. Second, gendered wage gaps exist within racial minorities: black women receive lower incomes than black men, and Hispanic women receive lower incomes than Hispanic men. Whether we examine gendered wage gaps within or across racial groupings, or racial wage gaps within and across gender groupings, white men are always at the top.

2. Trends

Most international research suggests that the wage gap has been narrowing since the 1960s—although this conclusion tends to be restricted to developed industrial capitalist countries, since much

Table 1.1
US MEDIAN INCOME BY GENDER AND RACE[41]

Population Group	Median Income	% of All Men's Income
All men	$ 22,508	100.0%
white men	23,114	102.7
black men	16,410	72.9
Hispanic men	16,389	72.8
All women	$ 14,479	64.3%
white women	14,677	65.2
black women	13,000	57.8
Hispanic women	11,874	52.8

less research has been done on the underdeveloped and developing world.[43] Mincer estimates that the average wage gap for seven European countries (Britain, Sweden, France, Germany, Italy, the Netherlands, and Spain), the USSR, Israel, Japan, Australia, and the US narrowed from 38 per cent in 1960 to 29 per cent in 1980; during this period, women's wages in these twelve countries grew by an average of 5.15 per cent per year and men's wages by 4.37 per cent.[44] The only exceptions to this trend were the US and the USSR, where the wage gap failed to narrow significantly over this period.[45] A closer inspection of the US pattern reveals a U-curve trend: from the early 1950s until the middle 1970s the wage gap widened and from the late 1970s until the present it has gradually narrowed. In the overall picture, therefore, the wage gap in the US has remained fairly stable, or failed to narrow, from the early 1950s until the 1980s. Expressed numerically, the wage gap of 42 per cent for full-time, year-round workers in 1939 narrowed to 36 per cent by the mid-1950s, then widened to 43 per cent by the early 1970s and narrowed again to 38 per cent by 1982.[46]

In Canada, as in much of the industrial world, women have been averaging a higher percentage of male wages, thereby narrowing—very slowly—the wage gap. For full-time, full-year workers, Canadian women earned 58 per cent of what men did in 1967, a figure that rose to 64 per cent by 1982; during this period, then, the wage gap in Canada narrowed slightly, from 42 to 36 per cent.[47] In Ontario the wage gap followed a US-style U-curve between the early 1950s and the 1980s: it narrowed from 35.9 per cent in 1946 to 25.8 per cent in 1952, after which it widened to 43.2 per cent in 1968, and then narrowed again to 29.9 per cent in 1981. There is some evidence that this narrowing slowed in the latter 1970s.[48] Thus Ontario and the US are latecomers to the well-established international trend of a steady two-decade decline in the wage gap; the reasons for this remain to be researched.

Research on trends in the wage gap among national sub-groups suggests variations on the overall patterns. In the US the wage gap among full-time, year-round black workers has narrowed substantially, from 42 per cent in 1955 to 22 per cent in 1982.[49] The familiar U-curve occurs in all age groups for full-time, year-round workers, but there are also some differences: for those under 35, the later narrowing of the wage gap between 1970 and 1982 is greater than the initial widening between 1955 and 1970, so that, overall, the wage gap narrows; for older groups, the initial widening is greater than the later narrowing, so that there is a net increase in the size of the wage gap between 1955 and 1982.[50]

FROM IDENTICAL WORK TO COMPARABLE WORK

1. Three stages of legislation

Historically, pay-equity legislation has been passed in three stages: equal pay for equal work; equal pay for similar or substantially similar work; and equal pay for work of equal or comparable value. In the first stage, equal-work legislation attempts to correct gender-based pay inequities between *identical* jobs held by women and men. It would be illegal under this legislation to pay women welders less than male welders, but quite legal to pay women welders less than male tool and die setters, and female nurses less than male truck drivers. In the second stage, equal pay for similar or substantially similar work, it might be illegal to pay women welders less than male welders and male tool and die setters, but still perfectly legal to pay female nurses less than male truck drivers. In the third stage, equal-value legislation goes one step further by correcting pay inequities between men's and women's jobs that may be substantially different but that can be compared in terms of the four criteria of skill, effort, responsibility, and working conditions (e.g., a nurse and a truck driver).

National societies, and the state or provincial jurisdictions within each society, are at different stages in the transition. For those jurisdictions now in the third stage, the first stage appears to have occurred before the 1960s, the second stage during the 1960s and early 1970s, and the third stage from the late 1970s onwards, although exceptions do exist. The US at the federal level is still wedged in the second stage, although some states (such as Minnesota, Washington, Iowa, Maryland, New Mexico, Connecticut, Hawaii, and Alaska) are entering the third stage. Canada at the federal level and the provinces of Prince Edward Island, Nova Scotia, Manitoba, Ontario, and Quebec have entered the third state; British Columbia, Alberta, and Saskatchewan are lodged in the second stage and at present have no intentions of entering the third. New Brunswick entered the first stage in 1961 with its Female Employees Fair Remuneration Act, but in 1976 repealed its equal-pay-for-the-same-work clause; it promised to introduce new pay-equity legislation. Newfoundland has taken a non-legislative approach through negotiations with public-sector trade unions.[51] The third stage may be sub-divided between two phases: an initial weaker phase in which equal pay for work of equal value is based only on a complaints model (as in the Quebec and Canadian federal government legislation), and a much stronger second phase in which equal pay for work of equal value is based on some degree of pro-activity (as in the Ontario, Manitoba, Prince Edward Island, and Nova Scotia laws) (see p. 28 below).

2. Class and gender struggles over the three stages

Before the completion of the first two stages, business opposes all forms of equal-pay laws; after the first two stages have been achieved, business moderates its demands by accepting laws regarding identical and similar or substantially similar work, but opposing their extension to equal pay for work of equal value, or comparable worth.[52] The basic argument of business has been that the legislation gained in the first two stages has been quite effective in handling sex discrimination in the workplace, and that no toughening of the law is required.[53] Trade-union and feminist organizations disagree completely: they want to move as quickly as possible to the third stage precisely because the laws regarding identical, similar, and substantially similar work have proved largely ineffective in reducing the gendered wage gap. Thus while business lobbying has been partly responsible for delaying the transition from the first to third stages, feminists and labourites can take some of the credit for speeding the passage to the third stage.

The neo-conservative anti-feminist movement in Canada opposes the transition from equal-work to equal-value legislation. Two of its organizational representatives, REAL Women and the National Citizens' Coalition, will be mentioned frequently throughout this book.

REAL Women—the initials stand for 'Realistic, Equal, Active, for Life'—accepts equal pay for identical or similar work but opposes equal pay for work of equal value.[54] Founded in 1983, it describes itself as a 'non-partisan, interdenominational organization of independent women' who come from 'all walks of life, occupations, social and economic backgrounds. Some members are employed full-time outside the home, some are employed in the home, some are both.'[55] There is a certain anti-radical-feminist consistency between the organization's position on pay equity and its stands on other issues. While REAL Women is pro-family, it is against abortion, pornography, prostitution, mandatory affirmative action, equal pay for work of equal value, and universal state-subsidized day-care. Its members are not against women working in the paid labour force, but think women should have the financial option to decide whether to do so or not. They do not oppose day-care for women who, out of economic necessity, must work in the paid labour force, but think women who want to take care of their children at home should be subsidized to do so; in other words, economic necessity should not force women out of the home. The group pushes for changes in state tax and other laws to give women the 'realistic' financial option of staying at home if that is what they want. Not surprisingly, REAL Women has created considerable controversy within the women's movement over the nature of women's equality and the family in Canadian society.[56]

The National Citizens' Coalition does not recognize even the first stage as valid. It completely rejects the terms 'pay equity', 'comparable worth', and 'equal pay'. It thus rejects equal pay whether for identical work, for substantially similar work, or for work of equal value.[57] A non-partisan, non-profit conservative Canadian business association, the Coalition claims a national membership of 36,000. Its pillars are the free market system, limited government, and the traditional patriarchal family. It opposes higher taxes for the rich, agricultural marketing boards, state-funded health care, and trade-union support for political and social causes such as the NDP and free-standing abortion clinics. It favours a reduction in social programs to balance the budget, extra billing for doctors, a 40 per cent reduction in unemployment-insurance benefits, white-only immigration, Canadian involvement in the US Star Wars program, and an energy policy favourable to multinational corporations. The Coalition receives strong backing from major corporations such as Canadian Pacific, the Canadian Imperial Bank of Commerce, Bell Canada, Stelco, Abitibi Paper, Brascan, Goodyear, Royal Trust, the Power Corporation, and the Bank of Montreal.[58]

3. Explanations

Why do some national, provincial, or state jurisdictions make the transition from 'equal work' to 'similar or substantially similar work' to 'equal pay for work of equal value' much sooner than others? There are at least four possible explanations.

RESERVE ARMY OF LABOUR. The very existence of women as a

cheap reserve army of labour and the demand for such workers in a capitalist system act as necessary—but not sufficient—conditions for women ultimately to put pressure on the state for equalization of pay rates by gender through legislation. The contradiction of the reserve army of labour is that it throws low-waged women into a labour force in which they can compare their rates with men's; this then leads to a demand for comparable job evaluations across occupational ghettos, and hence equal pay for work of equal value.

WAR. Some of the earliest agitation over equal-pay-for-equal-work legislation occurred during the Second World War in Great Britain, Australia, the US, and Canada. Governments were anxious to minimize the disruptions in war production caused by labour disputes over unequal pay rates between women and men. Male veterans returning from overseas were anxious to take up their former jobs at rates of pay that would not be diluted by women's low-wage competition. In addition, in the context of the immediate post-war boom, business did not strongly resist equal pay for equal work.

ELECTORAL COMPETITION. With the increasing participation of women in (low-) waged labour, political parties vie with one another for the women's vote; a popular platform for all political parties would be to support, at least in principle, equal pay for work of equal value, even though in practice support might be far from enthusiastic. However, this electoral competition has had to receive a stimulus from left-leaning labour, socialist, or social-democratic parties. In Manitoba it was the New Democratic Party that introduced the advanced stage of equal pay for work of equal value in the public sector in 1985. In Ontario too, it was mainly NDP pressure that enshrined the equal-value principle in the Liberal-NDP accord of 28 May 1985, which in turn put the Liberal Party of David Peterson into power. A direct result was the introduction of the province's public-sector equal-value bill, which was replaced in 1987 with combined public-and private-sector legislation. While it is possible that the Liberal Party on its own would have introduced this advanced type of pay equity, it is doubtful whether the Conservative Party would ever have done so, despite its recent support for the abstract notion of equal pay for work of equal value. Such legislation was introduced, however—though only for the public sector—in 1988 by the Liberal Party in Prince Edward Island and the Conservative Party in Nova

Scotia. The class and gender struggles over pay equity in Prince Edward Island took on dimensions similar to those in other jurisdictions, especially Manitoba and Ontario.[59]

FEMINIST AGITATION. The second wave of the women's movement (since the late 1960s), especially in its alliance with the labour movement, probably provided the final push needed to persuade governments to change their largely ineffective equal- and similar-work legislation in the direction of equal pay for work of equal value. The differences in the political strength of the women's movement in various jurisdictions may have much to do with the unevenness in the timing of equal-value legislation since the 1970s. As we shall see in this book, where the women's movement was strong both on its own and in a loose coalition with the labour movement, as in Ontario, governments during the 1980s experienced strong pressure to move to the pro-active phase of the third stage of pay equity. Where the women's movement was somewhat weaker, as in Alabama, governments did not experience the same pressure to institute equal-value legislation.

We now turn to a detailed examination of the gender and class struggles over pay-equity legislation. The capitalist workplace will be considered in Chapter 2, the marketplace in Chapter 3, and the household workplace in Chapter 4. Chapter 5 will examine the passive revolutions involved in sexism, racism, and classism, as well as the exemptions, loopholes, and defects embedded in pay-equity laws.

Notes

[1] *Globe and Mail*, 31 June 1984, p. 7. For the union context of this issue, see Confederation of Canadian Unions, *A Brief on the Green Paper on Pay Equity* (John Lang, Secretary-Treasurer, 27 March 1986).

[2] For example, see R.A. Holmes, 'Male-Female Earnings Differentials in Canada', *Journal of Human Resources* 11, no. 1 (1976), pp. 109-17; Roberta Edgecombe-Robb, 'Earnings Differentials Between Males and Females in Ontario, 1971', *Canadian Journal of Economics* 11, no. 2 (1978), pp. 350-9; John C. Goyder, 'Income Differences Between the Sexes: Findings from a National Canadian Survey', *Canadian Review of Sociology and Anthropology* 18, no. 3, (1981), pp. 321-42; Michael D. Ornstein, *Accounting for Gender Differentials in Job Income in Canada: Results from a 1981 Survey*, series A, no. 2, Labour Canada, Women's Bureau (Ottawa: Minister of

Supply and Services, 1983); Athena Petraki Kottis, 'Female-Male Earnings Dif-
ferentials in the Founder Countries of the European Economic Community: An
Econometric Investigation', *Die Economist* (Netherlands), 132, no. 2 (1984), pp.
204-23; June O'Neill, 'The Trend in the Male-Female Wage Gap in the United
States', *Journal of Labor Economics* 3, no. 1, part 2 (1985), pp. S91-S116; Peter Kuhn,
'Sex Discrimination in Labor Markets: The Role of Statistical Evidence', *American
Economic Review* 77, no. 4 (Sept. 1987), pp. 567-83; Paul W. Miller, 'Gender
Differences in Observed and Offered Wages in Canada, 1980', *Canadian Journal of
Economics* 20, no. 2 (May 1987), pp. 225-44.

[3]For example, see Roberta Edgecombe-Robb, 'Occupational Segregation and
Equal Pay for Work of Equal Value', *Relations Industrielles* 39, no. 1 (Spring 1984),
pp. 146-66; Morley Gunderson, 'Male-Female Wage Differentials and the Impact
of Equal Pay Legislation', *Review of Economics and Statistics* 62 (Nov. 1975), pp.
462-9; 'Spline Function Estimates of the Impact of Equal Pay Legislation: The
Ontario Experience', *Relations Industrielles* 40, no. 4 (1985), pp. 775-91; 'Dis-
crimination, Equal Pay, and Equal Opportunities in the Labour Market', pp.
219-65 in W. Craig Riddell, ed., *Work and Pay: The Canadian Labour Market*, vol. 17,
Collected Research Studies, Royal Commission on the Economic Union and
Development Prospects for Canada (Toronto: University of Toronto Press, 1985);
Robert Buchele and Mark Aldrich, 'How Much Difference Would Comparable
Worth Make?' *Industrial Relations* 24, no. 2 (1985), pp. 222-33; R.G. Gregory and
R.C. Duncan, 'Segmented Labour Market Theories and the Australian Experience
of Equal Pay for Women", *Journal of Post Keynesian Economics* 3, no. 3 (1981), pp.
403-28; D.M. Shapiro and M. Stelcner, 'The Persistence of the Male-Female
Earnings Gap in Canada, 1970-1980: The Impact of Equal Pay Laws and Language
Policies', *Canadian Public Policy* 13, no. 4 (1987), pp. 462-76.

[4]See Jane Goldman, 'Unions, Women and Economic Justice: Litigating Union Sex
Discrimination', *Women's Rights Law Reporter* 4, no. 1 (Fall 1977), pp. 3-26; H.C.
Jain, 'Canadian Legal Approaches to Sex Equality in the Workplace', *Monthly
Labor Review* 105 (Oct. 1982), pp. 38-42; Lynn C. Kaye, 'A Review of the Enforce-
ment of Equal Pay for Work of Equal Value Legislation in Canada' (Paper
presented to the Women, the Law and the Economy Conference in Banff, Alberta,
14-16 Oct. 1983); Barbara Warren and Carroll Boone, 'AFSCME v. State of
Washington: Title VII As a Winning Strategy to End Wage Discrimination',
Women's Rights Law Reporter 8, no. 1-2 (Winter 1984), pp. 17-49; and Janice R.
Bellace, 'Comparable Worth: Proving Sex-Based Wage Discrimination', *Iowa Law
Review* 69 (March 1984), pp. 655-703.

[5]In the US, see the economist June O'Neill, 'The "Comparable Worth" Trap', pp.
263-6 in Phyllis Schlafly, ed., *Equal Pay for Unequal Work: A Conference on Comparable Worth* (Washington, D.C.: Eagle Forum Education and Legal Defense
Fund, 1983). In Canada, see the political scientists Thomas Flanagan, 'Equal Pay
for Work of Equal Value: Some Theoretical Criticisms', *Canadian Public Policy* 13,
no. 4 (1987), pp. 435-44; and Christian Dick, *Pay Equity, Discrimination and Undervaluation*. Unpublished MA Thesis, McMaster University, 1987.

[6]Judy Scales-Trent, 'Comparable Worth: Is This a Theory for Black Workers?',
Women's Rights Law Reporter 8, no. 1-2 (Winter 1984), pp. 51-8.

[7]Immigrant Women's Information Centre, *Equal Pay for Work of Equal Value in
Ontario* (A response to the Green Paper on Pay Equity, presented to the [Ontario]
Consultation Panel on Pay Equity; Windsor, 11 March 1986); Women Working

With Immigrant Women, *Submission to the Ontario Consultation Panel on Pay Equity* (Toronto, 1986); Coalition of Visible Minority Women, *Submission to the Ontario Consultation Panel on Pay Equity* (Toronto, 14 May 1986); *Pay Equity: Its Potential Impact on and Relevance to Visible Minority and Immigrant Women* (Submission to the Ontario Standing Committee on the Administration of Justice, Toronto, 23 Feb. 1987).

[8] George Ehring, 'What About Class Equity?', *Our Times*, March 1989, p. 34.

[9] See Debra J. Lewis, *Just Give Us the Money: A Discussion of Wage Discrimination and Pay Equity* (Vancouver: Women's Research Centre, 1988), pp. 28-32. For example, the Ottawa-Carleton Board of Trade, in its brief to the Ontario Consultation Panel on Pay Equity, kept repeating that it supported pay equity without ever mentioning whether or not it meant 'equal pay for work of equal value'. See Ottawa-Carleton Board of Trade, *Brief to the Consultation Panel on Pay Equity* (Ottawa, 17 April 1986), pp. 1-2.

[10] Ontario, *Pay Equity Act, 1987*, Statutes of Ontario, 1987, ch. 34 (Toronto: Queen's Printer, 1988).

[11] Equal Pay Coalition, *Submission to the Standing Committee on the Administration of Justice Concerning Bill 154—The Pay Equity Act, 1986* (Toronto, 5 March 1987), p. 7.

[12] Ontario Pay Equity Commission, *How to Do Pay Equity Job Comparisons* (Toronto, March 1989), pp. 48, 50.

[13] For example, the Kitchener Chamber of Commerce used three different terms to describe the Ontario *Green Paper on Pay Equity*: pay equity, equal value, and equal pay for work of equal value. See Kitchener Chamber of Commerce, *Green Paper on Equal Pay for Work of Equal Value (Pay Equity)* (Kitchener, Ont., 27 Dec. 1985) The Board of Trade of Metropolitan Toronto simply equated 'equal pay for work of equal value' with 'equal value'. See its *Submission on Equal Pay for Work of Equal Value* (Toronto, Oct. 1985), p. 1.

[14] Equal Pay Coalition, *Submission* (1987), pp. 2, 5, 45. Some business groups also took the view that the exclusion of some workers (i.e., males) posed the possibility of a legal challenge to pay-equity acts under the Charter of Human Rights and Freedoms. See, for example, Board of Trade of Metropolitan Toronto, *Submission to the Consultation Panel on the Green Paper on Pay Equity* (Toronto, March 1986), p. 12.

[15] Ontario Mining Association, *Submission to Consultation Panel on Pay Equity on Equal Pay for Work of Equal Value* (24 Feb. 1986).

[16] Congress of Canadian Women, *Submission on Pay Equity Hearings* (Toronto, 14 May 1986), p. 2.

[17] US Congress, House Committee on Post Office and Civil Service, Subcommittee on Compensation and Employee Benefits, *Options for Conducting a Pay Equity Study of Federal Pay and Classification Systems: Hearings, March 28-June 18*, 99th Congress, 1st Session (Washington, D.C.: Government Printing Office, 1985), pp. 286, 814-16 (hereafter US Congress, *Options* [1985]).

[18] Equal Pay Coalition, *Response to the Ontario Government's Green Paper on Pay Equity* (Toronto, 24 Jan. 1986); *Submission* (1987), p. 1.

[19] Amalgamated Clothing and Textile Workers Union, *Implementing Pay Equity in a Workplace Which Has a Piece-Rate Compensation Structure* (Prepared for the Ontario Women's Directorate by Noella Martin under the Supervision of Heather Webster, Research Director, ACTWU; Aug. 1986); United Food and Commercial

Workers International Union, Regions 18 and 19, *Brief in Response to the Ontario Government Green Paper on Pay Equity*, March 1986).

[20] Pat McDermott, 'Pay Equity in Ontario: Coalition Politics', *Cayenne*, Fall 1987, p. 5.

[21] Ontario Public Service Employees Union, *Meeting the Challenge: Pay Equity in Ontario* (By James Clancy, President; 1 Oct. 1986), p. 14.

[22] Oral presentations by Pat McDermott, York University professor, and Isla Peters, Pay Equity Advisor, the Ontario Public Service Employees Union, 'Women and Unions Workshop', University of Ottawa, 7 April 1989. See also Ontario Public Service Employees Union and Human Resources Secretariat, *Pilot Test of the Pay Equity Survey* (Toronto, 16 Jan. 1989).

[23] For discussions of 'femocrats' and 'femocracy', see Sophie Watson ed., *Playing the State: Australian Feminist Interventions* (London: Verso, 1989).

[24] Sue Findlay, 'Equal Pay: Why No Debate?', *Cayenne*, Spring/Summer 1987, pp. 36-40.

[25] McDermott, 'Pay Equity' (1987), p. 7.

[26] Ibid., p. 5.

[27] Ibid., p. 8.

[28] Ibid.

[29] Ibid., p. 7; emphasis in original.

[30] Findlay, 'Equal Pay' (1987).

[31] McDermott, 'Pay Equity' (1987), p. 8.

[32] In one case that seems bizarre in a Canadian context, the Board of Trade of Metropolitan Toronto produced a 41-page document that cites American sources opposing comparable worth, and virtually ignores Canadian sources and experiences, despite its purpose to argue against equal pay for work of equal value in Canada. See its *Submission on Equal Pay* (1985).

[33] Ontario Coalition for Better Daycare, *Day Care Brief to Pay Equity Hearings*, (Toronto, March 1986), p.1; *Brief to the Standing Committee on Administration of Justice re Bill 154: An Act to Provide Pay Equity* (Susan Colley, Executive Director; Toronto, 1987), p. 2.

[34] Jacob Mincer, 'Intercountry Comparisons of Labor Force Trends and of Related Developments: An Overview', *Journal of Labor Economics* 3, no. 1, part 2 (1985), pp. S6, S22.

[35] Goyder, 'Income Differences' (1981), p. 327.

[36] Margaret Denton and Alfred A. Hunter, 'Economic Sectors and Gender Discrimination in Canada: A Critique and Test of Block and Walker . . . and Some New Evidence', no. 6 in series A: *Equality in the Workplace*, Labour Canada, Women's Bureau (Ottawa: Minister of Supply and Services, 1984), pp. 27, 30.

[37] Labour Canada, Women's Bureau, *Women in the Labour Force* (Ottawa: Minister of Supply and Services, various years).

[38] Ornstein, *Accounting for Gender Differentials* (1983), p. 1.

[39] Gunderson, 'Spline Function Estimates' (1985), p. 782.

[40] Kottis, 'Female-Male Earnings Differentials' (1984), p. 220.

[41] These are 1983 Bureau of the Census data presented by the National Organization of Women (NOW) to the Subcommittee on Compensation and Employee Benefits of the Committee on the Post Office and Civil Service in the US House of Representatives. See US Congress, *Options* (1985), p. 247.

[42] Ibid., p. 631.

[43]Mincer, 'Intercountry Comparisons' (1985), p. S2,; O'Neill, 'The Trend in the Male-Female Wage Gap' (1985), p. S96.

[44]Mincer, 'Intercountry Comparisons' (1985), pp. S1-S2, S11, S26.

[45]Ibid., p. S6.

[46]O'Neill, 'The Trend in the Male-Female Wage Gap' (1985), pp. S93-S94.

[47]W. Craig Riddell, 'Work and Pay: The Canadian Labour Market: An Overview', in Riddell, ed., *Work and Pay* (1985), p. 61.

[48]Gunderson, 'Spline Function Estimates' (1985), pp. 782, 784. See also Gunderson, 'Time Pattern of Male-Female Wage Differentials: Ontario 1946-1971', *Relations Industrielles* 31, no. 1 (1976), pp. 65-8.

[49]O'Neill, 'The Trend in the Male-Female Wage Gap' (1985), pp. S93-S94.

[50]Ibid., p. S95.

[51]Alberta, *Chapter 1-2: Individual's Rights Protection Act*. Revised Statutes of Alberta, 1980, vol. 3 (Edmonton: Queen's Printer), sec. 6; British Columbia, *Chapter 186: Human Rights Code*, enacted in 1973, Revised Statutes of BC, 1979, vol. 3 (Victoria: Queen's Printer), sec. 6(1); Prince Edward Island, *Chapter H-13: An Act Respecting Human Rights* [enacted in 1968], Revised Statutes of Prince Edward Island, 1974 (Charlottetown: Queen's Printer), sec. 7(1); Prince Edward Island Dept. of Labour, *Report of the Committee on Equal Pay for Work of Equal Value* (Charlottetown: 1987); Newfoundland, *Chapter 262: An Act to Establish the Newfoundland Human Rights Code and to Provide for its Implementation*, Revised Statutes of Newfoundland, 1970, vol. 6 (St John's: Queen's Printer), sec. 10(1); Nova Scotia, *Chapter L-1: An Act to Provide for a Labour Standards Code* [enacted in 1972], Consolidated Statutes of Nova Scotia, vol. 10 (Halifax: Queen's Printer, 1979), sec. 55(1); Nova Scotia, *Chapter 16: An Act to Provide for Pay Equity*, Statutes of the Province of Nova Scotia (Halifax: 1988); Saskatchewan, *Chapter L-1: An Act Respecting Annual Holidays, Hours of Work, Minimum Wages and Other Employment Standards*, June, Statutes of Saskatchewan, vol. 4 (Regina: Queen's Printer, 1980), sec. 17(1); New Brunswick Advisory Council on the Status of Women, *Equal Pay for Work of Equal Value* (Moncton: 1985), pp. 4-5; Ontario Pay Equity Commission, *Report to the Minister of Labour on Sectors of the Economy Which Are Predominantly Female, As Required Under the Pay Equity Act, Section 33(2)(e)* (Toronto: Jan. 1989), pp. 11-14.

[52]Several Canadian business associations told the Ontario government that they supported either equal pay for equal work or equal pay for substantially similar work, but opposed equal pay for work of equal value. See Kitchener and District Chamber of Commerce, *Green Paper* (1985), p. 1; Sudbury and District Chamber of Commerce, *Public Consultation on the Green Paper on Pay Equity* (Don Smith, President; 24 Feb. 1986), p. 1; Retail Council of Canada, *Submission to the Ontario Consultative Panel on Pay Equity* (By Alasdair J. McKichan, President; April 1986), pp. 2, 3, 19.

[53]The Board of Trade of Metropolitan Toronto argued that there was no need for legislating equal pay for work of equal value since there were sufficient legal remedies to sex discrimination in the Ontario Employment Standards Act and the Human Rights Code. See its *Submission on Equal Pay* (1985), pp. 11-12.

[54]REAL Women, *Equal Pay for UNequal Work*, Pamphlet no. 7 (Toronto, n.d.) p. 1; REAL Women, *Position Papers, Publication No. 3* (Toronto, n.d.) p. 4.

[55]See REAL Women, *Who We Are* (Brief to Members of Parliament; Toronto, 19 Nov. 1985) p. 1.

[56]Doris Anderson, 'REAL Women Don't Really Speak For Women'. *Toronto Star*, 7 Oct. 1985; Penni Mitchell, 'REAL Problems'. *Herizons* 4, no. 5 (July/Aug. 1986), pp. 4, 7; Charlotte Gray, 'Why Can't Women Get Their Act Together?', *Chatelaine*, Nov. 1988, pp. 82-3, 232-40; and Danielle Crittenden, 'Women Against Women: REAL Women Don't Eat Crow', *Saturday Night*, May 1988, pp. 27-35.

[57]National Citizens' Coalition, *Pay Discrimination: A Blueprint for the Radical Restructuring of Our Society: How It Will Demean Women, Help Break Down the Traditional Family and the Free Market System* (Brief submitted to the [Ontario] Consultation Panel on Pay Equity; 15 May 1986), pp. 3, 17.

[58]See National Citizens' Coalition, 'Here's How to Win the Next Election', *Globe and Mail*, 5 Nov. 1987, p. A11; Nick Fillmore, 'The Right Stuff: An Inside Look at the National Citizens' Coalition', *This Magazine* 20, no. 2 (June/July 1986), pp. 4-11, 19.

[59]E.g., see: Prince Edward Island Dept. of Labour, *Report of the Equal Pay for Work of Equal Value Committee* (Charlottetown, 1987); Prince Edward Island Federation of Labour, *Brief to the Pay Equity Committee* (Charlottetown, 1986); *The Guardian* (Charlottetown), 4 Dec. to 6 Dec., 12 Dec. 1986.

2

The Capitalist Workplace

The struggle over pay equity has affected most centrally the capitalist workplace: the offices, factories, and mines where women and men are employed to earn a measure of subsistence so that others may profit by their labour. Changes in the capitalist labour process (the way tools and equipment are combined with labour to produce commodities) have interacted with the way wages are divided up between women and men. This interaction occurs in three ways. First, under the strongest pro-active versions of 'equal pay for work of equal value', employers and union bargaining agents are mandated to negotiate pay-equity plans in the capitalist workplace itself. These plans attempt to define more precisely the value of work and how it is divided up between women and men. Second, unions interpret pay-equity legislation as holding out the possibility of increasing their control over the labour process, while employers regard such legislation as a threat to their control. Where unions have not existed in particular workplaces (and this has been typical for women), pay-equity plans reaffirm managerial control over workers by giving employers the right to unilaterally impose their own desired form of pay equity, subject to the approval of state pay-equity commissions or bureaus. Third, both unions and employers have contended that pay equity would have long-reaching implications for the structure of work. The labour-feminist alliance has argued that pay equity would increase the productivity of women by making them more satisfied with their level of monetary compensation; managers and employers have argued that equal pay for work of equal value would lead to a restructuring of the labour process in the direction of more part-time work, more subcontracting of work, and faster replacement of intensive labour with labour-saving technology. It will be argued in this chapter that the labour-feminist alliance has invited state intervention in the capitalist workplace primarily to redress women's lower wages, but in a form that would increase the control by women workers and unions over the labour process, while business has opposed state intervention in the paid workplace for this very reason.

MODELS: COMPLAINT, PRO-ACTIVE, INTEGRATED

There are three main pay-equity models: complaint, employer-initiated or pro-active, and integrated. In the *complaint* model, common in human-rights legislation, women employees are entitled to file complaints alleging that their jobs are not being paid on a basis equal to similar or comparable male jobs. This method exists in the 1978 Canadian Human Rights Act, the Employment Standards Acts of Manitoba and Ontario, and the Quebec Charter of Human Rights and Freedoms enacted in 1975. The *employer-initiated* or *pro-active* model requires the implementation of job-evaluation and pay-equity plans by the employer in non-unionized establishments and jointly by employees and employers through collective bargaining in unionized workplaces. This model is prominent in the legislation of Minnesota in the US, the Manitoba Pay Equity Act of 1985 (where disputes are referred to arbitration or the labour board), and the 1988 Nova Scotia Pay Equity Act (which has no dispute-settlement mechanism). The *integrated* model provides for combinations of the complaint and pro-active models. This was the approach adopted in the 1986 Ontario Public Service Pay Equity Bill, the 1987 Ontario Pay Equity Act, and the 1988 Prince Edward Island Pay Equity Act: the pro-active model is effective in an initial phase, when employers and employees are to negotiate a pay-equity plan; later, complaints could be lodged for failure to comply with the plan. Complaints may be made only about contraventions of the acts and are limited to how the acts define pay equity, its implementation, restrictions, and exemptions. A fully-integrated act would not impose such restrictions on the complaints that could be lodged.[1] Generally, business and the neo-conservatives, if they had to accept any type of equal-pay legislation, favoured the complaint model,[2] or one based on 'voluntary compliance', in which it was left up to employers to decide how best to equalize wages.[3] Managers and personnel officers in the new middle class fell in line with this position.[4] The feminist-labour alliance, on the other hand, favoured the pro-active model either by itself or in combination with the complaint procedure in the integration model. The Equal Pay Coalition of Ontario came up with a relatively innovative plan: the pro-active setting-up of pay-equity plans was to apply only to unionized workplaces and workplaces with 100 employees or more; workplaces with fewer than 100 employees and unorganized workplaces would only have to follow the complaint model.[5]

COVERAGE

In several national, Canadian provincial, and US state jurisdictions there are three issues variously at stake regarding the coverage of women by pay-equity legislation: *gender predominance*, (should job comparisons be made between female-dominated and male-dominated jobs, or between all jobs, regardless of their gender composition?); *establishment* (should job comparisons be made only within a single establishment of the same employer, or between establishments of the same and/or different employers?); and *sector* (should the legislation apply only to the public sector, or a subpart of that sector, or to the private sector as well?). Business has wanted to exclude as many women as possible from coverage, while feminist and trade-union organizations have wanted the broadest possible coverage. Each issue will be discussed in turn.

1. Gender predominance

In pro-active and integrated pay-equity legislation, gender predominance is usually specified, so that the law covers only 'women's positions', or those occupied mainly by women. The 1985 Manitoba Pay Equity Act applies only to those jobs in the public sector in which 70 per cent or more are women; comparisons can be made only with those jobs in which 70 per cent or more of the occupants are men. These levels can be changed through negotiations between employers and employees.[6] The 1988 Nova Scotia and Prince Edward Island Pay Equity Acts define both female and male predominance at the 60 per cent level.[7] In the Ontario *Green Paper on Pay Equity* it was suggested that pay-equity adjustments could be carried out only by comparing female-predominant with male-predominant jobs, but the question of determining gender predominance was left open. A number of methods from other jurisdictions were discussed: a sliding scale of 55 to 70 per cent, based on the number of employees per establishment, proposed by the Canadian Human

Rights Commission; a statistical formula proposed by a comparable-worth commission in New York State; consideration of historical patterns, especially in those occupations that were once female-predominant and consequently still receive low pay; or the arbitrary 70 per cent cut-off figure plus the possibility of negotiating other levels, as in the Manitoba legislation.[8] The Ontario Public Service Pay Equity bill and the 1987 Ontario Pay Equity Act provide for a 70 per cent cut-off for predominantly male jobs and a 60 per cent cut-off for predominantly female jobs unless these levels are changed through negotiation between employers and employees.[9] In many complaint-based human-rights and employment-standards acts, gender predominance is not formally defined or acknowledged.[10] However, in 1978 a Canadian Human Rights Commission Task Force recognized the issue of gender predominance in the case of group complaints.[11] In November 1986, the Canadian Human Rights Commission (CHRC) accepted a sliding scale based on the number of employees in a firm to determine gender predominance.[12] The cut-offs were as follows: fewer than 100 employees, 70 per cent; 100 to 500 employees, 60 per cent; and more than 500 employees, 55 per cent.[13] In smaller firms, because the cut-off is higher, there is a greater chance that women will not qualify for equal-pay adjustments. Regardless of firm size, the Canadian Human Rights Act applies to all persons in each occupation. It does not have the minimum-of-ten threshold found in the 1985 Manitoba and 1988 Nova Scotia Acts.

(a) The business position

Business interests have either rejected any definition of gender predominance or wanted the cut-off to be set as high as possible and made inflexible, so that very few women qualify for pay-equity adjustments. In Canada in 1986 the Automotive Parts Manufacturers Association opposed defining gender predominance in any way.[14] The Ontario Chamber of Commerce thought that the 60 per cent to 70 per cent contemplated by the government was too low, and wanted the levels for both male- and female-predominant jobs established at between 80 and 90 per cent.[15] Other business associations wanted a level higher than the 60 to 70 per cent range without specifying exact percentages.[16] Such employer groups as the Ontario Mining Association, Ontario Hydro, the Municipal Electric Association, and the Canadian Manufacturers' Association took the less extreme position of favouring the 70 per cent cut-off level.[17] The Board of Trade of Metropolitan Toronto wanted to have a phase-in period for gender predominance: during the first year of pay equity, the threshold for male- and female-predominant jobs would be set at 90 per cent, to fall 5 per cent in each subsequent year until it reached a 70 per cent plateau. To avoid the uncertain effects of fluctuations in the thresholds, it recommended a three-year stabilization period before a level could be established, and wanted a ban on any negotiations between unions and management to reduce the figure below 70 per cent.[18] The Day Care Advisory Committee of Metropolitan Toronto, which on other issues leaned more towards the business position than the feminist one, favoured a 50 per cent threshold for female predominance on the grounds that women's participation rate in the labour force would soon reach this level.[19] The Manufacturers' Association also wanted the 70 per cent figure, which it favoured, to be non-negotiable and applicable to groups of no less than 10 employees, with 'group' defined as 'occupational type rather than evaluated grade level', and a three-year stabilization period.[20]

(b) The labour-feminist position

In the Ontario and Manitoba debates, the feminist-labour alliance mounted seven responses to the neo-conservative business approach to gender predominance.

NO CUT-OFF. As one option, many in the feminist-labour alliance rejected completely any automatic numerical cut-off figure, whether applied to female- or male-predominant jobs.[21] The Ontario Equal Pay Coalition stated its objection graphically: 'A fixed percentage could work like a guillotine and automatically exclude large numbers of women who deserve the right to file a complaint.'[22] The National Action Committee on the Status of Women warned that automatic cut-off figures for gender predominance would give employers grounds to launch court appeals under the Canadian Charter of Human Rights and Freedoms, resulting in years of delays in implementing pay equity.[23] The Public Service Alliance of Canada argued that 'any threshold level that restricts the initiation of a complaint is a direct violation of Section 15 of the Canadian Charter of Rights and Freedoms'.[24]

LOWER CUT-OFF. As another option, several feminist and labour organizations suggested lower numerical figures than 70 per cent in the determination of gender predominance. The Charter of

Rights Coalition in Manitoba and the Manitoba Association of Women and the Law suggested a 60 per cent figure for both female- and male-dominated jobs.[25] Organized Working Women, the Ontario Equal Pay Coalition, the Ontario Coalition for Better Daycare, and the Federation of Women Teachers' Association of Ontario suggested that, since women make up 44 per cent of the labour force, gender predominance should be set at a level just above this figure.[26]

FLEXIBILITY. Trade unions and feminist groups wanted as much flexibility as possible in the determination of gender predominance.[27] In particular, they said, sex stereotypes and the historical patterns of gender predominance should be taken into account.[28] For example, some low-paying occupations that are now dominated by men were once dominated by women, and this historical pattern has influenced current wages.[29] Women in such occupations should be able to qualify for pay-equity adjustments despite the fact that they are not in female-predominant jobs.[30] The Ontario Equal Pay Coalition suggested a dual approach to gender predominance: in the pro-active setting-up of pay-equity plans, use a flexible approach that takes into account historical patterns and sex stereotyping of some occupations; in the complaint procedure, abandon the notion of gender predominance completely.[31]

COLLECTIVE BARGAINING. Trade unions more than feminist organizations pushed for the determination of gender predominance through collective bargaining rather than unilaterally, by management fiat.[32] Although many feminist organizations accepted collective bargaining as a means to achieve pay equity, some were suspicious of male domination in negotiations, resulting in the dropping of 'women's issues' (such as child care or affirmative action) from packages presented to employers in favour of general wage and benefits increases desired by male majorities in many unions.

SIZE OF BUSINESS. Feminists and labourites rejected higher gender-predominance thresholds for smaller places of business, since this would give employers an opportunity to avoid equal-pay legislation by hiring a few more men in women-dominated jobs.[33] In the Manitoba Pay Equity Act, job comparisons between female- and male-dominated jobs are allowed only if there are at least 10 employees in each job class. The Manitoba Equal Pay Coalition wanted a relaxation of this rule so that for public-sector employers with fewer than 500 employees, the numerical mark of

10 would not have to be reached in order to apply the act.[34] This would have broadened the application of the law to women in small workplaces and occupations with few employees.

NO MALE CUT-OFF. Since men are more finely distributed among a greater number of occupational categories than women, it would be difficult to achieve a male-predominance figure of 70 per cent, and many women would therefore be prevented from comparing their jobs with male categories.[35] As a result, the Ontario Equal Pay Coalition took the position that since 'women generally work in jobs which have more incumbents than men's jobs, women must be able to compare their work to any male-dominated job, regardless of the number of male incumbents.'[36]

PAY EQUITY FOR MEN. Finally, both trade unions and feminist organizations pushed to extend to men the right to demand pay adjustments under equal-pay legislation. The Ontario Secondary School Teachers' Federation and its Provincial Status of Women Committee argued in a joint pamphlet that 'many men are trapped in jobs which their employers consider "women's work" and suffer low wages as a result (a custodian in a nursing home is a good example). Any legislation must remedy their situation.'[37] Other examples are male switchboard operators and kitchen help (traditionally female-dominated occupations) in male penal institutions, or a sole male receptionist-typist (again a female-dominated job) in a manufacturing plant.[38] In its presentation to the Ontario Consultation Panel on Pay Equity, the Ontario Nurses Association stated that it 'strongly objects to the premise that "comparisons are to address the valuation of 'women's work' only" . . . the legislation should not preclude any possibility that men can have recourse to pay equity.'[39] Neo-conservative anti-feminist organizations, such as REAL Women of Canada, the National Citizens' Coalition, and the Manitoba Progressive Party, argued that pay-equity legislation is sexist because it would discriminate against men in denying them the right to lodge equal-pay complaints with human-rights commissions or pay-equity tribunals.[40]

2. Establishment

Practically all pay-equity legislation allows comparisons between jobs only *within* an employer's establishment. The difficulty concerns the definition of 'establishment'. In the Ontario *Green Paper on Pay Equity*, three options for defining the boundaries of an employer's establishment were discussed.[41]

1. Under the *geographic* definition, jobs could be compared only within a specific geographic boundary (such as a municipality) in an establishment of the company; if the company had establishments in different geographic localities, jobs could not be compared between these localities, even if they were of equal value to the employer. The Canadian Human Rights Commission adopted a geographic definition of 'establishment' in its interpretation guide to the Canadian Human Rights Act.[42] This example was followed by the Ontario government in its 1987 Pay Equity Act, although it left open the possibility of altering the geographic definition through agreement by management and labour.[43] In order to determine the boundaries of a geographic establishment, it is necessary to identify the employer (who is not defined in the Ontario Act). In 1989, the Ontario Pay Equity Hearings Tribunal—which was set up under the Act to hear complaints—decided that the following four criteria should be used for identifying the employer.

1. WHO HAS OVERALL FINANCIAL RESPONSIBILITY?
Who has responsibility for the budget? Who bears the financial burden of compensation practices, and the burden of wage adjustments under the Act? Who is responsible for the financial administration of the budget? What is the shareholder investment or ownership? Who bears the responsibility of picking up the deficit or benefiting from the surplus?

2. WHO HAS RESPONSIBILITY FOR COMPENSATION PRACTICES?
Who sets the overall policy for compensation practices? Who attaches the value of a job to its skill, effort, responsibility and working conditions? What is the labour relations reality, who negotiates the wages and benefits with the union or sets the wage rate in a non-unionized setting?

3. WHAT IS THE NATURE OF THE BUSINESS, THE SERVICE OR THE ENTERPRISE?
What is the core activity of the business, service or enterprise? Is the work in dispute integral to the organization or is it severable or dispensible? Who decides what labour is to be undertaken and attaches that responsibility to a particular job? What are the employees' perceptions of who is the employer?

4. WHAT IS MOST CONSISTENT WITH ACHIEVING THE PURPOSE OF [THE] PAY EQUITY ACT?
The purpose of this Act is to redress systemic gender discrimina-

tion in compensation for work performed by employees in female job classes. Systemic gender discrimination in compensation shall be identified by undertaking comparisons between each female job class in an establishment and the male job classes in the establishment in terms of compensation and in terms of the value of the work performed.[44]

2. According to the *functional* definition, jobs can be compared only between employees covered by a common set of company personnel and compensation policies; if employees within the same establishment are covered by different policies, they cannot compare their jobs for the purposes of achieving pay equity.

3. Under the *corporate* definition, the broadest comparison within a company is possible: the different operations of the same employer are treated as the same establishment, and comparisons can be conducted between such operations.

(a) The business position

Business has wanted to restrict the application of pay-equity legislation to comparisons between jobs within establishments defined as narrowly as possible, and has generally favoured a restrictive interpretation of the geographic definition. In the US, business has argued that departments and divisions within an employer's establishment constitute 'establishments' in their own right, so that comparisons between women's and men's jobs can be made only within those departments and divisions; given the gendered nature of the social division of labour within establishments, this would severely curtail the possibility of correcting women's low wages.[45] In Canada, business has made two arguments. First, some organizations representing specific business sectors, such as the auto-parts manufacturing industry, have rejected *any* definition of 'establishment' because they are so unalterably opposed to equal pay for work of equal value.[46] Second, business has proposed to locate the functional definition *within* the geographic one: job comparisons could be conducted only among employees covered by the same classification plan, common pay plan, and collective bargaining unit within a specific geographical region of the corporation.[47] Using this criterion, women in an office bargaining unit of a department store in one city could not compare their jobs to those of men in a sales bargaining unit either at the same store or at a different store of the same chain in another city. Such comparisons would cross both functional and geographic divisions, even though both divisions are still within the same 'corporate' firm. Personnel managers in the new middle class have aligned themselves with this second business position.[48]

(b) The labour-feminist position

Most feminist organizations and trade unions have rejected the geographic and functional definitions of 'establishment' and favoured a broad interpretation of the corporate definition.[49] Organizations such as the Ottawa Women's Lobby have suggested a broad corporate definition of 'establishment' defined by the boundaries of the province of Ontario, with no internal geographic division of the employer's establishment between regions of the province.[50] The reasons for this position are as follows.

GEOGRAPHIC DEFINITION. The geographic definition would not allow comparisons between women and men in different areas of a province, even between those working for the same employer. This would destroy the standardization of compensation systems institutionalized between regions—for example, within the Ontario government—and the centralized collective bargaining institutionalized in Ontario's seventy-two hospitals.[51] The geographic definition would also invite employers to engage in 'gerrymandering' by moving some divisions to a different location to avoid equal-pay comparisons between divisions.[52] Among women's organizations, perhaps the most accepting attitude towards the geographic definition was that of the Canadian Association of Women Executives, which was willing to restrict job comparisons to those between 'different locations of the same employer in the same geographic region'.[53]

FUNCTIONAL DEFINITION. Trade unions and feminist groups have opposed the functional definition because it would not allow job comparisons between bargaining units, between unionized and non-unionized workers, between full-time and part-time workers on a pro-rata basis, or between employees under different compensation plans within the same establishment. Often, in such cases, one group is predominantly female and its counterpart is predominantly male. There has been fear that employers could try to avoid pay-equity legislation by putting female part-time workers in different bargaining units from male full-time workers, a practice often condoned in the rulings of labour boards.[54]

RELATED ESTABLISHMENTS. Feminist and labour organizations

have been concerned about such establishments as banks, where most employees are women who cannot find any male workers in their workplace with whom to make comparisons for the purpose of pay equity.[55] To solve these kinds of problems, feminist organizations and trade unions in Ontario wanted a broad corporate definition of 'establishment', as in the Ontario Labour Relations and Employment Standards Acts, that would allow limited comparisons between establishments that are 'related';[56] such comparisons were intended to prevent employers from avoiding pay-equity legislation by restructuring their corporations.[57] Fear was expressed that employers might try to contract some work out; this would prevent women cleaners working for a private company from comparing their jobs with those of cleaners in a company with whom they have a contract. The 'related' definition was designed to allow such comparisons.[58] A special problem was presented by franchises: did franchises within the same chain constitute separate establishments or a single establishment? The Ottawa Women's Lobby took the position that this should be determined by the source of decisions about pay and the standardization of work across franchises. If decisions about pay were made locally, within each franchise, each would be treated as a separate establishment; if there was standardization of work across franchises within the same chain, they would be treated as a single establishment.[59] The linkage of work between different establishments was also used as a criterion for outside comparisons. In Toronto the Metro Action Committee on Public Violence Against Women and Children wanted comparisons 'outside establishments', and the exclusion of the exemption of small workplaces, so that women counsellors in small rape crisis centres and transition homes 'working with female victims of violence' could compare their jobs with those of male prison workers 'who guard the male assailants'.[60] The Ontario Nurses Association, which represented nurses 'employed in hospitals, public health units, nursing homes, homes for the aged, VON, medical clinics and industry', took special exception to the restrictive 'within establishment' comparisons, because 'a nurse is a nurse is a nurse', no matter what establishment she works in.[61] All such 'related' and 'outside' comparisons were rejected out of hand by business associations and individual employers.

CHILD-CARE CENTRES. As the Ontario Coalition for Better Daycare has pointed out, child-care centres present a special problem because 99 per cent of their workers are women.[62] How were women child-care workers, who in 1983 earned an average of $13,000 a year, expected to qualify for pay-equity adjustments when there were hardly any male jobs in their own establishments to use as a basis for comparison? In most cases, the only male jobs were janitor's or manager's, and these might not be used for comparison purposes because they were not equal or comparable in value to the child-care worker's (this point is taken up again in Chapter 5). Because of this (and the small size of many child-care centres), the Coalition estimated that 86 per cent of child-care workers would be excluded from the proposed Ontario pay-equity act.[63] To ensure that this did not happen, the Coalition asked the government to adopt the following measures. First, it should accept the broadest possible definition of 'corporate establishment'. Second, since even this would not help most child-care workers, the act should include a special provision in three parts. (a) Special funding would be provided by the government for pay-equity settlements in child-care centres. The reason for this was the danger that municipalities, faced with the increased costs associated with pay-equity settlements, would 'decide to reduce their purchase of day care services'.[64] (b) The definition of 'establishment' for child-care centres would be widened to include the 'broader public sector' on the grounds that all child-care centres received either direct or indirect funding from the government, and because child-care centres had been included under Ontario's 1976 wage-restraint agreement with the federal government as part of the 'broader public sector'. Defining the establishment for child-care centres as the broader public sector would make it relatively easy for women child-care workers to find male job classes to serve as bases of comparison in pay-equity cases. (c) 'Mechanisms could easily be introduced into the legislation to allow workers in all-female establishments the opportunity to receive pay adjustments equivalent to pay equity adjustments made to day care workers employed in a workplace where they were able to compare their job class to a male job class for pay equity purposes.'[65] The Ontario government adopted none of these measures (nor has any other government). The result was that in 1989, within a year after the Act came into force, the Ontario Pay Equity Commission had to go back to the government to ask for changes in the legislation to deal with predominantly female establishments such as child-care centres.[66]

3. Sector

(a) Legislation

Most pay-equity legislation, especially in North America, covers only the public sector or a part of it; it is still rare to find 'equal pay for work of equal value' applied to the private sector.[67] The equal-value provision contained in the Canadian Human Rights Act covers 'all federal government departments, agencies and Crown corporations and . . . businesses and industries under federal jurisdiction such as banks, airlines, interprovincial railway companies and trucking and uranium mining companies, and . . . the Canadian Armed Forces and the RCMP'.[68] These organizations employ about 10 per cent of the Canadian labour force. Thus only a tiny part of the private sector is covered by the Canadian federal legislation. The Manitoba Pay Equity Act of 1985 covers most but not all of the public sector. Included under the Act are the civil service, Crown entities, and such external agencies as four universities and the major hospitals; excluded are smaller health agencies, school boards, municipalities, and persons under contract to the provincial government, as well as the entire private sector.[69] In total, the act covers about 60,000 public-sector employees.[70] The 1988 Nova Scotia Pay Equity Act covers much of the public sector: 'civil servants, correctional service employees, highway workers and employees of the Victoria General and the Nova Scotia Hospitals'; other hospitals, Crown corporations (such as Sydney Steel Corporation), and school boards. The entire private sector is excluded. The 1988 Prince Edward Island pay-equity legislation is similar in that it covers the broader public sector: civil service, Crown corporations, hospitals, nursing homes that receive government funds, the University of Prince Edward Island, Holland College, the Charlottetown Area Development Corporation, the Summerside Waterfront Development Corporation, and any other organization receiving government funds. Again, the private sector is excluded. The non-legislative negotiated agreement between the public-sector unions and the Newfoundland government covers only provincial civil servants, the hospitals, and Crown corporations.[71] In Ontario the Liberal government of Premier David Peterson had been installed partly on the basis of the 1985 accord with the NDP, which promised to support the Liberals in power in return for their agreement to certain principles, one of which was the introduction of equal pay for work of equal value in both the public and private sectors.[72] In 1987 Ontario passed a single integrated pay-equity act that would eventually cover the entire public sector and much of the private sector. But the coverage is to be introduced only gradually: in 1990 for all of the public sector (see the definitions of 'state' in Appendix A); in 1991 for private-sector companies with 500 or more employees; in 1992 for private-sector firms with 100 to 499 employees; in 1993 for private-sector companies with between 50 and 99 employees; and in 1994 for private-sector businesses with 10 to 49 employees. Private-sector firms with fewer than 10 employees are exempt from the Ontario Pay Equity Act.[73] In considering together all of these acts, several specialists view the 1987 Ontario Act as the strongest because it is the only one to extend the principle of pro-activity to the private sector.

(b) Class and gender struggles

The first line of defence by business has been to oppose the application of pay-equity legislation to any sector of the economy; the second, to restrict it to the public or state sector; the third, suggested by small business, to restrict it to the largest corporations in the most concentrated sectors of the economy. Feminists and labourites have rejected all three defences with the argument that all women must be covered; this is particularly important given that many low-paid women are found in small corporations in the private sector.

THE BUSINESS POSITION. In the US, business associations have feared that the implementation of pay equity among government workers in several states as well as the possibility of its introduction at the federal level would create pressures for its later extension to the private sector. The National Association of Manufacturers called even the study of gender discrimination among federal government workers 'a misguided first step toward imposing comparable worth on the private sector'.[74] In support of this point, the American Society for Personnel Administration warned that job-evaluation studies imply the legal obligation to implement their findings through pay equity in the private sector.[75] In a 1985 article, a personnel consultant in Seattle, Washington, whose company had completed 150 job-evaluation studies, mostly for private-sector clients, stated that

> almost none of his clients have ever attempted to introduce equal-pay policies. 'I could count on the fingers of 1 hand the private firms

that have implemented pay-equity programs . . . . Most private employers see how much it would cost to eliminate the gaps, and back off . . . . implementing equal-pay legislation in the private sector is political dynamite. It's a public-sector issue.'[76]

In Canada some business associations, such as the Ottawa-Carleton Board of Trade, the Board of Trade of Metropolitan Toronto, and the Retail Council of Canada, argued that pay equity should be tried out in the public sector first, before any trial—at some indefinite point in the future—in the private sector.[77] Other business associations were completely against the extension of equal pay for work of equal value to the private sector. Fearing that the public-sector Manitoba Pay Equity Act might be interpreted as applying to the private sector, the Winnipeg Chamber of Commerce demanded that all references to the private sector be struck from the Act.[78] The Canadian Manufacturers' Association and REAL Women objected to the projected Ontario legislative acts on equal pay for work of equal value on the grounds that no comparable legislation existed in the private sector in the US; the Manufacturers' Association added that under Quebec's Charter of Human Rights and Freedoms, job evaluations in the private sector for the purposes of equal pay were extremely rare.[79] (However, job evaluations are normally done in the private sector under complaints-based legislation.) There was also an attempt by such organizations as the Canadian Federation of Independent Business and the Canadian Organization of Small Business to have small businesses in the private sector exempt from any pay-equity legislation on the grounds that they could not afford the cost of establishing job-evaluation systems.[80] This principle had already been enshrined in earlier bills on pay equity presented but not passed in the United States Congress.[81] The Retail Council of Canada proposed excluding from pay-equity acts businesses with fewer than 10 employees, and applying a very high gender predominance threshold on other small businesses, perhaps those with 10 to 100 employees.[82]

THE FEMINIST-LABOUR POSITION. In Ontario the feminist-labour alliance wanted pay-equity legislation to cover *all* workers, whether they were employed in the public or private sector, in large corporations or small businesses,[83] but in the United States there was not the same demand. Instead, the National Treasury Employees Union and Federally Employed Women argued in favour of a separate public-sector bill, partly on the grounds that it would provide a model that the private sector could follow.[84] This is not to imply, of course, that American trade unions or feminists were opposed to comparable worth in the private sector; rather, the opposition from business, the neo-conservatives, and many sectors of the state was so strong that the public-sector initiative was seen merely as a first step towards the more comprehensive implementation of comparable-worth legislation.

In Canada, perhaps because the principle of equal pay for work of equal value was somewhat more institutionalized, trade unions and feminist organizations demanded a single piece of legislation covering the broader public sector and the entire private sector.[85] In Ontario there was opposition to separate pieces of legislation for the civil service, the broader public sector, and the private sector, and a demand for a single piece of legislation covering all three. In particular, trade unions and feminist groups objected to the artificial exclusion from the Ontario Public Service Pay Equity Bill of such public-sector agencies as school boards, municipalities, hospitals, universities, and municipal day-care centres.[86] The Canadian Union of Public Employers (CUPE) feared that by initially presenting only the Public Sector Pay Equity Bill, the Ontario government would later lump public-sector CUPE workers in with the private sector.[87] The Service Employees International Union, although supporting the incorporation of the broader public sector in the original Ontario public-sector bill, was one of the few unions that did not demand a single bill incorporating both sectors.[88] In Manitoba there was feminist-labour opposition to the exclusion from the Pay Equity Act of small (especially rural) health agencies, school boards, local government districts, and municipalities.[89] Two reasons in particular were offered for objecting to the private-sector exclusions in Manitoba and Ontario. First, the wage gap is larger in the private than the public sector. Second, the wage gap is larger for non-unionized than unionized women; given the lower rate of unionization among women in the private sector, the latter are especially vulnerable and need some legislative assistance to gain equal pay.[90]

Feminist organizations and trade unions also worried about the possible exclusion of women in small workplaces, such as day-care centres and small social-service agencies, and in clerical and secretarial positions in small firms.[91] They offered three grounds for objecting to the exclusion of such workplaces. First, a large proportion of women work in such establishments: in Ontario, 30 per cent of women work in establishments with fewer than 20 employees, and 49 per cent in establishments with fewer than 100.[92] Second, neither the Canadian nor the Quebec equal-value legislation exempted small employers. Third, to exempt small businesses 'would encourage employers to fragment their business structures'.[93] The Federation of Women Teachers' Associations of Ontario bluntly pointed out that 'the very suggestion that small employers should be spared the necessity of paying women for the value of their work is an indication of the discriminatory attitudes which confront women in many aspects of their life in the work force'.[94]

EXEMPTIONS: ALLOWABLE GENDER DISCRIMINATION?[95]

Practically all pay-equity legislation in North America includes lists of exemptions allowing for different rates of pay for women and men, even if their jobs are of equal value or are similar or substantially similar.[96] For all exemptions, it is assumed that direct gender discrimination against women does not exist (i.e., 'gender neutrality'). At least twelve different categories of exemptions have been mentioned in different pieces of legislation: length of employment or gender-neutral seniority (it is quite acceptable for men with more years of uninterrupted employment or seniority to earn higher wages than women with fewer years);[97] overtime (women cannot use men's greater overtime earnings in pay-equity job comparisons);[98] job performance or merit systems (the earnings of men resulting from superior job performance or higher merit ratings cannot be a basis for job comparisons for the purposes of pay equity);[99] quantity and quality of production, or productivity (men's higher earnings resulting from bonus and piece-rate systems that reward greater productivity cannot be subject to pay-equity comparisons);[100] job experience (men's higher pay resulting from skills learned on the job cannot be a basis of pay-equity disputes);[101] regional labour-market conditions, or temporary labour shortages (employers are permitted to pay higher wages to certain male employees who are in temporary short supply or in certain regional labour markets);[102] physical or mental capacity of the worker (employers are allowed to pay higher wages to men with higher native talent or physical strength);[103] non-seasonal casual work amounting to less than one-third of normal full-time hours, temporary training positions, student positions, and rehabilitation positions (it is not discriminatory for employers to assign lower rates of pay to workers in these types of positions, even though the majority of them may be women);[104] 'red-circling' (in the context of technological change, employers may downgrade jobs and freeze or limit the increase in the wages of certain high-paid male workers by declaring their skills obsolete, thereby avoiding comparisons of their wages with lower-paid women's wages);[105] differences in bargaining strength between unions (after pay equity has been achieved, in Ontario it is legitimate for male job rates to increase faster than those of unionized and non-unionized women on the basis of the greater bargaining strength of the men's union);[106] factors 'other than sex' (this allows employers to introduce arguments not covered by the other exemptions);[107] and a discretionary power awarded to judges to deem any other factor an acceptable justification for paying unequal wages.[108]

Business generally wanted the longest possible list of exceptions written into equal-pay legislation; labour and feminist organizations, the shortest. The business point of view was succinctly stated by the Canadian Manufacturers' Association (with considerable backing from other business associations), which demanded that the Ontario legislation include the following exceptions: length of service or seniority, performance rating systems or merit, 'red circling', training assignments, regional rates of pay and temporary labour shortages, 'supply and demand for the skills in question, differences in relative bargaining strength, and any other non gender-based factors *which an employer may consider*'.[109] Personnel managers in the new middle class took almost the same position as business.[110] The feminist-labour alliance was generally opposed to the exemptions. In the words of the Ontario Equal Pay Coalition: 'These exemptions provide loopholes that employers will likely use to avoid paying women equally. Every exclusion denies thousands of women the protection of the legislation.'[111] Most trade unions and employee associations were willing to accept only one exception—seniority—provided it was gender-neutral—although the meaning and reality of 'gender-neutral' seniority were unclear.[112] The Public Service Alliance of Canada (PSAC) and the Ontario Nurses Association were two of the few unions in Canada to oppose *all* exemptions. PSAC took this position because of its unhappy experience with the exemptions listed under the guidelines of the Canadian Human Rights Act.[113]

There was a curious coming together of the labour movement and the anti-feminist neo-conservatives, and a split within the women's movement, on the question of 'red-circling' and merit. Trade unions and the anti-feminist neo-conservatives both wanted to protect male wages and prevent the demotion of men's jobs and wages to the level of women's, but for different reasons: the labour movement viewed this as a way of garnering support for pay-equity legislation from its largely male constituency; the anti-feminist neo-conservatives saw it as a means of preventing the passage of such legislation. Within the women's movement there was a class split: trade-union women, such as Organized Working Women, argued against merit as an exception, the demotion of male jobs, and freezing or reduction of men's wages;[114] business women agreed to accept both merit and demotion as legitimate exceptions to equal-value legislation. The NDP, one political expression of trade unions, pushed for two exceptions— seniority and quantity of production—when it tried several times in the early 1980s to introduce equal-value amendments to the Ontario Employment Standards Act.[115]

COLLECTIVE BARGAINING

Whether collective bargaining between employers and employees is incorporated in pay-equity legislation depends on the model adopted. In human-rights complaint-based laws, collective bargaining receives little official recognition. Responsibility for implementing equal pay for equal work or equal pay for work of equal value rests with the employer; the state acts as a monitoring agency to which employees may take their complaints. Trade unions may act as third-party interveners and launch complaints on behalf of employees, but they receive no legal sanction to negotiate job-evaluation or pay-equity plans with management.[116] In contrast, in both the pro-active and integration models, collective-bargaining negotiations are a central mechanism for implementing job-evaluation and pay-equity plans.[117] If a union does not exist in a particular establishment (which is the case for the majority of women in the private sector in Ontario), the employer herself/himself is obligated to devise a pay-equity plan.[118]

Business and the feminist-labour alliance took different positions on the extent and nature of the integration of collective bargaining in pay-equity legislation. Business wanted to protect the sanctity of the collective-bargaining process from any 'further state intervention'; it thus objected to any equal-pay legislation that could interfere with or override this process. It predicted that if equal-pay legislation were introduced, chaos would reign in collective negotiations between management and labour. Trade unions and feminist organizations, on the other hand, invited such intervention with open arms, on the grounds that in the past they had not been able to achieve pay equity through collective bargaining and needed some legislative teeth to back their demands. Six dimensions of this struggle will be outlined.

1. The union push for pay equity

In both Canada and the US, many trade unions have attempted to incorporate pay-equity clauses into their collective labour agreements, and at times have gone on strike over equal pay for work of equal value. On the other hand, it should be noted that this is a fairly recent phenomenon, dating back no further than the Second World War. It is difficult to know precisely how important pay equity is to trade unions in relation to other collective-bargaining issues. In the US it has been estimated that fewer than one-third of trade unions consider pay equity a major bargaining issue.[119] As early as the Second World War several American unions, such as the United Electrical Workers, were bargaining for the insertion of equal-pay-for-equal-work clauses in their contracts, though their demands did not extend to equal pay for work of equal value.[120] The most renowned case of American trade-union support for pay equity was the suit brought by the American Federation of State, County and Municipal Employees (AFSCME) against the State of Washington. To back up its collective-bargaining demand for pay equity, in 1982 AFSCME sued the state for discriminating against its women employees;[121] however, the state appealed the decision and had it overturned in 1985.[122] Other unions, such as the Communications Workers of America, the National Treasury Employees Union, and the Service Employees International Union, have won pay-equity adjustments for women employees through direct collective-bargaining negotiations with management.[123]

In Canada, after a history of negotiating collective agreements containing separate wage scales for women and men,[124] trade unions have become much more active and forceful in adopting *policies*, often in the form of convention resolutions, supporting pay equity at the bargaining table. But this is not the same as achieving actual pay-equity clauses in collective agreements. In 1980 the Canadian Labour Congress adopted a resolution encouraging its affiliates to negotiate equal starting rates between male- and female-dominated occupations covered by separate collective agreements in the same establishment.[125] In the same year, the British Columbia Federation of Labour adopted a resolution encouraging its affiliates to negotiate equal pay for work of equal value in their collective agreements.[126] The Canadian Union of Public Employees (CUPE) at its National Conventions adopted equal pay for equal work in 1971 and equal pay for work of equal value in 1975.[127] In 1981 it led 10,000 civic workers in the first strike over equal pay in Canadian history against the municipalities on the British Columbia lower mainland.[128] In 1986, in conferences and workshops across the country, CUPE made 'equal pay' a central priority for new negotiations.[129] By this time, the union had developed a national co-ordinated strategy on pay equity.[130] In 1975 the Civil Service Association of Ontario, the forerunner to the Ontario Public Service Employees Union, was unsuccessful in lobbying the provincial government to insert equal pay for substantially similar work in all provincial government contracts;[131] by the 1980s it was supporting equal pay for work of equal value. Before the Manitoba government introduced its Pay Equity Bill in 1985, the Government Employees Association successfully negotiated the setting up of a 'joint union-management committee to deal with the issue of pay equity in the Civil Service'.[132] The Women's Committee of the New Brunswick Federation of Labour successfully organized a workshop on equal pay for work of equal value in 1984. The Federation started a series of meetings with the New Brunswick Advisory Council on the Status of Women on ways of implementing equal pay for work of equal value, and between 1984 and 1986 pay equity became a central issue in collective negotiations with school boards and personal-care homes across the province.[133] Since the mid-1970s, the Newfoundland and Labrador Federation of Labour has supported equal pay for work of equal value.[134] Other labour organizations in Canada, such as the National Union of Provincial Government Employees, the United Steelworkers of America, the Canadian Auto Workers, and the Manitoba and Ontario Federations of Labour, strongly support the implementation of equal pay for work of equal value through direct collective negotiations.[135]

Convention resolutions and statements of intention concerning pay equity are one thing; their implementation in collective agreements is quite another, especially given the resistance shown by employers. Only 3.7 per cent (45 out of 1,231) of the contracts running from 1986 to 1988 and filed with Labour Canada's Bureau of Labour Information included pay-equity clauses (that is, either equal pay for equal work, or equal pay for work of equal value). These contracts covered all industries in Canada having 500 or more employees 'plus those under federal jurisdiction covering 200 to 499 employees'.[136] Seventy-three per cent of the 45 contracts containing pay-equity clauses were in the public sector, even though its workforce is smaller than the private sector's. Three unions in Canada had the lion's share of the pay-equity contracts: CUPE (33 per cent), the British Columbia Government Employees Union (20 per cent), and the United Food and Commercial Workers International Union (16 per cent); most of the latter union's pay-equity contract clauses were with Canada Safeway in Alberta. In the private sector, 67 per cent of all pay-equity contracts were in the retail sector, all in British Columbia, Alberta, and Saskatchewan. They were negotiated by the Retail, Wholesale and Department Store Union in Saskatchewan and the Retail-Wholesale Union in British Columbia (both of which are affiliated with the International Longshoremen's and Warehousemen's Union), or by the United Food and Commercial Workers International Union. In the public sector, the pay-equity contracts were distributed as follows: civil service (33 per cent), education (21 per cent), municipal (21 per cent), health (15 per cent), and Crown corporations (9 per cent). Only 20 per cent (9 out of 45) of all the pay-equity contracts had equal-pay-for-work-of-equal-value clauses, all of them in the public sector. With the exception of one contract in British Columbia, negotiated by CUPE at the University of British Columbia, all equal-value contracts were in provinces whose governments had moved in the direction of equal value: three each in Ontario and Newfoundland, and one each in Manitoba and Nova Scotia. This lends credence to the union argument that legislative support is important in negotiating equal-value clauses. CUPE negotiated five of them; the remaining four were negotiated by the Newfoundland Association of Public Employees, the Newfoundland and Labrador Nurses Union, the Manitoba Government Employees Association, and the Staff Association at Dalhousie College and University in Halifax, Nova

Scotia. In 1986 the Newfoundland Association of Public Employees negotiated 'a clause concerning equal pay for work of equal value between domestic workers (99% female) and janitors (99% male)'.[137] By subsector in the public sector, the equal-value contracts in Canada were in education (three), the civil service (two), health (two), housing (one), and at the municipal level (one). This meagre record suggests that unions face an uphill battle in order to win strong equal-value clauses in their collective agreements.

One union that has had a history of lodging equal-pay complaints under Section 11 of the Canadian Human Rights Act is the Public Service Alliance of Canada (PSAC). It has been forced to go this route because the federal government has resisted collective bargaining to institute equal pay for work of equal value for its employees. Because of the complaints model in the Canadian Human Rights Act, PSAC has had to lodge separate complaints for each occupational-group case of alleged discriminatory pay.[138] In many instances, after a long drawn-out conciliation process with the Human Rights Commission and the Treasury Board, it achieved success. For example, in 1979 PSAC launched a complaint that (female-predominant) government librarians were receiving 20 per cent less in salaries for performing work of value equal to that of (male-predominant) historical researchers. In 1980 the women librarians won equalization adjustments of between $500 and $2,500, with back-pay compensation of $5,900. Again in 1979, PSAC complained that workers in (female-predominant) food, laundry, and personal services were earning 30 per cent less than those in equal-valued (male-predominant) messenger, custodial, building, and store services jobs. It was not until 1982 that the complaint was settled, with 2,300 women workers receiving an average of $5,000 in increased pay. Ultimately, over 9,000 women benefitted from this settlement.[139] In 1985 the Treasury Board and PSAC set up a joint Union Management Committee to make recommendations on equal pay for work of equal value in the federal sector. PSAC pushed for a re-evaluation of all 67 occupational groups in the federal government sector. Although the Treasury Board remained resistant to bargaining and implementing equal pay for work of equal value in the federal government, the Human Rights Commission and the Women's Bureau of Labour Canada have been more supportive.[140]

2. Separate negotiations

Trade unions and feminist organizations such as Organized Working Women wanted equal pay for work of equal value to be negotiated separately, outside the regular collective-bargaining negotiation process, because they feared that employers would play off pay equity against other bargaining chips.[141] The Ontario Equal Pay Coalition suggested that the separate pay-equity settlement, after being reached across all bargaining units within an establishment, could then be integrated into the regular collective-bargaining process of each unit.[142] Encountering resistance to these proposals from employers, however, unions realized that they would have to lobby the state in order to create an equal-value law to back up their bargaining demands.[143] In this campaign feminists and trade unions demanded a separate piece of pay-equity legislation (rather than the insertion of pay-equity clauses in human-rights and employment-standards laws, as had been the practice in the past) and the amendment of provincial labour and first-contract arbitration laws to ensure that equal-value clauses would appear in all collective labour agreements.[144]

One of the few trade unions in Canada to oppose the integration of collective bargaining and legislation on equal pay for work of equal value is the Christian Labour Association of Canada (CLAC).[145] To the right of the majority of the Canadian labour movement (with the exception of the craft unions in the Canadian Federation of Labour), the CLAC is a tiny independent quasi-trade union with 6,513 members spread among 61 locals, mainly in Ontario, British Columbia, and Alberta.[146] Its locals are found in construction, transportation, food distribution, forestry, manufacturing, and nursing and rest homes.[147] The Association advocates Christian principles based on the Bible in the workplace, harmony and partnership between labour and management, limited government, and protection of marriage and the family. It opposes the right to strike[148] and is against equal-value legislation mainly on the grounds that in implementing it, the state would be overreaching the limits of its authority and destroying non-state 'intermediate' institutions such as business, family, and the church.[149]

This position of the CLAC is consistent with the anti-feminist neo-conservatives represented by such groups as the National Citizens' Coalition and REAL Women of Canada, and by several business associations. Business predicted that pay-equity legislation would disrupt the 'normal' collective-bargaining process, and sought to limit as much as possible the extent to which the two could be integrated.[150] For example, the Ontario Chamber of Commerce, the Ontario Mining Association, and the Canadian Manufacturers' Association wanted all workers covered by collective-bargaining agreements to be *excluded* from pay-equity legislation.[151] Employers such as the Metropolitan Toronto Board of Trade, Cummings Signs, Workwear Corporation, and the London University Hospital warned that if they were forced to carry out pay-equity negotiations, either as part of the normal collective-bargaining process or separate from it, they would simply hold back an amount of money for pay equity and make it unavailable for general wage increases.[152] The Metropolitan Toronto Board of Trade warned that the consequences of this would be 'the possibility of heightening tensions, inter- and intra-union conflict, delays in reaching settlements, more and longer strikes and the resultant loss of productivity.'[153] Personnel managers in the new middle class also wanted all employees covered by collective agreements, and thus all unionized employees, to be excluded from equal pay for work of equal value.[154]

3. Separate bargaining units

There was a deep split in Ontario between the feminist-labour alliance and business over the question of bargaining units. One problem was that bargaining units, often because of state labour-board rulings, frequently mirror the marked gendered division of labour within an establishment: separate bargaining units are often set up between office and clerical workers (women) and shop-floor manual workers (men); between inside workers (women) and outside workers (men); between nursing assistants (women) and technical workers (men); and between cleaners (women) and janitors and maintenance workers (men). In addition, more than one union may represent employees in an establishment, with one union containing mostly women and another mostly men, and non-unionized employees are more likely to be women than are unionized employees in the same establishment. Pay inequities cross these divisions so that female-predominant units receive less pay than comparable male units.[155] Pay-equity legislation is of little use in correcting such inequities unless it is applied across bargaining units and between organized and unorganized workers.

The Ontario government, in its *Green Paper on Pay Equity*, initially suggested a solution to this problem through a phase-in plan in which job comparisons would be allowed only within each bargaining unit and within groups of non-unionized workers in a first stage; in a second stage, comparisons would be allowed across these categories within the same establishment.[156] The feminist-labour alliance rejected any suggestion of a phase-in plan: it wanted immediate collective-bargaining negotiations across all bargaining units to achieve job-evaluation and pay-equity plans that would be applicable to all workers in an establishment, regardless of which bargaining unit they were in or whether they were organized or unorganized; where agreement on these plans could not be reached, arbitration was to be used.[157]

Business and employer groups, however, including the Ontario Chamber of Commerce, the Metropolitan Toronto Board of Trade, the Apparel Manufacturers' Association, Polysar, and the Canadian Manufacturers' Association, argued against bargaining over pay equity across units and between organized and unorganized workers.[158] If the state was determined to incorporate across-unit comparisons, then public-sector employers such as the North York Board of Education and the Municipality of Metropolitan Toronto wanted it brought in by phases, as suggested in the Ontario *Green Paper on Pay Equity*.[159] Business offered two main reasons for opposing such job comparisons. First, on a philosophical level, it argued that the integration of collective bargaining and pay equity across bargaining units and between organized and unorganized workers violated employees' 'freedom of choice': such comparisons would 'undermine our entire democratic history of freedom of association' because some bargaining units would have contracts imposed on them by other bargaining units with whom they did not particularly want to be associated and whose priorities they did not share.[160] Second, on a more practical level, business predicted that the integration of collective bargaining and pay equity across bargaining units would lead to economic chaos in the form of wage spirals. If predominantly female bargaining units or unorganized workers had their pay raised 'artificially' through pay-equity legislation, stronger male-dominated bargaining units might respond by increasing their wage demands in order to maintain the traditional wage gap. The result would be an unchecked wage spiral.[161] The Ontario Chamber of Commerce foresaw a 'whipsawing and leapfrogging of wage rates between groups', whether organized or unorganized.[162]

4. Relative bargaining power

Business and the feminist-labour alliance have also disagreed over the role of trade unions and their 'relative bargaining power' in correcting pay inequities. Three quite contradictory arguments have come from the business side. One is that unions might be responsible for unequal pay because they have not tried hard enough to eliminate the wage gap in unionized establishments.[163] Another is that equal-pay legislation is unnecessary, since the mechanism to negotiate the end of the wage gap already exists in the form of unions![164] The third is that the 'relative bargaining power' of unions has to be curbed because they are responsible for the wage spirals discussed in the preceding paragraph. Some Canadian business associations proposed making 'relative bargaining power' an exception to pay-equity legislation.[165] The feminist-labour alliance argued strongly against such an exception, contending that 'relative bargaining power' is gender-related in two respects: first, male bargaining units often have more marketable skills, which enhance their bargaining power; second, male bargaining units and unions are often more militant than women's because of (a) the longer tradition of trade unionism among men, (b) the historical exclusion of women from unions until recent times, (c) women's double work load of wage work and homework, which reduces their participation in unions, and (d) the lower wages of women, which reduce the bargaining power of their units.[166]

In Manitoba and Ontario there was a curious implicit alliance between business and one part of the women's movement over the role of trade unions and their 'relative bargaining power' in addressing pay inequities. Both wanted to remove any reference to unions' right of collective bargaining from pay-equity legislation, but for different reasons: from the business viewpoint, unions would eat into profits and undermine the reserve army of labour; in the view of some women's groups, unions had not used their 'relative bargaining power' sufficiently to correct the gendered wage gap. This latter opinion grew out of a resentment in the women's movement over the way 'women's issues' have historically been shunted aside or given low priority by patriarchal-oriented trade unions. Thus in Ontario the North York

Women Teachers' Association and in Manitoba the Association for Women and the Law (MARL) argued against collective bargaining negotiations over pay equity.[167] MARL requested an amendment to Section 8 of the Manitoba Pay Equity Act so that unions (in this case, the Manitoba Association of Government Employees) would not have the right to collectively negotiate a pay-equity plan with employers; instead, responsibility for implementing such a plan would be placed solely in the hands of the government and the civil service commission. MARL took this position because 'it would be naive to believe that women's interests are always best protected by their unions'. Its co-chairperson, Deborah Carlson, stated that, especially in unions where women do not have very much power, pay equity could be negotiated away for other bargaining items. MARL was not opposed to unions' negotiating the mechanics of the implementation of pay equity, but believed they should not have the legal right to negotiate what constitutes such equity in the first place.[168] It obviously thought women's interests in the area of pay equity were better protected by the state than by unions.

5. Unions' role in reducing the wage gap

The evidence on the role of unions in reducing the gendered wage gap is at best ambiguous. On the one hand, it has been suggested that unions and unionization are positive factors helping to close the wage gap, especially given the recent rapid increase in the unionization of women, the establishment of women's committees and caucuses (which have more effect on union policies regarding women's issues than does the mere election of women officers), and the support by many trade unions for equal pay for work of equal value. Kottis suggests that the reason Italy has the lowest wage gap of six European Economic Community members is its strong trade-union movement, which since 1957 has strongly supported equal pay for women.[169] Ornstein reports that in 1981 women in Canada earned 76 per cent of what men did among unionized workers, but only 56 per cent among non-unionized employees.[170] Using different data, Aach has suggested a smaller wage gap for the same year: among full-year, full-time workers, women earn 86 per cent of men among union members, but only 74 per cent among non-union members.[171] In 1986 the Canadian Auto Workers argued that unions have been beneficial for women, since women in their union made 72 per cent of what men did, in contrast to 62 per cent for non-union women.[172] Ironically, these data seem consistent with both the feminist-labour contention that unions have contributed to the closing of the wage gap and the business contention that male-dominated unions, because of their 'relative bargaining power', manage to maintain the wage-gap differential between themselves and the large number of unorganized women. Although the data do not appear to support other businessmen and the minority of feminists in the women's movement who argue that unions are a negative factor, when statistical controls are introduced (such as industry, occupation, education, job experience, etc.), the union role in closing the wage gap does appear much less significant.[173]

6. Control over the labour process

The fundamental factor underlying the above discussion on the role of unions and collective bargaining in pay equity is the control of the labour process itself. The feminist-labour alliance implicitly recognized that legislated pay equity offered a golden opportunity to wrest greater control over the labour process from management in two ways. First, rather than have employers unilaterally impose job-classification and wage systems on employees, unions would take on a direct role in determining with management the goals and content of both job-evaluation and pay-equity plans and the way they would be implemented in the workplace.[174] Second, individual workers at the grass-roots level would decide on the relative worth of their jobs in any job-evaluation plan that was to form the basis of pay-equity adjustments. This idea was promoted in Canada by the Ontario Federation of Labour, CUPE, and the National Union of Provincial Government Employees, and in the US by the Communications Workers of America.[175] On the other hand, business and neo-conservative sections of the new middle class have suspected that pay equity is a thinly disguised plan by labourites, feminists, and some government bureaucrats to gain control over that part of the labour process dealing with wage determination and job classification.[176]

REORGANIZATION OF WORK: A CAPITAL STRIKE?

The ultimate ace-in-the-hole that business has held over labour is its proprietary control of the means of production. With a loud echo among its anti-feminist neo-conservative allies, it has threatened to reorganize the labour process and even shut production down and move elsewhere in retaliation for any attempt to legislate equal pay for work of equal value. The labour-feminist alliance has responded to several of these threats, but has been curiously silent on others.

1. Investments

One business argument is that the higher costs of labour entailed by pay-equity legislation would scare away new investments in plant and equipment. The Canadian Manufacturers' Association, for instance, warned that the Ontario pay equity legislation would discourage investment in the province,[177] while the Automotive Parts Manufacturers' Association of Canada backed up this statement with an example from its own sector:

> Investment in the parts industry has increased from an average of under $100 million in the late 70s to over $300 million per year currently. The government will potentially be sending a very serious negative message to every foreign investor in the world, especially in the automotive sector where literally dozens of foreign parts companies are currently examining joint ventures, licensing arrangements and equity positions in Canada. We know these foreign companies are concerned because they ask us wherever we go about the chances of Equal Value legislation being implemented.[178]

In 1987 the neo-conservative National Citizens' Coalition warned that pay equity would force investment out of Canada and into the US.[179] The Cornwall Women's Network cited a case within Canada where investment had already moved because of pay-equity legislation. After the enactment in 1975 of the Quebec Charter of Human Rights and Freedoms, containing an equal-value provision, several sewing companies moved from Quebec to the Cornwall area in eastern Ontario to take advantage of the now-cheaper francophone female labour there willing to work at below-minimum wages in factories or in the cottage industry at home. Referring to the Quebec factories that made this move, the Women's Network told the Ontario government: 'They all have openly admitted the reason for moving is to avoid the legislation.' The Network urged speedy passage of pay-equity legislation in Ontario to deal with this situation.[180]

2. Plant shut-downs

On a closely related issue, business has warned that equal pay for work of equal value would force some employers, especially those on the margin of survival, either to go bankrupt or to move their production to the southern US or the Third World.[181] Tony Carlson, Director of Members' Services and Assistant Director of Communications at the Canadian Federation of Independent Business, argued that pay-equity legislation for employers 'could mean packing up the tent and leaving for an area—the United States comes to mind—where supply and demand still have clout'.[182] It is surprising that the labour-feminist alliance has not responded to this threatened link between pay equity and plant shut-downs by suggesting state ownership and/or the socialization of production.

3. Technology

Business and the neo-conservatives have also warned that pay equity would accelerate automation as employers introduce new labour-saving technology to replace higher-priced female labour.[183] The Auto Parts Manufacturers' Association threatened: 'As the total wage bill goes up, employers will substitute capital for labour which will increase unemployment.'[184] Tony Carlson of the Canadian Federation of Independent Business argued that

> employers have only so much money to spend on wages. If they're forced to pay one section of their operation more, without an increase in productivity, they'll look for alternatives to save costs. That could mean high tech to replace workers.[185]

To the author's knowledge, there have been no studies of the possible link between the introduction of pay-equity legislation and automation and labour-saving technologies. In the absence of such data, it is surprising that several economists have warned that the substitution of technology for labour may be one of the effects of pay equity.[186] The labour-feminist alliance, for its part, has had little to say on the subject.

4. Unemployment

Business and the anti-feminist neo-conservatives have stated repeatedly that pay equity would have three serious effects on employment: it would (a) increase unemployment among both women and men as employers seek to reduce the total size of their workforce to pay for the more highly priced women on their payrolls; (b) reduce job opportunities for women; and (c) reduce the rate of increase in women's labour-force participation.[187] The Winnipeg Chamber of Commerce succinctly summarized the dilemma between income and jobs for women, noting that the Manitoba Pay Equity Act 'could force some organizations to reduce the numbers of these jobs available to women, creating more unemployment among the very group that the legislation is attempting to help. How does a women benefit, if her $20,000 a year job is evaluated at $30,000 a year, but then disappears?'[188] Walter Block, senior economist at Vancouver's neo-conservative Fraser Institute, argued that once equal-pay legislation takes away the competitive advantage that their cheap labour confers on women, their employment opportunities will be severely reduced; female unemployment rates will be pushed 'up through the roof' and the effect will be 'to drive women "back into the kitchen"'.[189] Labour and feminist organizations in general have argued that equal-pay laws would not increase unemployment;[190] they contend that a more buoyant economy, based on a better standard of living and greater purchasing power among women, would create more jobs.

Several employers and anti-feminist neo-conservative commentators have pointed out that five years after Australia introduced equal pay for work of equal value, the unemployment rate among women had increased and the rate of their labour-force participation had slowed down.[191] But Gregory and Duncan found that Australia's equal-work law of 1969 and equal-value legislation of 1972 did not increase unemployment for women in relation to men; in fact, women's employment grew in relation to men's, although part of the reason was the increasing participation of women in the labour force and the growth of industries in which they were well represented. However, because equal pay results in higher wages for women, it did reduce the rate of employment growth in the female labour force.[192]

In general, there is little consensus among economists as to the effects of pay-equity legislation on employment.[193] Some economists have argued that it increases unemployment.[194] With regard to the 1978 Canadian Human Rights Act's provision of equal pay for work of equal value, Edgecombe-Robb suggested in 1984 that female unemployment might result from pay adjustments awarded incorrectly on alleged grounds of gender-based wage discrimination, when in fact low pay may be the result of women's 'oversupply' or preference for specific jobs because of the flexibility they allow in balancing domestic and labour-force duties.[195] Other economists have shown that pay equity leads to greater growth in women's employment.[196] There is an interesting parallel between the majority in the economics profession and the business and neo-conservative anti-feminist alliance in their opposition to equal pay for work of equal value.[197] A few economists, however, favour pay-equity legislation whether or not they detect some negative employment consequences for women.[198]

5. Part-time work

Another argument from business and the anti-feminist neo-conservatives is that pay-equity legislation would accelerate the conversion from full-time to part-time work among women workers,[199] especially since employers find part-time jobs cheaper and more efficient in terms of the total work performed within a standard set of hours.[200] To ensure that pay equity would not be extended to the part-time work that employers would create in response to pay-equity legislation, the Canadian Manufacturers' Association demanded that such laws exempt casual part-time work, temporary training positions, and student positions, though not regular part-time work.[201] Some governments were more than willing to satisfy business on this point: the guidelines to the Canadian Human Rights Act permit different pay scales for rehabilitation assignments and temporary training positions;[202] the 1987 Ontario Pay Equity Act exempts non-seasonal casual work of less than one-third of normal full-time work and temporary training positions.[203] To drive home the 'inevitable' link between pay-equity laws and part-time work, several business associations and anti-feminist commentators alleged that five years after the introduction of equal-value legislation, part-time work in Australia had increased.[204]

The labour movement has been campaigning for years against the erosion of full-time jobs into exploitative part-time work, regardless of any possible link to pay-equity legislation.[205] Trade unions have opposed the exemption of part-time work and training positions from pay-equity legislation because it would allow employers to subvert equal pay for women; this was especially important as women constitute 72 per cent of all part-time workers.[206] The feminist-labour alliance, noting the position of business, feared that the exclusion of casual part-time work from pay-equity legislation would provide 'an incentive for employers to convert regularly scheduled part-time jobs to casual positions'.[207] In 1986 CUPE pointed out that training positions are often created by employers when women begin applying for male-dominated jobs. For example, when women at the Hamilton Board of Education won the right to apply for the position of assistant caretaker (a male-dominated position), extra skills (such as maintenance of boilers and air conditioners) and a year of training were attached to this position.[208] The labour movement wanted such practices prohibited in Ontario's equal-pay legislation. The Ontario Coalition for Better Daycare was particularly opposed to the casual part-time exemption because all day-care workers, whether casual part-time, permanent part-time, or full-time, perform essentially the same functions, and giving pay equity to permanent part-time and full-time workers but not to casual part-timers would establish different rates of pay for the same work. In addition, 'commercial day care centres, where profit is the primary motive for offering the service', and which constitute 86 per cent of all day-care centres, would attempt to avoid pay-equity adjustments by hiring more casual part-timers: 'This would undermine the attempts of the day care movement to provide high quality day care which relies on stable, regular staff.'[209]

6. Subcontracting

Business and anti-feminists in Ontario warned that contracting out or subcontracting work would increase in response to pay equity as employers searched for ways to avoid the legislation.[210] For example, if job comparisons were allowed only within establishments and not between 'related employers', as the feminist-labour alliance had suggested (see the section on 'establishment' above, p. 33-8), contracting-out would be a way around the law. For business, there was a peculiar interaction between the gender mix of an establishment and the opportunities for subcontracting to avoid pay equity. The effect of the legislation would be much greater on a firm that had a few high-paid male-dominated positions and a large proportion of low-paid female-dominated positions (comparisons could be made between the two sets of jobs) than in another firm that also had a large number of female-dominated positions but that had contracted out its high-paid male-dominated positions (no comparisons could occur in this case).[211] The definitions of 'establishment' and 'gender-predominance' in pay-equity legislation would obviously encourage employers to accelerate subcontracting. The labour-feminist alliance was generally opposed to subcontracting. As Organized Working Women (OWW), a group of trade-union women in Ontario, told the provincial government in 1986: 'For years the union movement has been fighting employers who contract out bargaining unit work. OWW is concerned that similar moves could be taken to circumvent a pay equity scheme. This could possibly be done as an "exclusion" . . . or potentially the employer could contract out of the "establishment" the male group, to which a female group of workers is attempting to compare themselves.'[212]

7. Productivity and intensification of work

Business has also argued that pay-equity laws would lead to an intensification of work, since employers would seek to extract greater productivity from its labour force to meet the increased labour costs.[213] This is particularly the case because, according to the Winnipeg Chamber of Commerce, pay equity would raise the wages of many women without a corresponding rise in their productivity.[214] In the US, the American Retail Federation took this argument one step further in suggesting that pay equity would destroy workers' productivity by taking away their incentive to achieve excellence on the job, since the link between wages and job performance would be loosened.[215] State bureaucrats who favoured pay-equity legislation, as well as the labour movement, argued on the contrary that pay equity would increase productivity because women workers would be more satisfied and thus devote themselves more energetically to their duties.[216] This rationale was even built into the 1963 United States Equal Pay Act, in which pay equity was justified partly on the grounds that a wage differential based on sex 'prevents the maximum utilization of the available labour resources'.[217]

The issue of productivity took another twist in several pay-equity debates. Pay differences based on differences in productivity were listed as an exemption to pay equity in British Columbia and Quebec, at the federal level in the US, and under the Employment Standards Act in Ontario.[218] They were not specifically listed as an exemption under the 1987 Ontario Pay Equity Act; however, the merit exemption was worded in such a way that an employer could exempt a job rate ('the highest rate of compensation for a job class') from a pay-equity job comparison on the grounds of gender-neutral 'formal performance ratings', a provision that sounded ominously similar to a productivity exemption.[219] This was a concern to organizations speaking on behalf of workers in the clothing and textile industry, which employed a large number of immigrant women at piece rates determined by productivity and performance levels. A piece rate is commonly calculated as a percentage of a base rate, which in non-unionized clothing firms is often set at the minimum-wage level: 'For instance, a base rate of five dollars an hour corresponds with a certain level of output. If an employee attains 130% of that base output then she would receive 130 x the base rate of 5 dollars. In this case, she would receive $6.50/hour ($5 base rate x 130 output = $6.50).'[220] The Amalgamated Clothing and Textile Workers Union (ACTWU) wanted this piece-rate system to be included under the Ontario Pay Equity Act for both garment and textile factories and the home cottage industry, even though some unions opposed the latter extension on the grounds that it would condone the continuation of exploitative homework. The ACTWU admitted that job evaluations of piece-work would be difficult to do because of the tremendous variations in effort, one of the four factors in job-evaluation methodology: 'workers may increase their output for a short time but work much less strenuously in another time period.'[221] Its solution to this problem was to take the *average* wages in job comparisons: 'There will be those piece rate workers who earn only the base rate while a very few others might earn up to 180-190 per cent of the base rate. . . . Taking the average level of earnings for piece-rate workers evens out these highs and lows and leaves a figure most likely to be the closest possible estimate of what the experienced operator earns.'[222] The Cornwall Women's Network also wanted pay equity to cover piece-work because of the concentration of women in southeastern Ontario performing this type of labour. It was particularly disturbed by the number of women doing piece-work whose earnings were falling below the minimum wage as they went without pay while they waited for their broken-down machines to be repaired.[223] It is interesting to note that the employers' association of those women workers, the Apparel Manufacturers Association of Ontario, used the term 'performance' rather than 'productivity' to argue for the exemption of piece-rates from the Pay Equity Act.[224] This is exactly the same language used in the merit exemption in the Act.

8. The wage gap and 'red-circling'

(a) The business and neo-conservative arguments

Business and neo-conservative interests have warned that, despite the stated aims of legislation, pay equity will either have little effect on the wage gap or else even increase it. The relationship between pay-equity legislation and the size of the wage gap is complex because it can be affected by such separate factors as changes in women's and/or men's wages, business cycles, unemployment rates, employment opportunities, union strength, export and import markets, and technological innovations. Business and the neo-conservatives suggested that pay-equity legislation would help to close the wage gap only for the minority of highly skilled women who manage to keep their jobs; REAL Women put this figure at 2.5 to 3 per cent of all women in the paid labour force.[225] The Winnipeg Chamber of Commerce went further by suggesting that women with high-paying jobs would see their wages frozen to pay for the salaries of women in low-paying positions.[226] Others have argued that, for the majority of less-skilled women employees, incomes would fall in relation to men's because they would be forced (a) out of their old jobs into lower-paying job markets where competition would be stiffer, or (b) into unemployment or welfare, or back into the home on a full-time basis. Employee benefits, part of the broader conception of pay, will be reduced for women, according to the business scenario: one example would be the right of women to interrupt their careers to have babies without loss of seniority.[227] In 1986 the Canadian Manufacturers' Association pointed to two indicators underlining the modest effect that pay-equity legislation would have on women's wages: first, large groups of women would be untouched by the legislation because of the absence of comparable male-dominated positions in their establishments;[228] second, the Ontario government itself had indicated that legislation would at best close only about one-quarter of the wage gap.[229] In addition, the Association recommended that any pay-adjustment comparisons 'should be to the minimum rate or to the minimum of the range paid to those employees in male-predominated jobs which are deemed to be of equal value.'[230] To dampen enthusiasm for pay equity, business and anti-feminist spokespersons in Canada and the US have drawn analogies between equal-pay and mini-mum-wage laws, which, they argue, decrease the wages of women, minorities, and the unskilled by dequalifying them for 'covered' jobs and forcing them into lower-paid, unprotected jobs; equal-pay laws would have the same effect, though on a broader scale.[231]

Business converted the argument that it should have the *right* to reduce the wages of (male) employees to finance pay equity into the argument that pay-equity legislation would have the *result* of either freezing or lowering male wages to meet the increased costs of women employees.[232] In order to ensure that this conversion took place, business groups such as the Canadian Federation of Independent Business, the Canadian Manufacturers' Association, and the Board of Trade of Metropolitan Toronto argued for treat-ing 'red-circling' as exempt from pay-equity legislation.[233] This would allow employers to downgrade male jobs while freezing their wages and offering lower rates of pay to new employees coming into the new de-valued positions. The Retail Council of Canada threw down the gauntlet to all 'high-priced' male workers: 'why should it be assumed that the high paying [male] job category is "correct" rather than the lower paying [female] job category. . . . some male-dominant jobs could be overvalued. . . . the arbitrary commitment to a levelling up of wages cannot be justified.'[234] The anti-feminist neo-conservatives took the question of male wages one step further by using it in a campaign against pay equity on the grounds of reverse discrimination against men. In the US, Phyllis Schlafly, president of the anti-feminist, right-wing Eagle Forum Education and Legal Defense Fund, sought to characterize comparable worth as constituting a freeze on male wages.[235] In Canada, REAL Women suggested that equal-value legislation, since it applies to the characteristics of jobs rather than of job-holders, would increase the number of men lodging reverse-discrimination complaints.[236] It alleged that the US had already had trouble implementing equal pay through collective bargain-ing because of rank-and-file trade-union men's fear that the wage package would be used to boost only women's wages.[237] The National Citizens' Coalition complained that pay equity would discriminate against men, who would not be able to have their wages redressed.[238] Similarly, the Manitoba Progressive Party characterized the Manitoba Pay Equity Act as 'sexist' on the grounds that it discriminated against males by not allowing them to seek pay adjustments.[239]

(b) The feminist-labour response

Trade unions and feminist organizations in Canada and the US have rejected the business and neo-conservative argument that pay-equity legislation would have a negligible or negative effect on the wage gap, arguing that such legislation is essential to close even part of the gap. The threat to male wages could be removed by legally prohibiting employers from lowering any worker's wages in order to comply with equal-pay laws.[240] The Ontario Equal Pay Coalition stated: 'It is the employers who have been reaping the benefits of the wage discrimination faced by women and it is employers who should pay, not men. We believe that any suggestion that it is the men who should pay is one which is calculated to divide workers against each other rather than focusing on the real culprit.'[241] Concern was expressed that employers could effect a wage reduction by reducing general wage increases and transferring the savings to pay equity.[242] The United Steelworkers expressed well the sentiments felt on this score throughout much of the labour and women's movements:

> The problem in the workplace is not the over-valuation of men's work, but the under-valuation of women's work. Employers have profited from this state of affairs in the past, and they must not be permitted to correct historical inequities by emptying the pockets of male workers. It would be totally unjust if money which otherwise would have gone to improve the standard of living of other workers were redirected to achieve equal value.[243]

In order to prevent general wage increases from being reduced to meet the costs of pay equity, feminists and labourites suggested that a separate pay-equity fund be set up and that the two be negotiated separately.[244] To prevent the use of red-circling to reduce male workers' wages, feminists and trade unions suggested that it *not* be exempt from pay-equity legislation.[245] The Ontario Federation of Labour objected to red-circling for the same reason the labour and women's movement objected to male wage reductions to achieve pay equity: 'Red-circling is . . . a mechanism which attempts to have men pay for women's equal wage, when the wage bill should more appropriately fall to he who has profited from underpayment, i.e., the employer.'[246] The feminist-labour alliance was especially suspicious of employers' arguments that, in the context of technological change and the reorganization of work, men's work was 'overpaid': 'Hence, women's rates of pay become the "appropriate" rate of pay and men's rates are the "anomalous" ones.[247]

(c) Legislation

Governments typically deal with red-circling and wage reduction under separate clauses in pay-equity legislation. In the Canadian Human Rights Act, wage reductions to achieve pay equity are prohibited under Section 11(5), but red-circling is permitted under the Commission's guidelines.[248] Under the 1987 Ontario Pay Equi-ty Act, wage reductions to achieve pay equity are prohibited under Section 9(1), but red-circling is permitted under Section 8(1)(d).[249] The Quebec and US pay-equity laws prohibit wage reductions to achieve equal pay, but are silent on red-circling.[250] Red-circling could be permitted in the United States Equal Pay Act under the 'any other factor other than sex' clause (Section 3[d][1]). This separation of wage-reduction and red-circling clauses allows the state some latitude in dealing with the contradictions of class and gender struggles: it tilts towards working-class men and women in prohibiting wage reductions in one clause, but tilts towards male business interests by permitting red-circling either directly, in special clauses for this purpose, or indirectly through 'kitchen sink' clauses; the overall effect is to forbid wage reduc-tion with one hand and permit it with the other, thus favouring business.

(d) Studies

Although social-scientific studies indicate only an ambiguous relationship between pay-equity legislation and the size of the gendered wage gap, several other studies provide evidence that pay-equity legislation does what it is intended to do: decrease the size of the wage gap.[251] Some economists have argued that there would be a wage increase at least for those women who managed to keep their jobs after the implementation of legislation;[252] Gunderson suggests that this might happen because the costs of discrimination (in the form of wage settlements, fines, penalties, and image problems) would increase for employers.[253]

Economists differ over the proportion of the wage gap that can be closed through pay-equity legislation. Some argue that the gap would be completely closed for jobs that are comparable in value.[254] In the US, on the basis of an analysis of the characteristics of jobs (rather than those of workers), Buchele and Aldrich find that comparable-worth legislation would close 98 per cent of the wage gap if it were applied to job comparisons between establishments (which, as we saw above, no legislation even contemplates).[255] Other economists suggest that equal-pay laws could be expected to wipe out at best only about half of the wage gap, which would leave women's wages still at only about 80 per cent of men's.[256] Gregory and Duncan show that in Australia, as a result of that country's equal-work legislation in 1969 and equal-value law in 1972, the wage gap declined from 42 per cent in 1969 to 23 per cent in 1977.[257] Zabalza and Tzannatos show that in Great Britain women's pay rose in relation to men's by 19 per cent during the 1970s as a result of the 1970 Equal Pay Act and the 1975 Sex Discrimination Act.[258]

Other economists suggest that pay-equity laws have little effect on the wage gap and may even increase it. Gunderson, for example, found that the equal-pay provision of Ontario's Employment Standards Act of 1969 failed to narrow the wage gap and was more often associated with its widening in the nine occupations studied.[259] This widening may be due to a variety of factors: (a) because employers lay off or refuse to hire any more high-priced women(!) in the protected sector, these women are forced to compete with other women and men for lower-waged jobs in the unprotected areas, thereby increasing the size of the wage gap; (b) employers may introduce labour-saving technology in response to equal-pay legislation (although little research has been done on this possible outcome); (c) much equal-pay legislation is narrowly applied to comparisons between identical or substantially similar jobs in the same establishment, which is likely to leave untouched the substantial wage differences between different jobs of equivalent value in separate establishments; (d) resources for enforcing equal pay provisions are often few; and (e) as already indicated, employers may avoid equal-pay provisions by subcontracting out at wages even lower than those they paid before equal-pay legislation was introduced.[260] Gunderson argues that the majority of studies show that equal-pay laws have virtually no effect on the wage gap.[261]

(e) Male unionist fear of cheap female labour

It has not been any appreciation of feminism or anger over women's oppression that has led male unionists to lobby for equal-pay legislation. Rather, the labour movement has seen equal-pay legislation as presenting less of a threat to male wages than would low wages for women. Especially following each of the two world wars, male unionists feared that their jobs would be taken over by women at lower rates of pay. In many cases, the skill level of those jobs had been diluted and the men were being forced to accept the 'women's rate of pay'.[262] In Canada the labour movement has historically argued in favour of equal-pay legislation as a defence against women's cheap labour and protection for higher male wages. In the late 1800s, equal pay for equal work was supported by the Trades and Labour Congress of Canada, the Knights of Labour, the International Typographical Union, and the Montreal Federated Trades and Labour Council, although it is not clear whether this support was general throughout the Canadian labour movement.[263] During the First World War, the British Columbia Federation of Labour argued: 'We will not only benefit [women] by helping them to secure equal pay for equal work but we shall . . . prevent our own wages and conditions from being drawn down to the lower standard by any successful efforts of the employers to use female labour at a lower price.'[264] The motives for male unionists to support equal pay in the late nineteenth and early twentieth centuries are perhaps best indicated by the fact that at the same time they advocated the removal of women from the labour force because they posed a threat to male jobs.[265] The principle of equal pay was adopted by the Vancouver Trades and Labour Council and the Trades and Labour Congress of Canada during the Second World War with an eye to returning male veterans who would want to re-enter their old jobs at the same rates of pay.[266] What accounts for the labour movement's current support of equal pay for work of equal value—whether outrage over the undervaluation of women's jobs or the threat to male wages posed by women's low wages—is difficult to determine. The truth probably lies somewhere in the middle.

CONCLUSIONS

The struggles over pay equity, simultaneously through the state and in the capitalist workplace, have served as proxies for the struggles between capital and labour, and women and men, over control of the labour process and the right to make managerial decisions about the shape and direction of that process. In unionized workplaces, a strong pay-equity plan would force employers to share decisions about wage-setting with union representatives. In non-unionized workplaces, employers would have more absolute authority over the shape of such plans, but still have to submit them to the state for final approval. In both types of workplaces, equal pay for work of equal value would interfere with the freedom of employers to use women as part of a cheap reserve army of labour. This strongest version of pay equity is thus a direct attack on the ability of capitalists to exploit women workers, and thus to extract from them the surplus value that has formed the basis of their continued accumulation of capital.

The capitalist workplace, however, does not exist in a vacuum. Workers have to get to the workplace through the labour market. The labour power that they sell in the marketplace is produced and reproduced both within the capitalist workplace and outside it, especially in the household and educational institutions. The question of earning a 'fair day's wage' is deeply affected by these institutions. It is therefore not surprising that the struggles over pay equity have continued outside the capitalist workplace. It is to the marketplace and the household that we turn in the next two chapters.

Notes

[1] Ontario, *Green Paper on Pay Equity* (Hon. Ian Scott, Attorney General and Minister Responsible for Women's Issues, Toronto, 1985), pp. 29-38; Ontario, *Debates. Hansard* (Legislative Assembly of Ontario), 19 Nov. 1985, p. 1595; 11 Feb. 1986, p. 4000; Ontario, *Pay Equity Act, 1987* (1988), chap. 34, sec. 22; Manitoba, *The Pay Equity Act*, Chapter P13 (Winnipeg, 1985), sec. 10, 15; Nova Scotia, *An Act to Provide for Pay Equity*, Chapter 16 (Halifax, 1988); Prince Edward Island, *Pay Equity Act* (Charlottetown, 1988), sec. 6.

[2] For example, see Ottawa-Carleton Board of Trade, *Brief* (1986), pp. 6-7; Ontario Chamber of Commerce, *Submission to the Consultation Hearings Panel on the Green Paper on Pay Equity* (15 May 1986), pp. 10-11; Board of Trade of Metropolitan Toronto, *Submission to the Consultation Panel* (1986), p. 22.

[3] For example, see Retail Council of Canada, *Submission* (1986), p. 17.

[4] Personnel Association of Ontario, *Submission to the Consultation Panel on the Government of Ontario Green Paper on Pay Equity* (14 May 1986), pp. 18-19.

[5] Equal Pay Coalition, *Submission* (1987), p. 19.

[6]Manitoba, *The Pay Equity Act. Chapter P13* (Winnipeg: Queen's Printer, 1985), sec. 1.

[7]Nova Scotia, *An Act to Provide for Pay Equity* (1988), sec. 3 (1) (j) and (m); Prince Edward Island, *Pay Equity Act* (1988), sec. 1 (g) and (h).

[8]Ontario, *Green Paper* (1985), pp. 18-19.

[9]Ontario, *Bill 105, An Act to Provide Pay Equity for Employees in Predominantly Female Groups of Jobs in the Public Service* (Toronto: Queen's Printer, 1986), sec. 1; *Debates*, 11 Feb. 1986, p. 4000; *Pay Equity Act, 1987* (1988), chap. 34, sec. 1(1).

[10]For example, see US Congress, *Statutes At Large, Public Law 88-38, An Act to Prohibit Discrimination on Account of Sex in the Payment of Wages by Employers Engaged in Commerce or in the Production of Goods for Commerce*, vol. 77 (Washington, D.C.: Government Printing Office, 1964), sec. 3; Canada, *Acts of the Parliament of Canada*, 2nd Session, 30th Parliament, 1976-77 (Ottawa: Queen's Printer, 1977), chap. C-33, sec. 11; Quebec, *Revised Statutes of Quebec* (Quebec: Éditeur officiel du Québec, 1979), chap. C-12, sec. 19.

[11]Canadian Human Rights Commission, *Equal Pay for Work of Value. Report of the Task Force* (Ottawa, March 1978), p. 15.

[12]Equal Pay Coalition, *Response* (1986), p. 15. The date referred to in this brief is December 1985, which is incorrect.

[13]Ontario, *Green Paper* (1985), p. 18.

[14]Automotive Parts Manufacturers Association of Canada, *Statement to the [Ontario] Consultation Panel on Equal Pay for Work of Equal Value* (27 March 1986), p. 6.

[15]Ontario Chamber of Commerce, *Submission* (1986), pp. 3-4.

[16]For example, see Retail Council of Canada, *Submission* (1986), p. 10.

[17]C. David Clark, Gail C.A. Cook, and William A. Dimma, *The Report of the Consultation Panel on Pay Equity* (Toronto: Ontario Women's Directorate, 1986), p. 17; Canadian Manufacturers' Association, Ontario Division, *Submission to the Consultation Panel on the Green Paper on Pay Equity* (Toronto, March 1986), pp. 7-8; Ontario Mining Association, *Submission* (1986), p. 5.

[18]Board of Trade of Metropolitan Toronto, *Submission to the Consultation Panel* (1986), pp. 10-11.

[19]Day Care Advisory Committee of Metropolitan Toronto, *Submission to the Ontario Consultation Panel on Pay Equity* (Toronto, 1986), p. 2.

[20]Canadian Manufacturers' Association, *Submission* (1986), pp. 7-8. An identical position on a minimum number of employees in the occupation was taken by the Ontario Chamber of Commerce, *Submission* (1986), p. 3.

[21]For example, Congress of Canadian Women, *Submission* (1986), p. 1; Canadian Association of Women Executives, Legislative Committee, Subcommittee on Pay Equity, *Response to the Government of Ontario Green Paper on Pay Equity* (Feb. 1986), pp. 3, 5; Ottawa Women's Lobby, *Submission to the Consultation Panel on Pay Equity* (Sharon Katz; 7 April 1986), pp. 6-7; United Food and Commercial Workers International Union, *Brief* (1986), p. 8; Confederation of Canadian Unions, *A Brief* (1986), p. 5.

[22]Equal Pay Coalition, *Response* (1986), p. 15. See also Canadian Human Rights Commission, *Equal Pay Casebook*, 1978-1984 (Ottawa, 1984), pp. 5-7, 8-9; Federation of Women Teachers' Associations of Ontario, FWTAO *Response to the Green Paper on Pay Equity* (Feb. 1986), pp. 8-9; Ontario Federation of Labour, *Brief by the Ontario Federation of Labour in Response to the Ontario Government Green Paper on Pay Equity* (Presented by Cliff Pilkey, President, Julie Griffin, Vice-President, and

Wally Majesky, Secretary-Treasurer; Feb. 1986), pp. 8-9; and Equal Pay Coalition, *Response* (1986), p. 16.

23 National Action Committee on the Status of Women, *Brief to the [Ontario] Consultation Panel on the Green Paper on Pay Equity* (Michelle Swenarchuk; 14 May 1986), pp. 11-12.

24 Public Service Alliance of Canada, *Submission to the Ontario Government Consultation Panel on Pay Equity* (April 1986), p. 5.

25 Charter of Rights Coalition (Manitoba), *Submission on Bill 53, The Pay Equity Act* (July 1985), p. 2; and Manitoba, Legislative Assembly, Standing Committee on Industrial Relations, *Oral Presentations on Bill No. 53, The Pay Equity Act* (Winnipeg: Queen's Printer, 1985), p. 5.

26 Ontario Coalition for Better Daycare, *Brief to the Standing Committee* (1987), p. 5; Organized Working Women, *Brief to the Green Paper Hearings* (Toronto, 27 March 1986), p. 5; Equal Pay Coalition, *Response* (1986), p. 16; Federation of Women Teachers' Associations of Ontario, FWTAO *Response* (1986), pp. 8-9.

27 National Union of Provincial Government Employees, *Brief Presented to the [Ontario] Consultative Panel on Pay Equity* (17 April 1986), p. 5; Congress of Canadian Women, *Submission* (1986), p. 2; Service Employees International Union, *Presentation to the Consultation Panel on Pay Equity* (S. E. [Ted] Roscoe, International Vice-President; 15 May 1986), pp. 5-6; United Food and Commercial Workers International Union, *Brief* (1986), p. 8; Confederation of Canadian Unions, *A Brief* (1986), pp. 5-6.

28 Ontario Nurses Association, *Submission to the Consultion Panel on Pay Equity* (March 1986), pp. 22-3; Ontario Public Service Employees Union, *Submission to the Consultation Panel on Pay Equity* (May 1986), p. 10; Equal Pay Coalition, 'The Equal Pay Coalition's Media Release: Legislative Proposals for Equal Pay for Work of Equal Value', *Canadian Woman Studies* 6, no. 4 (Winter 1985), p. 38; Ontario Secondary School Teachers' Federation, *The Response to the [Ontario] Green Paper on Pay Equity To the Commission on Public Hearings* (22 Jan. 1986), pp. 8-9.

29 Federation of Women Teachers' Associations of Ontario, FWTAO *Response* (1986), pp. 8-9.

30 Canadian Union of Public Employees, Ontario Division, *Response to the Ontario Government Green Paper on Pay Equity* (Toronto, 14 May 1986), pp. 14-15.

31 Equal Pay Coalition, *Submission* (1987), p. 10.

32 United Steelworkers of America, *Brief to the [Ontario] Consultation Panel on Pay Equity* (Presented by Leo Gerard, Director, District 6, and Carrol Anne Sceviour, Local 6624; 27 March 1986), pp. 8-9; Ontario Federation of Labour, *Brief* (1986), pp. 8-9; Service Employees International Union, *Presentation* (1986), pp. 5-6; Ontario Nurses Association, *Submission* (1986), pp. 22-3.

33 Confederation of Canadian Unions, *A Brief* (1986), pp. 1-2; Federation of Women Teachers' Associations of Ontario, FWTAO *Response* (1986), pp. 8-9; Ontario Federation of Labour, *Brief* (1986), pp. 8-9; Equal Pay Coalition, *Response* (1986), p. 17.

34 Manitoba, *Oral Presentations* (1985), p. 14.

35 Equal Pay Coalition, *Response* (1986), p. 16.

36 Equal Pay Coalition, *Equal Pay for Work of Equal Value: Media Release* (Toronto, 4 Oct. 1985), p. 4.

37 Ontario Secondary School Teachers Federation, District 31 (Sudbury), Status of

Women Committee, *A Response to the [Ontario] Green Paper on Pay Equity* (Charlotte Ure; Sudbury, 24 Feb. 1986). See also Canadian Association of Women Executives, *Response* (1986), pp. 3, 5; Canadian Union of Public Employees, *Response* (1986), pp. 7-8; and Clark, Cook, and Dimma, *Report* (1986), p. 20.

[38] Equal Pay Coalition, *Response* (1986), p. 9.

[39] Ontario Nurses Association, *Submission* (1986), p. 8.

[40] REAL Women, *Green Paper on Pay Equity—Province of Ontario* (15 May 1986), pp. 7, 9; National Citizens' Coalition, *Pay Discrimination* (1986), p. 17; Manitoba, *Oral Presentations* (1985), pp. 6-7.

[41] Ontario, *Green Paper* (1985), pp. 16-17.

[42] Canadian Human Rights Commission, *Equal Pay for Work of Equal Value: Interpretation Guide for Section 11 of the Canadian Human Rights Act* (Ottawa, 1984).

[43] Ontario, *Pay Equity Act, 1987* (Toronto, 1988), secs. 1, 14, 15; Ontario Pay Equity Commission, *Definition of Establishment*, Implementation Series #4 (March 1988), p. 1.

[44] Ontario Pay Equity Commission. *Decisions of the Pay Equity Hearings Tribunal*, File 0001-89 (30 June 1989), paragraphs 51 and (for criterion #4) 41.

[45] 'Equal Pay For Women Hits Retailers', *Business Week*, 29 Jan. 1972, p. 76.

[46] Automotive Parts Manufacturers Association, *Statement* (1986), pp. 5-6.

[47] Ontario Chamber of Commerce, *Submission* (1986), pp. 4-6; Ontario Mining Association, *Submission* (1986), p. 4; Board of Trade of Metropolitan Toronto, *Submission to the Consultation Panel* (1986), pp 8-9; Canadian Manufacturers' Association, *Submission* (1986), p. 7. The Retail Council of Canada either favoured the functional definition or wanted the decision as to the best definition of 'establishment' left up to each individual business. See Retail Council of Canada, *Submission* (1986), p. 9.

[48] Personnel Association of Ontario, *Submission* (1986), pp. 5-6.

[49] Ontario Nurses Association, *Submission* (1986), pp. 8, 16-18; Ontario Public Service Employees Union, *Submission* (1986), pp. 6-7; United Food and Commercial Workers International Union, *Brief* (1986), p. 8; Federation of Women Teachers' Associations of Ontario, *FWTAO Response* (1986), pp. 6-7; Ontario Federation of Labour, *Brief* (1986), pp. 5-6; Canadian Union of Public Employees, *Response* (1986), pp. 10-13; Service Employees International Union, *Presentation* (1986), p. 3.

[50] Ottawa Women's Lobby, *Submission* (1986), p. 15.

[51] Canadian Union of Public Employees, *Response* (1986), pp. 10-12.

[52] United Steelworkers of America, *Brief* (1986), p. 9; Equal Pay Coalition, *Response* (1986), p. 13.

[53] Canadian Association of Women Executives, *Equal Pay, Equal Value, Equal Opportunity* (A brief to the Ontario Minister of Labour; Oct. 1978), p. 3; *Submission to the [Ontario] Standing General Committee: Consideration of Bill 3, An Act to Amend the Employment Standards Act, 1974* (29 Jan. 1980), p. 4; *Response* (1986), p. 6.

[54] Canadian Union of Public Employees, *Response* (1986), pp. 12-13; Norene Pupo and Ann Doris Duffy, 'The Ontario Labour Relations Board and the Part Time Workers', *Relations Industrielles* 43, no. 3 (1988), pp. 660-85; Equal Pay Coalition, *Response* (1986), p. 14.

[55] Equal Pay Coalition, *Response* (1986), p. 8; New Brunswick Advisory Council on the Status of Women, *Equal Pay* (1985), pp. 7, 12-3; Canadian Union of Public Employees, *Response* (1986), p. 8.

[56]Organized Working Women, *Brief* (1986), p. 5; Ottawa Women's Lobby, *Submission* (1986), p. 15; Canadian Union of Public Employees, *Response* (1986), p. 13; Equal Pay Coalition, *Response* (1986), p. 14; Service Employees International Union, *Presentation* (1986), pp. 4-5. See also New Brunswick Advisory Council on the Status of Women, *Equal Pay* (1985), p. 13.

[57]National Union of Provincial Government Employees, *Brief* (1986), p. 5.

[58]Canadian Union of Public Employees, *Response* (1986), p. 14.

[59]Ottawa Women's Lobby, *Submission* (1986), p. 15.

[60]Metro Action Committee on Public Violence Against Women and Children, *Submission to the Standing Committee on the Administration of Justice Concerning Bill 154* (Pat Marshall, Executive Director; Toronto, 4 March 1987) p. 1; for a similar opposition to 'within establishment' comparisons, see Public Service Alliance of Canada, *Submission* (1986), pp. 8-9.

[61]Ontario Nurses Association, *Submission* (1986), pp. 1, 8.

[62]Ontario Coalition for Better Daycare, *Day Care Brief* (1986), p. 1; *Brief to the Standing Committee* (1987), p. 2.

[63]Ontario Coalition for Better Daycare, *Brief* (1987), p. 7.

[64]Ontario Coalition for Better Daycare, *Day Care Brief* (1986), p. 4; *Brief* (1987), pp. 7-8; Day Care Advisory Committee of Metropolitan Toronto, *Submission* (1986), pp. 8-9; see also Equal Pay Coalition, *Submission* (1987), pp. 32-3.

[65]Ontario Coalition for Better Daycare, *Brief* (1987), p. 7; see also Equal Pay Coalition, *Submission* (1987), p. 17.

[66]Ontario Pay Equity Commission, *Report to the Minister of Labour on Sectors of the Economy Which Are Predominantly Female, As Required Under the Pay Equity Act, Section 33 (2)(e)* (Toronto, Jan. 1989).

[67]Bruce McDougall, 'Here Comes Equal Pay: Under Proposed Laws, You'll Not Only Have to Pay Employees Equally for Work of Equal Value, You'll Have to Prove It', *Small Business* 4, no. 8 (Oct. 1985), pp. 33-8. But see Quebec, *Revised Statutes*, chap. C-12 (1979).

[68]Canadian Human Rights Commission, *Canadian Human Rights Act—Employer Guide* (1981), p. 5.

[69]Manitoba, *Pay Equity Act* (1985), sec. 1, 3 and Schedule A.

[70]McDougall, 'Here Comes Equal Pay' (1985), p. 33.

[71]Ontario Pay Equity Commission, *Report* (1989), pp. 12-13; Nova Scotia, *Chapter 16: An Act to Provide for Pay Equity*, Statutes of the Province of Nova Scotia (Halifax, 1988); sec. 4; Prince Edward Island, *Pay Equity Act* (1988), sec. 1(k).

[72]Ontario, *Debates* 2 July 1985, p. 414; 15 Oct. 1985, p. 789.

[73]Ontario Pay Equity Commission, *Questions and Answers: Pay Equity in the Workplace* (March 1988), p. 3; *Globe and Mail*, 4 Jan. 1988, p. A10; Ontario, *Pay Equity Act, 1987* (1988).

[74]US Congress, *Options* (1985), p. 396.

[75]Ibid., pp. 260-1.

[76]McDougall, 'Here Comes Equal Pay' (1985), pp. 33, 38.

[77]Ottawa-Carleton Board of Trade, *Brief* (1986), p. 5; Retail Council of Canada, *Submission* (1986), pp. 20-1; Board of Trade of Metropolitan Toronto, *Submission to the Consultation Panel* (1986), p. 24.

[78]Manitoba, *Oral Presentations* (1985), pp. 3, 17.

[79]Canadian Manufacturers' Association, *Submission* (1986), p. 19; REAL Women, *Green Paper* (1986), pp. 5-6.

[80] Canadian Federation of Independent Business, *Equal Pay for Work of Equal Value: An Address to the Corpus Information Services Conference* (By Judith Andrew, Director, Provincial Affairs Ontario, CFIB; Scarborough, Ont., 19 March 1986), pp. 12-13; Clark, Cook, and Dimma, *Report* (1986), pp. 24-5; Canadian Manufacturers' Association, *Submission* (1986), p. 10.

[81] US Congress, *Hearings* (1946), p. 22.

[82] Retail Council of Canada, *Submission* (1986), pp. 16-17.

[83] Clark, Cook, and Dimma, *Report* (1986), pp. 23-4; Ottawa Women's Lobby, *Submission* (1986), p. 8.

[84] US Congress, *Options* (1985), pp. 444, 553.

[85] New Brunswick Advisory Council on the Status of Women, *Equal Pay* (1985), p. 11; Canadian Association of Women Executives, *Response* (1986), p. 5; Congress of Canadian Women, *Submission* (1986), p. 1; Federation of Women Teachers' Associations of Ontario, FWTAO *Response* (1986), p. 4; Charter of Rights Coalition (Manitoba), *Submission* (1985), p. 1; Manitoba, *Oral Presentations* (1985), pp. 4-5, 14; Ontario Federation of Labour, *Brief* (1986), p. 7; United Auto Workers Canada, Local 1980, *Equal Pay for Work of Equal Value: On the Issue of 'Merit'* (Submission to the Public Consultation on Pay Equity; 15 May 1986), p. 1; United Steelworkers of America, *Brief* (1986), pp. 3, 7.

[86] Ontario Coalition for Better Daycare, *Brief* (1987), p. 7; Ontario Nurses Association, *Submission* (1986), pp. 5, 18; Federation of Women Teachers' Associations of Ontario, FWTAO *Response* (1986), p. 4; Equal Pay Coalition, *Equal Pay for Work of Equal Value: Media Release*, (1985), p. 7; 'The Equal Pay Coalition's Media Release: Legislative Proposals' (1985), p. 39; *Response* (1986), pp. 6-7.

[87] Canadian Union of Public Employees, *Response* (1986), p. 6.

[88] Service Employees International Union, *Presentation* (1986), pp. 2, 10.

[89] Manitoba Federation of Labour, *Response to the Law Amendments Committee: The Pay Equity Act (Bill 53)* (July 1985), p. 1; Charter of Rights Coalition (Manitoba), *Submission* (1985), p. 2; Manitoba, *Oral Presentations* (1985), pp. 4-5, 14.

[90] For example, see Manitoba, *Oral Presentations* (1985), p. 14.

[91] Ontario Coalition for Better Daycare, *Brief* (1986), p. 5; Equal Pay Coalition, *Response* (1986), p. 8; United Steelworkers of America, *Brief* (1986), pp. 3, 7; Ontario Federation of Labour, *Brief* (1986), p. 7.

[92] Ontario, *Green Paper* (1985), p. 65.

[93] Equal Pay Coalition, *Response* (1986), p. 27.

[94] Federation of Women Teachers' Associations of Ontario, FWTAO *Response* (1986), p. 17.

[95] The Ontario Public Service Employees Union discusses the exemptions in the 1987 Ontario Pay Equity Act in terms of the highly-specific term '*job rates*' ('the highest rate of compensation for a job class'). (See OPSEU, *Equity at Work* [1987], pp. 94-5.) This concept is taken from the Act, although section 8, which spells out the exemptions, does not use it. The acts in other jurisdictions do not employ the Ontario terminology, preferring instead 'wages' (federal US), 'wages' and 'benefits' (federal Canada), 'salary or wages' (Quebec), 'average pay or wages' (Manitoba), 'wages' or 'compensation' (Prince Edward Island), or simply 'pay' (Nova Scotia). Although the Ontario terminology is the most precise, it would be inappropriate to use it when comparing jurisdictions, as much of this book does. Unless otherwise noted, throughout the book I do not use the term 'job rate' but the less legally precise 'wages' or 'pay'; this was the term used most often in the

debates between business and the labour-feminist alliance preceding the implementation of legislation. Although such debates, rather than legal analyses of legislation, are the book's focus, to achieve a sufficient degree of clarity and precision, legal terms cannot be avoided completely.

[96] The 1985 Manitoba Pay Equity Act does not have a formal list of exemptions. See Manitoba, *The Pay Equity Act* (1985). The Canadian Human Rights Act gives the Human Rights Commission authority to decide on exceptions. See Canada, *Acts of the Parliament of Canada*, 1977, chap. 33, sec. 11(3); Canadian Human Rights Commission, *The Canadian Human Rights Act: Employer Guide* (1981), pp. 29-30; *Equal Pay for Work of Equal Value: Interpretation Guide* (1984). The 1987 Ontario Act allows seven differences in the job rates between female and male job classes if the employer can show that they are not based on gender discrimination. See Ontario, *The Pay Equity Act, 1987* (1988), chap. 34, sec. 8(1) (a) to (d); Ontario Pay Equity Commission, *Permissible Differences in Compensation*, Implementation Series #13 (Nov. 1988). A *job class* 'means those positions in an establishment that have similar duties and responsibilities and require similar qualifications, are filled by similar recruiting procedures and have the same compensation schedule, salary grade or range of salary rates' (Ontario, *The Pay Equity Act, 1987* [1988], sec. 1[1]).

[97] E.g., Canadian Human Rights Commission, *The Canadian Human Rights Act: Employer Guide* (1981), p. 29; *Equal Pay for Work of Equal Value: Interpretation Guide* (1984); Manitoba, Acts of the Legislature of the Province of Manitoba, *Chapter 18: An Act to Prevent Discrimination Between the Sexes in the Payment of Wages for the Doing of Similar Work*, Third Session, Twenty-Fourth Legislature (Winnipeg: Queen's Printer, 1956), sec. 3(3); US Congress, *Statutes At Large, Public Law 88-38* (1964), sec. 3; Ontario, Statutes of the Province of Ontario, chap. 112: *The Employment Standards Act*, 22-23 Elizabeth II (Toronto: Queen's Printer), sec. 33(1); *The Pay Equity Act, 1987* (1988), chap. 34, sec. 8(1)(a); Ontario Pay Equity Commission, *Permissible Differences in Compensation*, Implementation Series #13 (Nov. 1988), pp. 2-3; British Columbia, *Chapter 186* (1979), sec. 6(2); Quebec, *Revised Statutes*, chap. C-12 (1979), sec. 19; Saskatchewan, *Chapter L-1* (1980) sec. 17(1); Prince Edward Island, *Pay Equity Act* (1988), sec. 8(1)(b); Nova Scotia, *An Act to Provide For Pay Equity* (1988), sec. 4(a).

[98] Overtime was not mentioned very often. For example, see Quebec, *Revised Statutes*, chap. C-12 (1979), sec. 19.

[99] For example, see US Congress, *Statutes At Large, Public Law 88-38* (1964), sec. 3; Canadian Human Rights Commission, *The Canadian Human Rights Act: Employer Guide* (1981), p. 29; *Equal Pay for Work of Equal Value: Interpretation Guide for Section 11* (1984); Ontario, *Employment Standards Act* (1974), sec. 33 (1); Ontario, *Pay Equity Act, 1987* (1988), chap. 34, sec. 8 (1c); Ontario, Pay Equity Commission, *Permissible Differences in Compensation*, Implementation Series #13 (Nov. 1988), p. 4; British Columbia, *Chapter 186* (1979), sec. 6(2); Quebec, *Revised Statutes*, chap. C-12 (1979), sec. 19; Saskatchewan, *Chapter L-1* (1980), sec. 17(1); Prince Edward Island, *Pay Equity Act* (1988), sec. 8(1)(a); Nova Scotia, *An Act to Provide For Pay Equity* (1988), sec. 4(c).

[100] For example, see US Congress, *Statutes At Large, Public Law 88-38* (1964), sec. 3; Ontario, *Employment Standards Act* (1974), sec. 33 (1); British Columbia, *Chapter 186* (1979), sec. 6(2); Quebec, *Revised Statutes*, chap. C-12 (1979), sec. 19.

[101] Job experience was not mentioned very often. For example, see Quebec, *Revised*

Statutes, chap. C-12, (1979), sec. 19. It is probably similar to length of employment and seniority.

[102] For example, see Manitoba, *Chapter 18* (1956), sec. 3(3); Ontario, *Bill 105* (1986), sec. 8; Ontario, *Pay Equity Act, 1987* (1988), sec. 8(1e); Ontario Pay Equity Commission, *Permissible Differences in Compensation,* Implementation Series #13 (Nov. 1988), p. 5; Canadian Human Rights Commission, *Equal Pay for Work of Equal Value: Interpretation Guide* (1984); Prince Edward Island, *Pay Equity Act* (1988), sec. 8(1)(c), 8(2); Nova Scotia, *An Act to Provide For Pay Equity* (1988), sec. 4(d).

[103] For example, see Manitoba, *Chapter 18* (1956), sec. 3(3); Canadian Human Rights Commission, *Equal Pay for Work of Equal Value: Interpretation Guide* (1984).

[104] These part-time positions were mentioned in the new Ontario legislation. See Ontario, *Bill 105* (1986), sec. 8; Ontario, *Pay Equity Act, 1987* (1988), sec. 8(1b)(3), (4). However, a casual position (and its job rate) does not constitute an exception to pay equity if it 'is performed on a regular and continuing basis, although for less than one-third of the normal work period that applies to similar full-time work'. In addition, the guidelines to the Canadian Human Rights Act permit different pay scales for rehabilitation assignments and temporary training positions. See Canadian Human Rights Commission, *The Canadian Human Rights Act: Employer Guide* (1981), pp. 29-30; *Equal Pay for Work of Equal Value: Interpretation Guide* (1984); for an identical exception, see Ontario Pay Equity Commission, *Permissible Differences in Compensation,* Implementation Series #13 (Nov. 1988), p. 3; and Nova Scotia, *An Act to Provide For Pay Equity* (1988), sec. 4 (b).

[105] This exception to equal pay is contained in the guidelines accompanying the Canadian Human Rights Act. See *Canadian Human Rights Commission, The Canadian Human Rights Act: Employer Guide* (1981), p. 29; and *Equal Pay for Work of Equal Value: Interpretation Guide* (1984). Gender-neutral red-circling is also to be found in the most recent Ontario Act. See Ontario, Pay *Equity Act, 1987* (1988), chap. 34, sec. 8(1d); Ontario Pay Equity Commission, *Permissible Differences in Compensation,* Implementation Series #13 (Nov. 1988), p. 4.

[106] Ontario, *Pay Equity Act, 1987* (1988), chap. 34, sec. 8(2).

[107] For example, see Manitoba, *Chapter 18* (1956), sec. 3(3); US Congress, *Statutes At Large, Public Law 88-38* (1964), sec. 3; Ontario, *Employment Standards Act,* (1974), sec. 33(1); Newfoundland, Chapter 262 (1970), sec. 10(2); British Columbia, *Chapter 186* (1979), sec. 6(3); Alberta, *Chapter 1-2* (1980), sec. 6(4); Prince Edward Island, *Chapter H-13* (1974), sec. 7(2); Nova Scotia, *Chapter L-1* (1979), sec. 55(2).

[108] This was not listed very often. For example, see Manitoba, *Chapter 18* (1956), sec. 3(3).

[109] Canadian Manufacturers' Association, *Submission* (1986), p. 11 (emphasis added); see also Ontario Chamber of Commerce, *Submission* (1986), p. 9; Retail Council of Canada, *Submission* (1986), p. 13; Board of Trade of Metropolitan Toronto, *Submission to the Consultation Panel* (1986), pp. 14-16.

[110] Personnel Association of Ontario, *Submission* (1986), pp. 14-16.

[111] Equal Pay Coalition, *Submission* (1987), p. 24.

[112] For example, see Ontario Public Service Employees Union, *Submission* (1986), p. 14; United Food and Commercial Workers International Union, *Brief* (1986), p. 9; Ontario Secondary School Teachers' Federation, *Response* (1986), p. 12; National Union of Provincial Government Employees, *Brief* (1986), p. 7; Canadian Union of Public Employees, *Response* (1986), p. 18; United Steelworkers of America, *Brief* (1986), p. 10; Equal Pay Coalition, *Submission* (1987), *p. 24.*

[113]Public Service Alliance of Canada, *Submission* (1986), p. 4; Ontario Nurses Association, *Submission* (1986), p. 29.

[114]Organized Working Women and the Ottawa and District Labour Council, *Response to the Green Paper on Pay Equity* (Ottawa, 17 April 1986), p. 8; Organized Working Women, *Brief* (1986), p. 3.

[115]Ontario, *Bill 3 (Private Member's Bill): An Act to Amend The Employment Standards Act, 1974 (Mr Bounsall)*, 4th Session, 31st Legislature (Not Passed), (Toronto: Queen's Park, 1980), sec. 33(1); Ontario, *Private Member's Bill 82: An Act to Provide for Equal Pay for Work of Equal Value (Ms Bryden)*, 3rd Session, 32nd Legislature (Toronto: Queen's Printer, 1983), sec. 33(1); Ontario, *Private Member's Bill 15: An Act to Provide for Affirmative Action and Equal Pay for Work of Equal Value (Bob Rae)*, 4th Session, 32nd Legislature (Toronto: Queen's Printer, 1984), sec. 33(1).

[116]For example, Canada, *Acts of the Parliament of Canada* (1977).

[117]Manitoba, *Pay Equity Act* (1985), secs. 8, 13; Ontario, *Bill 105* (1986), sec. 12.

[118]Ontario, *Bill 105* (1986), sec. 14; Federation of Women Teachers' Associations of Ontario, FWTAO *Response* (1986), p. 22.

[119]Bureau of National Affairs, *Pay Equity and Comparable Worth* (Washington, D.C., 1984), p. 9.

[120]US Congress, *Hearings* (1946), p. 161.

[121]Alice H. Cook, *Comparable Worth: A Case Book of Experiences in States and Localities* (Manoa, Hawaii: Industrial Relations Center at University of Hawaii at Manoa, 1985), pp. 222-8; Warren and Boone, 'AFSCME v. State of Washington', (1984).

[122]Ted Gest, Carey English, and Micheline Maynard, 'Fair-Pay Drive By Women Hits a Legal Detour', *U.S. News & World Report* (16 Sept. 1985), p. 31.

[123]US Congress, *Options* (1985), pp. 420, 422-3, 427, 546-7, 690.

[124]Joan McFarland, 'Women and Unions: Help or Hindrance', *Atlantis* 4, no. 2 (Spring 1979), pp. 48-70.

[125]Hana Aach, *Unions and Affirmative Action* (Ottawa: Canadian Labour Congress, Women's Bureau, n.d.), p. 2.

[126]British Columbia Federation of Labour, *Policy Statement: Equal Pay For Work Of Equal Value* (1980).

[127]Canadian Union of Public Employees, 'Workplace Inequality: It Will Persist Until We Get Equal Pay for Work of Equal Value', *The Factsheet*, Dec.-Jan. 1985); *Response* (1986), Appendix C.

[128]But for a 1977 strike over pay equity, see Stella Lord, 'The Struggle for Equal Pay for Work of Equal Value: A Case Study', *Alternate Routes* 4 (1980), pp. 21-52. Also see Aach, *Unions and Affirmative Action*, pp. 53-60.

[129]Canadian Union of Public Employees, Equal Opportunities Office, *A Co-ordinated National Strategy for CUPE Members on Pay Equity/Equal Pay for Work of Equal Value* (Adopted by the CUPE National Executive Board; Ottawa, 15 March 1986), pp. 17-19.

[130]Canadian Union of Public Employees, *Policy #3: Women's Economic Equality* (1985); *A Co-ordinated National Strategy* (1986), pp. 19-22.

[131]*CSAO News*, Feb. 1975, p. 2.

[132]Manitoba, *Oral Presentations* (1985), p. 12.

[133]New Brunswick Advisory Council on the Status of Women, *Equal Pay* (1985), pp. 6-7.

[134]Newfoundland and Labrador Federation of Labour, *Policy Statements* (n.d.).

[135]National Union of Provincial Government Employees, *Brief* (1986), p. 9; United

Steelworkers of America, *Brief* (1986), pp. 5-6, 12-14; *Toronto Star*, 6 Feb. 1980, p. C3; United Auto Workers Canada, *UAW Response to the Ontario Government Green Paper on Pay Equity* (Submitted by Robert White, President; 11 March 1986).

[136] These calculations are based on an analysis of a computer printout of contracts containing pay-equity clauses supplied to me by Kate Humpage, Women's Bureau, Labour Canada, Ottawa, 11 April 1989.

[137] National Union of Provincial Government Employees, *Brief* (1986), p. 2.

[138] For a listing of many of its complaints and their status, see Public Service Alliance of Canada, *Equal Pay for Work of Equal Value: Do You Have It?* (Ottawa, n.d.) pp. 3-18; see also Canadian Human Rights Commission, *Equal Pay Casebook* (1984).

[139] Public Service Alliance of Canada, *Equal Pay* (n.d.) pp. 3-4; Canadian Human Rights Commission, *Equal Pay Casebook* (1984), pp. 5-9. See also Ottawa Women's Lobby, *Submission* (1986), pp. 3-4.

[140] Public Service Alliance of Canada, *Equal Pay* (n.d.), p. 19; oral presentations by Rosemary Warskett and Penny Bertrand at the *Women and Unions Workshop* (University of Ottawa, 7-8 April 1989).

[141] See Organized Working Women and Ottawa and District Labour Council, *Response* (1986), p. 14; Ontario Federation of Labour, *Brief* (1986), pp. 13-16; Canadian Union of Public Employees, *Response* (1986), p. 30; United Steelworkers of America, *Brief*, (1986), p. 14; Equal Pay Coalition, *Equal Pay for Work of Equal Value: Media Release* (1985), p. 8; *Response* (1986), pp. 11, 24-5; Clark, Cook, and Dimma, *Report* (1986), p. 71.

[142] Equal Pay Coalition, *Response* (1986), pp. 34-6.

[143] For example, Ontario Secondary School Teachers' Federation, *Response* (1986), p. 10; Clark, Cook, and Dimma, *Report* (1986), p. 68.

[144] New Brunswick Advisory Council on the Status of Women, *Equal Pay* (1985), p. 13; Ontario Federation of Labour, *Brief* (1986), pp. 18-19; Equal Pay Coalition, *Equal Pay for Work of Equal Value: Media Release* (1985), p. 10; *The Equal Pay Coalition's Media Release: Legislative Proposals* (1985), p. 39; *Response* (1986), pp. 34-5; Clark, Cook, and Dimma, *Report* (1986), p. 69.

[145] Christian Labour Association of Canada, *Letter on Equal Pay* to the Honourable Ian Scott, Attorney General and Minister Responsible for Women's Issues, from Ed Vanderkloet, Executive Secretary (13 Nov. 1985), p. 7.

[146] Labour Canada, *Directory of Labour Organizations in Canada* (Ottawa 1985), pp. 62-3.

[147] Christian Labour Association of Canada, *Affirmative Action: The Perils of Social Engineering* (London, Ont., 1985), p. 1.

[148] Harry Antinodes, *Renewal in the Workplace: A Critical Look at Collective Bargaining* (London: Christian Labour Association of Canada, 1982).

[149] Christian Labour Association of Canada, *Letter on Equal Pay* (1985).

[150] Clark, Cook, and Dimma, *Report* (1986), p. 69.

[151] Ontario Chamber of Commerce, *Submission* (1986), p. 5; Canadian Manufacturers' Association, *Submission* (1986), pp. 7, 15; Ontario Mining Association, *Submission* (1986), pp. 3, 8.

[152] Clark, Cook and Dimma, *Report* (1986), p. 71.

[153] Board of Trade of Metropolitan Toronto, *Submission to the Consultation Panel* (1986), p. 33.

[154] Personnel Association of Ontario, *Submission* (1986), pp. 23-4.

[155] See Equal Pay Coalition, *Response* (1986), p. 32; Canadian Union of Public

Employees, *Response* (1986), p. 27-30; and Pupo and Duffy, 'Ontario Labour
Relations Board' (1988).
[156]Ontario, *Green Paper* (1985), p. 40. See also Ontario, *Bill 105* (1986), secs. 12-16;
Ontario *Pay Equity Act, 1987* (1988), sec. 4(4)-(5).
[157]See Congress of Canadian Women, *Submission* (1986), p. 2; Federation of Women
Teachers' Associations of Ontario, FWTAO *Response* (1986), p. 22; Ontario Secondary School Teachers' Federation, *Response* (1986), p. 6; Canadian Union of Public
Employees, *Response* (1986), pp. 24, 29; United Auto Workers Canada, Local 89,
Presentation to the Pay Equity Hearings (Submitted by Judith Decou; 11 March
1986); United Steelworkers of America, *Brief* (1986), pp. 9-10; Ontario Federation
of Labour, *Brief* (1986), p. 6; Equal Pay Coalition, *Response* (1986), pp. 32-4;
Submission (1987), p. 15; Clark, Cook, and Dimma, *Report* (1986), pp. 66-7.
[158]Ontario Chamber of Commerce, *Submission* (1986), p. 5; Canadian Manufacturers' Association, *Submission* (1986), pp. 7, 15-16; Clark, Cook, and Dimma,
Report (1986), p. 67; Board of Trade of Metropolitan Toronto, *Submission to the
Consultation Panel* (1986), p. 33.
[159]Clark, Cook, and Dimma, *Report* (1986), p. 66.
[160]For example, see Canadian Manufacturers' Association, *Submission* (1986), p. 16.
[161]See Clark, Cook, and Dimma, *Report* (1986), pp. 67-8, 70; Ottawa-Carleton Board
of Trade, *Brief* (1986), p. 9; Retail Council of Canada, *Submission* (1986), p. 15;
Automotive Parts Manufacturers Association, *Statement* (1986), pp. 3-5; Canadian
Manufacturers' Association, *Submission* (1986), p. 16; Day Care Advisory Committee of Metropolitan Toronto, *Submission* (1986), p. 12; Board of Trade of
Metropolitan Toronto, *Submission to the Consultation Panel* (1986), p. 15.
[162]Ontario Chamber of Commerce, *Submission* (1986), p. 6.
[163]Clark, Cook, and Dimma, Report (1986), p. 70; US Congress, Options, (1985), p. 670.
[164]Canadian Union of Public Employees, *Response* (1986), p. 5; US Congress, Senate
Committee on Labor and Public Welfare Subcommittee on Labor, *Equal Pay Act
of 1962: Hearings, August 1, on S. 2494 and H.R. 11677, To Provide Equal Pay for Equal
Work Regardless of Sex: Statements Submitted In Lieu of Oral Testimony*, 87th Congress, 2nd Session (Washington, D.C.: Superintendent of Documents, 1962), p. 70
(hereafter US Congress, *Hearings* [1962]).
[165]Canadian Manufacturers' Association, *Submission* (1986), p. 11.
[166]Equal Pay Coalition, *Response* (1986), pp. 33-4.
[167]Clark, Cook, and Dimma, *Report* (1986), p. 68; Manitoba, *Oral Presentations* (1985),
pp. 5-6.
[168]Manitoba, *Oral Presentations* (1985), pp. 5-6.
[169]Kottis, 'Female-Male Earnings Differentials' (1984), p. 215.
[170]Ornstein, *Accounting for Gender Differentials* (1983), p. 20.
[171]Aach, *Unions and Affirmative Action*, p. ii; see also Gunderson, 'Male-Female Wage
Differentials' (1975), pp. 467-8.
[172]United Auto Workers Canada, *UAW Response* (1986), p. 6.
[173]Michael D. Ornstein, *Gender Wage Differentials in Canada: A Review of Previous
Research and Theoretical Framework*, Series A, No. 1, Labour Canada, Women's
Bureau (Ottawa: Minister of Supply and Services, 1982), pp. 26-7; *Accounting for
Gender Differentials* (1983), p. 39; but see Gunderson, 'Male-Female Wage
Differentials' (1975), p. 467.
[174]Equal Pay Coalition, *Response* (1986), p. 34; US Congress, *Options* (1985), p. 428.
[175]Canadian Union of Public Employees, *Policy #3* (1985); *A Co-ordinated National*

Strategy (1986); US Congress, *Options* (1985), p. 428; National Union of Provincial Government Employees, *Brief* (1986), p. 6; Ontario Federation of Labour, *Brief* (1986), p. 13.

[176] US Congress, *Options* (1985), p. 272.

[177] Canadian Manufacturers' Association, *Submission* (1986), p. 19. See also National Citizen's Coalition, *Letter on Bill 154 to Coalition Supporters* (By Colin M. Brown, Chairman; 26 Jan. 1987), p. 2.

[178] Automotive Parts Manufacturers Association, *Statement* (1986), pp. 1-2.

[179] National Citizens' Coalition, *Brief on Bill 154 to the Standing Committee on Administration of Justice of the Legislature of Ontario* (25 Feb. 1987), p. 3; *Pay Discrimination* (1986), pp. 21-2.

[180] Cornwall Women's Network, *Response to the Green Paper* (Submitted by Marilyn Lawrie, Vice President; Cornwall, Ont., 1986), p. 2.

[181] Canadian Manufacturers' Association, *Submission* (1986), pp. 17-18; National Citizens' Coalition, *Pay Discrimination* (1986), p. 19.

[182] Tony Carlson, *Mainstream Canada: The Bitter Fruit of Comparable Worth* (Toronto: Canadian Federation of Independent Business Feature Service, n.d.).

[183] Sudbury and District Chamber of Commerce, *Public Consultation* (1986), p. 3; Retail Council of Canada, *Submission* (1986), p. 20; John S. McCallum, 'Does Equal Pay for Work of Equal Value Impose Costs on Women?' *Business Quarterly* 50, no. 3 (Autumn 1985), pp. 8-9; McDougall, 'Here Comes Equal Pay' (1985), p. 38; Canadian Manufacturers' Association, *Submission* (1986), pp. 17-18; National Citizens' Coalition, *Pay Discrimination* (1986), p. 19; REAL Women, *Equal Pay for UNequal Work* (n.d.), p. 5; *Green Paper* (1986), p. 8; Clark, Cook and Dimma, *Report* (1986), p. 76.

[184] Automotive Parts Manufacturers Association, *Statement* (1986), p. 8.

[185] Carlson, *Mainstream Canada* (n.d.).

[186] For example, Riddell, 'Work and Pay' (1985), p. 64.

[187] Ottawa-Carleton Board of Trade, *Brief* (1986), p. 8; Kitchener Chamber of Commerce, *Green Paper* (1985), pp. 1-2; Board of Trade of Metropolitan Toronto, *Submission* (1985), pp. 27-9; Carlson, *Mainstream Canada* (n.d.); Canadian Manufacturers' Association, *Submission* (1986), pp. 17-18; Retail Council of Canada, *Submission* (1986), pp. 18, 20; Automotive Parts Manufacturers Association, *Statement* (1986), p. 4; McDougall, 'Here Comes Equal Pay', (1985), p. 35; National Citizens' Coalition, *Pay Discrimination* (1986), p. 19; *Letter on Bill 154* (1987), p. 2; REAL Women, *Equal Pay for Unequal Work* (n.d.), p. 5; Christian Labour Association of Canada, *Letter on Equal Pay* (1985), p. 6; Clark, Cook, and Dimma, *Report* (1986), p. 76.

[188] Manitoba, *Oral Presentations* (1985), p. 17.

[189] Walter Block, 'Economic Intervention, Discrimination and Unforeseen Consequences,' in W.E. Block and M.A. Walker, eds, *Discrimination, Affirmative Action and Equal Opportunity* (Vancouver: Fraser Institute, 1981), p. 106. See also National Citizens' Coalition, 'NCC Backs "Men and Women for a Fair Market Wage" Group', News release (Toronto, n.d.).

[190] For example, see Times Change Women's Employment Service, *Brief to the [Ontario] Pay Equity Consultations* (Toronto, 10 Feb. 1986), p. 3; National Union of Provincial Government Employees, *Equal Value, Equal Pay* (1987), p. 50; United Food and Commercial Workers International Union, *Brief* (1986), p. 10.

[191] Kitchener Chamber of Commerce, *Green Paper* (1985), p. 2; McCallum, 'Does

Equal Pay' (1985), pp. 8-9; McDougall, 'Here Comes Equal Pay' (1985), p. 38; Carlson, *Mainstream Canada* (n.d.); Manitoba, *Oral Presentations* (1985), p. 17; REAL Women, *Equal Pay for UNequal Work* (n.d.), p. 5; *Green Paper* (1986), p. 8.

[192] Gregory and Duncan, 'Segmented Labour Market Theories' (1981), pp. 413-25.

[193] Ibid., pp. 413-25; Riddell, 'Work and Pay' (1985), p. 64; Edgecombe-Robb, 'Occupational Segregation' (1984), pp. 159-63; A. Zabalza and Z. Tzannatos, *Women and Equal Pay: The Effects of Legislation on Female Employment and Wages in Britain* (Cambridge: Cambridge University Press, 1985).

[194] Riddell, 'Work and Pay' (1985), p. 64.

[195] Edgecombe-Robb, 'Occupational Segregation' (1984), pp. 159-63.

[196] For example, Zabalza and Tzannatos, *Women and Equal Pay* (1985); Gregory and Duncan, 'Segmented Labour Markets' (1981).

[197] For example, see Riddell, 'Work and Pay' (1985), pp. 64, 66-7.

[198] For example, see Edgecombe-Robb, 'Occupational Segregation' (1984), p. 163; Buchele and Aldrich, 'How Much Difference' (1985), p. 232.

[199] Sudbury and District Chamber of Commerce, *Public Consultation* (1986), p. 3; McCallum, 'Does Equal Pay' (1985), pp. 8-9; McDougall, 'Here Comes Equal Pay' (1985), p. 38; REAL Women, *Green Paper* (1986), p. 8; Clark, Cook, and Dimma, *Report* (1986), p. 76.

[200] Julie White, *Women and Part-Time Work* (Ottawa: Canadian Advisory Council on the Status of Women, 1983), p. 41.

[201] Canadian Manufacturers' Association, *Submission* (1986), p. 11.

[202] Canadian Human Rights Commission, *The Canadian Human Rights Act: Employer Guide* (1981), pp. 29-30; *Equal Pay for Work of Equal Value: Interpretation Guide* (1984).

[203] Ontario, *Pay Equity Act, 1987* (1988), sec. 8 (1) (b), (3), and (4). See n. 104 above.

[204] McCallum, 'Does Equal Pay' (1985), pp. 8-9. See also McDougall, 'Here Comes Equal Pay' (1985), p. 38; Manitoba, *Oral Presentations* (1985), p. 17; REAL Women, *Equal Pay for UNequal Work*, (n.d.), p. 5; *Green Paper* (1986), p. 8.

[205] White, *Women and Part-Time Work* (1983), pp. 49-95; National Union of Provincial Government Employees, *Bargaining for Equality* (Researched and written by Susan Attenborough; Ottawa, 1982); Patricia Morrison, 'Part-Time Organizing', *Labour Ottawa Syndical* (Ottawa: Ottawa and District Labour Council, 1986), p. 33; Newfoundland and Labrador Federation of Labour, *Policy Statements* (n.d.); Ontario Federation of Labour, *Making Up The Difference: Ontario Women Speak Out: Brief to the Government of Ontario on the Results of the Ontario Federation of Labour Campaign on Women and Affirmative Action* (Compiled by Shelly Acheson and Janis Sarra; Toronto, April 1984), pp. 24-6.

[206] White, *Women and Part-Time Work* (1983), p. 26; United Steelworkers of America, *Brief* (1986), p. 8.

[207] Equal Pay Coalition, *Submission* (1987), p. 27.

[208] Canadian Union of Public Employees, *Response* (1986), pp. 20-1.

[209] Ontario Coalition for Better Daycare, *Brief* (1987), p. 4.

[210] Canadian Manufacturers' Association, *Submission* (1986), pp. 17-18; National Citizens' Coalition, *Pay Discrimination* (1986), p. 19; REAL Women, *Equal Pay for UNequal Work* (n.d.), p. 5; *Green Paper* (1986), p. 8; Clark, Cook, and Dimma, *Report* (1986), p. 76.

[211] See Canadian Manufacturers' Association, *Submission* (1986), p. 18.

[212] Organized Working Women, *Brief* (1986), p. 6.

[213] National Citizens' Coalition, *Letter on Bill 154* (1987), pp. 2-3; McCallum, 'Does Equal Pay' (1985), pp. 8-9; McDougall, 'Here Comes Equal Pay' (1985), p. 38.

[214] Manitoba, *Oral Presentations* (1985), p. 17.

[215] US Congress, *Options* (1985), pp. 672-81.

[216] Ontario, *Green Paper* (1985), p. 48; US Congress, *Hearings* (1946), pp. 166-7; Ontario, *Debates*, 19 Nov. 1985, p. 1594. See also NAC, *Brief* (1986), p. 9.

[217] US Congress, *Statutes At Large. Public Law 88-38* (1964), sec. 2 (a).

[218] Ibid., sec. 3; Ontario, Employment Standards Act (1974), sec. 33(1); British Columbia, Chapter 186 (1979), sec. 6(2); Quebec, Revised Statutes, chap. C-12 (1979), sec. 19.

[219] Ontario, *Pay Equity Act, 1987* (1988), sec. 8 (1c).

[220] Amalgamated Clothing and Textile Workers Union, *Implementing Pay Equity* (1986), p. 4.

[221] Ibid., p. 32.

[222] Ibid., pp. 33-4.

[223] Cornwall Women's Network, *Response to the Green Paper* (Submitted by Marilyn Lawrie, Vice President; Cornwall, Ont., 1986), pp. 1-2; see also Ottawa Women's Lobby, *Submission* (1986), p. 11.

[224] Apparel Manufacturers Association of Ontario, *Pay Equity* (Submission to the Ontario Consultation Panel on Pay Equity; Toronto, 1986), p. 3.

[225] REAL Women, *Equal Pay for UNequal Work* (n.d.), p. 5; *Position Papers, Publication No. 3* (n.d.), p. 5.

[226] Manitoba, *Oral Presentations* (1985), p. 17.

[227] McCallum, 'Does Equal Pay' (1985), pp. 8-9; McDougall, 'Here Comes Equal Pay' (1985), p. 38.

[228] Canadian Manufacturers' Association, *Submission* (1986), p. 20.

[229] Ibid., p. i; Ontario, *Green Paper* (1985), p. 12.

[230] Canadian Manufacturers' Association, *Submission* (1986), pp. v, 12.

[231] See Gary North, 'The Feminine Mistake: The Economics of Women's Liberation', *The Freeman* 21, no. 1 (Jan. 1971), pp. 8-11; McCallum, 'Does Equal Pay' (1985), p. 6; US Congress, *Options* (1985), p. 165.

[232] For example, Canadian Manufacturers' Association, *Submission* (1986), p. 4.

[233] Clark, Cook, and Dimma, *Report* (1986), p. 49.

[234] Retail Council of Canada, *Submission* (1986), p. 14.

[235] Schlafly, ed., *Equal Pay for UNequal Work* (1984); 'Shall I Compare Thee to a Plumber's Pay?' *Policy Review* 31 (Winter 1984), pp. 76-8; US Congress, *Options* (1985), p. 453.

[236] REAL Women, *Green Paper* (1986), p. 7.

[237] Ibid., p. 9; see also US Congress, *Options* (1985), p. 508.

[238] National Citizens' Coalition, *Pay Discrimination* (1986), p. 17.

[239] Manitoba, *Oral Presentations* (1985), pp. 6, 7.

[240] See Canadian Association of Women Executives, *Response* (1986), p. 4; Equal Pay Coalition, *Equal Pay for Work of Equal Value: Media Release* (1985), p. 3; Manitoba, Oral Presentations (1985), p. 13; US Congress, *Options* (1985), pp. 428, 630.

[241] Equal Pay Coalition, *Response* (1986), p. 11. For an identical argument from feminist organizations, see Congress of Canadian Women, *Submission* (1986), p. 1; and Organized Working Women, *Brief* (1986), p. 3.

[242] Canadian Union of Public Employees, Response (1986), p. 10; United Auto Workers Canada, UAW Response (1986), p. 4; Ontario Federation of Labour, Brief (1986), p. 6.

[243] United Steelworkers of America, *Brief* (1986), p. 10; see also United Food and Commercial Workers International Union, *Brief* (1986), p. 8.

[244] National Union of Provincial Government Employees, *Brief* (1986), p. 4; Equal Pay Coalition, *Response* (1986), p. 11.

[245] Ontario Secondary School Teachers' Federation, *Response* (1986), p. 12; District 31 (Sudbury), *Response* (1986); United Steelworkers of America, *Brief* (1986), p. 10.

[246] Ontario Federation of Labour, *Brief* (1986), p. 6. See also Ontario Public Service Employees Union, *Meeting the Challenge* (1986), p. 10; *Submission* (1986), pp. 8-9; *A Rose Is Not Enough: Pay Equity in Ontario* (May 1986), p. 5.

[247] Canadian Union of Public Employees, *Response* (1986), pp. 19-20; Equal Pay Coalition, *Response* (1986), pp. 22-3; Confederation of Canadian Unions, *A Brief* (1986), p. 5.

[248] Canada, *Acts of the Parliament of Canada* (1977), chap. 33; Canadian Human Rights Commission, *The Canadian Human Rights Act: Employer Guide* (1981), p. 29; *Equal Pay for Work of Equal Value: Interpretation Guide* (1984).

[249] Ontario, *Pay Equity Act, 1987* (1988).

[250] Quebec, *Revised Statutes*, chap. C-12 (1979), sec. 19; US Congress, *Statutes At Large, Public Law 88-38* (1964), sec. 3(d)(1).

[251] For example, Buchele and Aldrich, 'How Much Difference' (1985).

[252] For example, Edgecombe-Robb, 'Occupational Segregation' (1984), p. 159.

[253] Gunderson, 'Time Pattern' (1976), p. 63; 'Spline Function' (1985), p. 777.

[254] E.g., Edgecombe-Robb, 'Occupational Segregation' (1984), p. 159.

[255] Buchele and Aldrich, 'How Much Difference' (1985).

[256] E.g., Riddell, 'Work and Pay' (1985), p. 62.

[257] Gregory and Duncan, 'Segmented Labour Market Theories' (1981), pp. 408-13.

[258] Zabalza and Tzannatos, *Women and Equal Pay* (1985); see also B. Chiplin, M.M. Curran and C.J. Parsley, 'Relative Female Earnings in Great Britain and the Impact of Legislation', in Peter J. Sloane, ed., *Women and Low Pay* (London: Macmillan, 1980), pp. 106-18.

[259] Gunderson, 'Spline Function' (1985), p. 781; see also Gunderson, 'Time Pattern' (1976), pp. 67-8.

[260] Gunderson, 'Spline Function' (1985), pp. 777, 788; see also Gunderson, 'Male-Female Wage Differentials' (1975).

[261] Gunderson, 'Spline Function' (1985), pp. 784-9; 'Discrimination, Equal Pay' (1985), pp. 249-51.

[262] US Congress, *Hearings* (1946), pp. 161, 171.

[263] See Eugene Forsey, *Trade Unions in Canada, 1812-1902* (Toronto: University of Toronto Press, 1982), pp. 139, 221, 401, 444-5; Gregory Kealey, *Toronto Workers Respond to Industrial Capitalism, 1867-1892* (Toronto: University of Toronto Press, 1980), p. 228; Gregory Kealey and Bryan Palmer, *Dreaming of What Might Be: The Knights of Labour in Ontario, 1880-1900* (Cambridge: Cambridge University Press, 1982), pp. 318, 320-1.

[264] Marie Campbell, 'Sexism in British Columbia Trade Unions, 1900-1920', in Barbara Latham and Cathy Kess, eds., *In Her Own Right: Selected Essays on Women's History in British Columbia*. (Victoria, BC: Camosun College, 1980), p. 183.

[265] Paul Phillips and Erin Phillips, *Women and Work: Inequality in the Labour Market* (Toronto: James Lorimer, 1983), pp. 141-2.

[266] Muszynski, 'The Organization of Women' (1984), pp. 90, 92-3.

3

The Marketplace

A marketplace is a sphere in which goods and services are exchanged, either on a barter basis or for money. In the consumer market, workers purchase commodities essential for their physical and cultural survival. In capital markets, businesses buy and sell money, stocks, commodities, and their own means of production, such as machines and buildings, in order to expand their corporations and realize profits. In the labour market, workers sell their labour power, or capacity to work, to businesses in exchange for a wage so that they can gain some monetary means of subsistence. Much of this chapter concerns the labour market.

Gender and class struggles around four main issues will be discussed: whether gender discrimination exists in the labour market; the acceptability of state intervention in the marketplace in the form of job evaluations and equal pay for work of equal value; whether pay equity strengthens or weakens gender barriers to the mobility of women and men among occupations; and the likely economic consequences of pay equity for the marketplace. Feminist organizations and trade unions have favoured state intervention in the marketplace to erase gendered wage discrimination, while business associations and anti-feminist and neo-conservative organizations have opposed such efforts to correct a problem that in their minds does not exist.

HUMAN CAPITAL VS. DISCRIMINATION

1. Social-scientific studies

Economists and sociologists have discovered that anywhere from one-third to two-thirds of the gendered wage gap can be explained by a variety of labour-market, human-capital, productivity-related, and demographic factors (such as job experience, seniority, age, training or education, full- vs. part-time work, hours of work, unionization, the gendered segregation of occupations and industries, labour-force attachment, and desire for work flexibility).

Thus part of the explanation of why women are paid less then men lies in the fact that (a) they normally have less job experience and seniority; (b) they leave the labour force for temporary periods to have children or for other reasons; (c) they are less highly unionized than men (unionized employees are paid more highly than non-union employees); (d) they are segregated into low-paying occupations and economic sectors; and (e) they have less specialized education in non-traditional areas, such as engineering and dentistry. The proportion of the gendered wage gap that these factors explain is called the 'explained variance'. But the rest is left unexplained.

This 'unexplained variance' is large: from about one-third to two-thirds of the total size of the wage gap.[1] The difficulty comes when we attempt to explain its size and identify its components. One popular interpretation is that the unexplained variance consists of technical mistakes called 'measurement errors'; another attributes it to job- and family-related factors that were not measured or taken into account; a third points to discrimination by employers in the hiring, promotion, and payment of women. We don't know what proportion of the unexplained variance consists of each of these three factors, since none of them is measured or taken into account.[2] It is precisely because of this ambiguity that, in the political conflict surrounding pay-equity legislation, interpretation of the unexplained variance has given rise to such heated gender and class struggles.

2. Class and gender struggles over explained and unexplained variances

(a) Feminist-labour positions

The feminist-labour alliance has taken four different positions on closing the wage gap by legislation. One argument has been that the unexplained variance consists of gender-related factors that cannot be explained by so-called non-gender-related variables within the marketplace, such as education and job experience: all of it is attributable to discrimination, which should be corrected through legislation. In the US this position has been popular among feminists within the Communications Workers of America, the Public Employees Department of the AFL-CIO, and the American Federation of State, County and Municipal Employees.[3] Other elements in the alliance began to broaden the meaning of discrimination to include factors contained within the explained variance, such as gendered occupational segregation,[4] and women's unequal access to the specialized education that leads to high-paying jobs. In other words, they began to see systemic discrimination in almost all aspects of the wage gap, and to demand legislation to correct it. This position was adopted in the US by the National Organization of Women (NOW) and Federally Employed Women, an organization dedicated to advancing equal opportunity for working women employed by the federal government and foreign service.[5] A third argument has attacked human-capital explanations of the gendered wage gap, rejecting claims that women's lower education and job experience explain the wage gap with the counter-argument that the wage gap persists even where women have comparable education and experience. Finally, attempts were made to introduce race discrimination into the pay-equity debate alongside the question of gender discrimination. The Service Employees International Union in the US conducted a study of gender and race discrimination among Los Angeles County employees whom it represented. It found that women were paid $6,000 to $10,000 less than men, minority men were paid $6,000 less than white men, and minority women were paid $10,000 less than white men. It called for comparable-worth legislation that would raise the wages both of minority women and men and of white women to the level of white men's wages.[6]

(b) The business and anti-feminist response

The opponents of equal-value legislation responded with the following arguments.

ABSENCE OF DISCRIMINATION. The coalition of neo-conservative anti-feminists and businessmen have used two arguments to 'prove' the absence of discrimination. First, they have denied that employers discriminate against their women employees by paying them a lower wage than their male employees.[7] The reason is simple:

> If a firm underpaid workers in women's occupations, in the sense that their wages were held below their real contributions to the firm's receipts, other firms would have a strong incentive to hire workers in these occupations away, bidding up the wages in these occupations. . . . This process could only be thwarted by collusion,

an unrealistic prospect considering the hundreds of thousands of firms.[8]

Second, business organizations have argued that, since the portion of the wage gap attributable to discrimination by employers cannot be scientifically measured, it does not exist. Therefore no equal-value or comparable-worth legislation should be introduced to correct it. This view has been popular in the US within the National Association of Manufacturers, the Chamber of Commerce, the Civil Rights Commission, and the anti-feminist Eagle Forum,[9] and in Canada within the Ontario Chamber of Commerce.[10]

UNEXPLAINED VARIANCE DOES NOT EQUAL DISCRIMINATION. Neo-conservative anti-feminists, along with many economists, have argued that it is risky to associate the unexplained variance with discrimination; it can just as easily consist of measurement error and factors outside the marketplace that have not been taken into account.[11] REAL Women of Canada tried to 'prove' this through a puzzling analogy with Jews that borders on anti-Semitism. It cited a study by Chiswick, who found that non-Jewish white males earned only 64 per cent as much as Jewish males; this amounted to a wage gap of 36 per cent. Standard statistical controls for such human-capital factors as education and job experience, common in the economics literature, showed that 16 percentage points still remained unexplained. REAL Women stated: 'Based on "discrimination" theory, the conclusion is that nearly one-half of the Jewish earning advantage would be due to discrimination against non-Jewish white males.'[12] REAL Women suggested that, since this obviously was not the case, 'cultural characteristics' enabling Jews to attain more human capital than non-Jews were probably at work. The implication was that the unexplained variance in the wage gap between women and men is due not to discrimination, but to 'cultural characteristics' that enable men to attain greater human capital than women.

EXPLAINED VARIANCE DOES NOT EQUAL DISCRIMINATION. Business and its neo-conservative anti-feminist allies have rejected the labour-feminist argument that the explained variance contains hidden discriminatory factors. Instead, they have argued that most of the wage gap can be explained by non-gender factors that are neither explicitly nor implicitly discriminatory, and that therefore equal-value or comparable-worth legislation, designed to correct the discriminatory part of the wage gap, should not be introduced. In 1962 the National Association of Manufacturers in the US suggested that the wage gap could be explained by differences between women and men in human-capital and other factors, such as bargaining agreements, labour-market conditions, job performance, time and piece rates, hourly rates, levels of productivity, length of the working week, amount of overtime pay, education, training, skill, and job seniority and experience. This view was echoed by the National Federation of Independent Business and the Chamber of Commerce in the US,[13] and in Canada by the Atlantic Provinces Chamber of Commerce.[14] The neo-conservative anti-feminist organizations in Canada echoed the views of US and Canadian business on this question. The National Citizens' Coalition cited Toronto economist Morley Gunderson to argue that almost all of the wage gap was due to gender-based occupational differences and productivity-related factors, such as education, job experience, time worked, training, location, occupation, and industry.[15] REAL Women suggested that the wage gap was caused by women's lower education, job seniority, hours of work, and labour-force commitment, and greater desire for flexibility in labour-force arrangements.[16] On the right fringe of the labour movement, the Christian Labour Association of Canada argued that proponents of equal-value legislation did not take sufficient account of 'education, experience, attachment to the workforce, job satisfaction, hours of work and working conditions'.[17]

PAY EQUITY EQUALS PAY DISCRIMINATION. In Ontario the National Citizens' Coalition argued that equal-pay laws would themselves constitute discrimination:

> One of the worst effects which Pay Discrimination [Pay Equity] will have on women will be to demean them and to sap their sense of self-worth. If the policy of Pay Discrimination [Pay Equity] is implemented, there will be groups of women in the private sector who will know that the only reason that they're getting a part of their income is because they're women—not because they deserve it, or have worked for it, but solely because of their sex.

For the Coalition, pay equity effectively meant that the state response to women would be to 'Coddle them! They [proponents of pay equity] are effectively ensuring appointment of many women as a reward for being born female.'[18] In addition, the

Coalition argued that pay equity would discriminate against men because they would not be allowed to lodge unequal-pay complaints under the legislation.[19]

THE EDUCATION SOLUTION TO UNEQUAL WAGES. As an alternative to pay-equity legislation, some opponents have suggested improved education and training for women—a logical sequel to their emphasis on education as one explanation of the gendered wage gap. Six interrelated proposals have been put forward. First, young women at an early age in elementary schools should be taught the importance of pursuing non-traditional occupations.[20] Second, selected women presently in non-traditional jobs, such as welding and engineering, should be sent into the schools to provide role models for female students; in the US, the National Association of Manufacturers had already set up such a program 'to explain to our nation's youth the wide range of opportunities for women in corporate America'.[21] Third, programs should be set up in the workplace to train women on the job.[22] Fourth, special re-training programs should be established for women re-entering the labour force.[23] Fifth, as a substitute for the 'rigid' job-classification systems set up under pay-equity legislation, merit should be used more often as a principle in job promotions.[24] Finally, more state funds should be poured into special training and educational programs for women to increase their opportunities in the paid labour market.[25]

FREEDOM OF MARKETPLACE VS. STATE INTERVENTION

The labour-feminist alliance has locked horns with business, and its anti-feminist and neo-conservative allies, over three interrelated issues concerning the relationship of the state to the marketplace: the freedom of the market to operate according to objective laws of supply and demand; the merits of state intervention, in the form of equal-value legislation, in the private marketplace; and the merits of job-evaluation methodology as the particular form of state intervention to implement equal pay for work of equal value or comparable worth. The class and gender lines of struggle over these issues are clear-cut: the labour-feminist alliance does not believe that the marketplace is free; it supports state intervention in the marketplace; and, with some reservations, it supports the use of job-evaluation methodology. In contrast, the business community and its anti-feminist allies believe that the marketplace can and should be free from external interference; they object to state intervention in the form of comparable-worth legislation; and they detect a number of flaws in the ways state job-evaluation methodology is to be implemented. The freedom of the marketplace and state intervention will be discussed in this section, and job evaluations will be treated in the next.

1. Freedom of the marketplace

In both Canada and the US, business and neo-conservative anti-feminist organizations have thought it important to preserve the sanctity of a free marketplace. They believe that the labour market operates according to objective laws of supply and demand: wages are set objectively by the confluence of the supply of labour-power and the demand that exists for certain kinds of skills in particular occupations and industries. According to the US Chamber of Commerce,

> what the market does is process information on the scarcity of talents, the tastes of heterogeneous individuals, the demands of consumers and the availability and cost of other resources and technology. Market wages primarily reflect a balance between what employers are willing to pay for workers' services and how much is needed to induce workers to supply the labour for particular jobs.[26]

Similarly in Canada, associations such as the Sudbury and District Chamber of Commerce, the Ottawa-Carleton Board of Trade, REAL Women, and the National Citizens' Coalition (NCC) held that the forces of supply and demand were sacred and had to be preserved.[27] Concern over the possible negative effects of pay-equity laws prompted the NCC and REAL Women to join with the Ontario section of the Retail Merchants' Association, the Canadian Organization of Small Business, and Berwich Ferguson Payroll of Toronto[28] in a coalition called Men and Women For A Fair Market Wage to protect the freedom of the marketplace.[29] Within the universities, some economists sided with business in believing that pay equity would interfere with the freedom of the marketplace; others, however, thought that pay equity would not seriously hamper the laws of supply and demand.[30]

The labour-feminist alliance has argued that the marketplace has never been free and has never followed, exclusively and simply, the objective laws of supply and demand. In the US,

Barbara Hutchinson, a representative of the American Federation of Government Employees, argued that

> labour markets are an amalgam of supply and demand, bargaining power, expectations of career commitments, historical understanding of fair wages, social valuation of relative wages, and individual prejudices. As a result, there are numerous opportunities for discriminatory wage-setting practices to become established and engrained in any pay system.[31]

Feminists and labourites have deeply resented what they see as attempts by employers to hide behind the myth of the objective marketplace to mask their own discriminatory wage practices. This viewpoint was forcefully put forward by the National Organization of Women in the US in 1985. The strength of its statement makes it worth quoting at some length:

> Opponents of pay equity may glorify the so-called 'free market' as the proper determiner of wages in this economy, but we know that *employers* set wages. . . . The market is . . . manipulated by employers through price controls and wage-fixing. For instance, employer associations in larger cities are widely known to meet periodically to *set* the 'prevailing' market wage for nurses and secretaries in their area. We cannot allow ourselves to be fooled by the disingenuous professions of loyalty to the free market by those who profit from discrimination. . . . To those anti-pay equity doomsayers of the Reagan Administration who say that fairness is an impossible ideal in the labour market which operates 'freely', we reply that the marketplace is ruled by very visible corporate hands which mold its operation to maximize profit. Women will bear the high cost of sex-based wage discrimination no longer.[32]

In Canada, similarly, the Congress of Canadian Women, a member of the Ontario Equal Pay Coalition, told the Ontario Consultation Panel on Pay Equity:

> when the free market fails to deliver the rightful demands of the citizenry, the citizenry have every right to modify it with rules and regulations. Left to itself, the free market might well be employing children in the mines to this day. The privilege of the free market is an argument put forward only by those for whom the free market is an advantage. For the overwhelming majority, it impinges on their lives in the form of inequity, unemployment, over-priced housing and products. This is our country, and the population are under no constraint to accept lowering standards of living in the name of some mythical and virtually non-existent free market.[33]

2. State intervention

(a) The patriarchal capitalist objections

Business and neo-conservative arguments that the attempt to legislate equal pay for work of equal value or comparable worth constitutes an unwarranted intervention in the private marketplace have taken six forms.

INTERFERENCE IN PRIVATE DECISIONS OF CAPITAL. In the business view, legislating pay equity represents an interference in the private right of employers to set the wages for their employees. In 1962, the National Association of Manufacturers in the US complained that legislating pay equity would 'involve undue interference in the work relationship in a manner which would cause serious and numerous operating difficulties, interference with efficient management, and prove disruptive to good relations between employers and employees'.[34] Similar sentiments were expressed in 1985 by the American Farm Bureau Federation, representing 75 per cent of the commercial farms and ranches in the US.[35] In Canada, precisely the same grounds for opposing pay equity have been voiced by such business organizations as the Canadian Federation of Independent Business, the Winnipeg Chamber of Commerce, the Canadian Manufacturers' Association, and the Automotive Parts Manufacturers Association.[36]

INTERFERENCE IN THE RIGHT OF WORKING WOMEN TO COMPETE. A second argument is that pay-equity legislation represents interference with the right of working women to compete in the open market by offering their labour services at cheaper rates than men. In 1969 a British corporate woman, the director of a multi-million-dollar labour-exchange organization supplying woman-power to corporations, was asked on a Los Angeles talk show 'what she thought of the fact that women get paid less than men for their labour. "Well," she replied, "the best form of competition we women have is our willingness to work at lower wages. If you were to eliminate that, you would remove our most effective weapon."'[37] Neo-conservative anti-feminist organizations have elevated women's cheap labour to the level of an individual right to be protected against intervention by the state and feminists. One such organization in the US was the Foundation for Economic Education, which believed in the triple pillars of limited or no government intervention, private property, and the free market with open competition among all wage earners. Writing for this organization in 1971, Gary North suggested that

> what the competent woman needs, especially the woman who is not loaded down with paper qualifications, is that initial shot at the job that will serve as her testing ground, regardless of whether she gets a paycheck as large as a man's. What she does not need, and what those of us who benefit from her greater productivity do not need, is the establishment of the WFL's [Women's Liberation Front's] neomedieval principle, 'equal pay for equal work'.[38]

Displaying the patriarchal sexism common to such anti-feminist organizations, North suggested ways in which women can keep their labour cheap:

> A woman who is seriously concerned with getting fair pay for her contribution—mental, physical, or simply resembling Raquel Welch—has to ask this question: *What would it cost this company to replace me?* If a woman knows that there are five other women ready and willing to take her secretarial job at $350 a month, then she would be wise not to demand very much more than $350 a month in wages. She can demand a bit more, given the costs of training a new girl, the difficulties involved in all bureaucratic changes, and the tastes of her boss with regard to what constitutes someone who is sweet, cute, and so forth. But she must limit her demands.[39]

OVEREXTENDED STATE. Legislating pay equity, its opponents claim, would result in the growth of yet another division in the state bureaucracy at considerable cost to the taxpayer. In the US, the Chamber of Commerce estimated that passing the 1963 Equal Pay Act would create '"another vast Federal Bureaucracy" with an annual budget beginning at more than $1 million and the addition of 240 employees to Uncle Sam's payroll'.[40] In 1986, the Canadian Manufacturers' Association argued that 'equal pay for work of equal value legislation would impose an additional layer of government regulations and complexity for manufacturers who are already overwhelmed by legislative requirements'.[41] REAL Women of Canada predicted that equal pay for work of equal value would create 'a huge bureaucracy which must carry out this exhaustive, long-term classification of jobs—the cost to be paid by the taxpayers'.[42] The National Citizens' Coalition drew an analogy between central state planning in Soviet agriculture and state legislation of pay equity in Canada: in both cases an overextended state distorts the private marketplace.[43]

STATE BURDEN ON SMALL BUSINESS. Another argument has been

that legislating pay equity would weigh particularly heavily on the small business sector, already suffering from ambiguous over-regulation. Small business has generally been resentful of what it perceives as the growing burden of state intervention in its 'free enterprise sector'. In a survey of the members of the Canadian Federation of Independent Business, over half the business owners in Ontario were said to 'regard government regulation, red tape and paperwork to be a significant problem, second in importance only to the problem of total tax burden'.[44] Especially where such regulations were not in the interest of small business, the Federation looked with disdain on government bureaucracy, referring to the state as the 'regulatory morass which bears so heavily on small business'.[45] In its 1986 submission it complained that government regulations were often unclear in their application to small businesses, resulting in penalties for violations of laws they could not interpret or understand.[46] It claimed that the ambiguity surrounding the meaning of job evaluation, the basis of many equal-value laws, would be a further frustration for small and medium-sized businesses.

STATE 'PAY POLICE'. Business has also claimed that legislating equal pay for work of equal value would place a considerable amount of dictatorial and arbitrary power in the hands of in-dividual state bureaucrats who know nothing about running a business. Calling such officials 'pay police', the National Citizens' Coalition complained that the Ontario Act gives 'pay police a wide range of powers which include entering business premises without a warrant, and searching, seizing and removing private records'. The 'pay police' would be able to 'impose wages upon businesses [and] determine those wages using arbitrary guidelines to "value" jobs. . . . there will be no appeal of decisions by the pay police beyond the Pay Equity Commission of On-tario.'[47] Although not using the term 'pay police', the National Association of Manufacturers in the US also complained that, under the 1963 Pay Equity Act,

the Secretary of Labour becomes prosecutor, judge and legislator. He is given extensive authority to intervene and interfere in employer-employee relations. . . . There is no limit to the inter-ference with efficient operations or the amount of snooping which may result in an effort to uncover evidence concerning existing or possible future wage discrimination.[48]

Similarly, the US Chamber of Commerce complained that the Secretary of Labour would be given 'vast new powers over private industry with authority to investigate complaints, conduct hearings, issue orders, regulations and interpretations, and initiate legal actions to enforce complaints.'[49] Similar business resentment of new pay-equity bureaucrats was voiced in Canada.[50] Don King, partner and Vice-President of Thorne Stevenson and Kellogg, management consultants in Toronto, argued that equal-value legislation was 'a legalistic nightmare. We could end up with an army of bureaucrats armed with statistical tables, dictionaries and computers invading the private sector. It would be costly to society and costly to business, and it would accomplish nothing.'[51]

PARASITIC NEW MIDDLE CLASS. Finally, according to its opponents, the legislation of equal pay for work of equal value would increase the size of a parasitic new middle class of consultants and experts who would benefit from the legal and technical problems involved in trying to implement the law. The National Citizens' Coalition suggested that the main beneficiaries would be the professional bureaucrats and consultants for whom such legislation would create jobs, and it cited Nadine Winter, director of the equal-employment planning group at Hay Management Consultants in Toronto, who stated that 'consultants who say that jobs cannot be compared "are undermining their reason for existence"'.[52] The Manitoba Progressive Party, a neo-conservative organization, exhibited distrust and cynicism toward both state bureaucrats and the new middle class of private-sector consultants and job-evaluation experts. Party spokesperson Sidney Green complained to the Standing Committee of Industrial Relations in the Manitoba Legislative Assembly about the middle-class 'bureaucrat who never did an honest day's work in his life, never produced anything of value, and is now going to say what other people should earn'.[53]

(b) The feminist-labour response

The labour-feminist alliance has made two basic responses to these objections to equal pay for work of equal value. First, arguing that state intervention is the only way to eliminate gender discrimination in the marketplace caused by employers' hiring and promotion practices, it has proposed that two state institutions—legislative bodies and the courts—be used for these purposes. (a) Legislative assemblies, Parliament, or Congress should be lobbied to pass strong versions of equal pay for work of equal value. Collective bargaining without legislative support is not adequate to redress unequal wages; as Susan Hart, executive secretary of the Manitoba Federation of Labour, argued: 'The private sector won't respond to demands for equal pay for work of equal value without legislation.'[54] (b) Then the courts should be used to seek redress and compensation. In the US, public-sector trade unions such as the American Federation of State, County and Municipal Employees and the National Association of Government Employees have not hesitated to use the courts to win pay-equity settlements.[55]

The second response of trade unionists and women's organizations has been to make light of the business fear of state intervention in the marketplace. In 1978, for instance, the Canadian Association of Women Executives, in a brief on pay equity to the Ontario Minister of Labour, noted that the state was already involved in 'intervention in the workplace. . . . the Province is already involved in legislating, monitoring and penalizing, where necessary, employers under the Employment Standards Act and Human Rights Code.'[56] Using a quite different example, in 1986 the Congress of Canadian Women pointed to the huge bureaucracy in the criminal justice system: 'yet no one suggests that crime should not be punished because it involves such lengthy procedures.'[57] Unionists and feminists also argued that the business community, and to a lesser extent labour, had benefitted considerably in the past from state intervention. The Ontario Federation of Labour pointed out that 'business and workers alike have benefited for years from "intrusions" into the marketplace—the abolition of child labour, health and safety laws, minimum wage laws, are all protections for workers just as tax write-offs, preferential interest rates, tax free business loans have allowed business to profit.'[58] Similarly, the Federation of Women Teachers' Associations of Ontario observed that employers did not object to state intervention where they were the beneficiaries.[59]

JOB-EVALUATION METHODOLOGY

The implementation of equal pay for work of equal value requires some kind of methodology or procedure by which the characteristics of female- and male-predominant jobs may be evaluated. Because such methodologies are the bases for the adjustment of women's wages, they represent the most direct intervention by the state in the marketplace in the matter of pay equity. In this section four issues will be discussed: four types of job evaluation; the meaning of 'value' or 'worth' of a job; gender and class conflict over the subjectivity or objectivity of job-evaluation methodologies; and the possibility of hidden gender biases in these methodologies.

1. Types of job evaluations

Job-evaluation systems were first developed in the early 1930s.[60] There are four main types: job ranking, job classification or grade description, points rating, and factor comparison.[61] Each will be briefly described, and then all four will be compared.

JOB RANKING. In this system, entire or whole jobs (rather than their separate characteristics) in an organization are ranked (often by sorting cards listing the jobs) from the highest to the lowest on the basis of a set of job descriptions. Often only two criteria, such as responsibility and skill, are used by the raters. In one variation of this method, each job is ranked by pairing it off against every other job. Job ranking is feasible in small organizations or businesses with roughly a hundred jobs or fewer. But because complete information on the jobs' characteristics may be lacking, their ranking may be highly subject to the uncontrolled and unconscious biases of the raters.[62] However, the Ontario Pay Equity Commission has recommended its adoption in small businesses if all four criteria are used: skill, effort, responsibility, and working conditions.[63]

JOB CLASSIFICATION OR GRADE DESCRIPTION. In the job-classification method, similar jobs are divided into groups, such as shop, clerical, administrative, and research and teaching; in the grade description method, each group may consist of dissimilar jobs that nevertheless have similar value to the employer. In both methods, each group is subdivided into a number of job classes, and each class is then given a description. On the basis of these descriptions, specific jobs are slotted into these classes. The drawback of the job-classification method is that groups tend to be gender-specific and, since they include only broadly similar jobs (e.g., clerical or production jobs) cannot be used internally to compare dissimilar jobs.[64] The weakness of the grade-description method is that, since whole jobs are slotted into classes and their separate factors are not weighted, quite dissimilar jobs may be lumped together. In

Lemons vs. *City and County of Denver* in the US, for instance, nurses complained that dissimilar health-care jobs were classified in the same group.[65]

POINT RATING. Rather then examining whole jobs, this method breaks each job down into separate factors, such as skill, effort, responsibility, and working conditions. Each of these factors is then divided into sub-factors, as shown in Appendix B. Skill may be divided into on-the-job experience and educational qualifications; effort may be subdivided into physical and mental; responsibility may be subdivided into money, determination of company policy, equipment, contact with the public, and supervision of others; working conditions may be subdivided into danger, monotony, interruptions, and time pressure. Each job receives a certain number of points on each subfactor. Each subfactor is also weighted according to its importance to the employer or in the marketplace, or some other criterion. All the points of each job are then totalled, and the jobs are plotted on a graph accordingly. If the ranking represents too radical a departure from the present job hierarchy or from market rates, the company can change the weights assigned to the subfactors. This is a widely used job-evaluation plan.

FACTOR COMPARISON. Key or benchmark jobs are broken down into separate compensable factors, such as skill, working conditions, and physical requirements. To each factor is assigned a numerical score for each job and a weight reflecting the relative importance of the factor to the organization and thus meriting compensation. All the key jobs are ranked and the non-key jobs are slotted between the key jobs.[66] This method is often considered to be subjective and to reflect too closely the market rates for jobs.[67]

COMMENTS. Four general comparative comments may be offered about these job-evaluation methodologies. First, job ranking and job classification are qualitative. They are used more often in small organizations, and less often for equal pay for work of equal value. The point-rating and factor-comparison systems are quantitative. They are used more often in large organizations, and in the context of equal pay for work of equal value. However, the Ontario Pay Equity Commission does not recommend the use of factor comparison for pay-equity purposes, partly because it often employs current salaries to rank jobs and thus reflects gender biases.[68] Second, factor comparisons and point ratings are employed most often for management and clerical or white-collar positions.

Manual or blue-collar jobs are the least likely to be the subjects of formal evaluations. Third, in most applications a single job-evaluation system does not exist for all occupations within an establishment; several different methodologies and systems are usually used in combination in the same establishment (a point to which we will return below). Fourth, most job-evaluation plans do employ the four factors of skill, effort, responsibility, and working conditions.[69]

2. 'Value' or 'worth' of a job

The 'value' or 'worth' of a job has been the most difficult concept to define in the struggle over equal pay. Business and neo-conservative anti-feminists have argued that 'value' should be established according to either (a) the objective laws of the marketplace or (b) the worth of the job to the employer. Rejecting the first of these arguments, feminists and trade unionists have implied that 'value' either (c) is intrinsic to the job content in some undefinable but objective sense, or (d) could be based on the Marxian labour theory of value or the costs of the means of subsistence of the workers filling the job. (This is what feminists refer to when they argue that women work in the paid labour force out of 'economic necessity', and should therefore be paid a 'fair' wage rather than 'pin' money.)

Since these four considerations are rather elusive, the 'value' or 'worth' of a job has in practice been established by comparing it with other jobs, usually in terms of skill, effort, responsibility, and working conditions. The assumption in the pay-equity debates has been that women in jobs with a majority of women (female-predominant) are paid below their 'value'—that is, they are discriminated against in the sense that part of the wage for their jobs is determined negatively by female gender predominance. As a result, a common technique that arose in many pay-equity applications was to compare the jobs in which women predominated (e.g., in which 60 per cent or more were women) with jobs in which men predominated (e.g., in which 70 per cent or more were men).[70] Job 'worth' or 'value' became a composite comparative score usually combining effort, skill, responsibility, and working conditions. If the composite score, or total points, for a female-predominant job was equivalent to the composite score of a male-predominant job, then the women were to be paid as much as the men. But what weightings should be applied to the four criteria? Should skill be more heavily weighted than working conditions? Should responsibility be more heavily weighted than effort? It is around such questions that disputes have broke out over the objectivity of job-evaluation methodology.

3. Subjectivity vs. objectivity

(a) Business, neo-conservative and anti-feminist positions

Representatives of the bourgeoisie and anti-feminist and neo-conservative organizations have argued that the attempt to assign numbers to the value of jobs is unscientific, subjective, and arbitrary, reflecting the personal biases of the evaluator rather than the objective realities of the marketplace. In the US the National Association of Manufacturers complained that in an Iowa job evaluation, the results indicated that 'bosses should be paid less than their employees, and that some part-time employees should be paid the same as full-time employees doing the same job'. It also complained that a Wisconsin job evaluation found that 'secretaries endured more stress than airline pilots'.[71] In mounting the biased-subjectivity argument, the business communities of Canada and US apparently co-operated to a considerable degree. In 1985, the National Association of Manufacturers in the US presented a table (see Table 3.1 below) to the Subcommittee on Compensation and Employee Benefits of the Committee on Post Office and Civil Service in the Congressional House of Representatives.[72] It is a comparison, among four studies in four different states, of the job-evaluation scores of four female-predominant jobs (practical duty nurse, dental assistant, telephone operator, and data entry operator I) with one male-predominant job (electrician). Sharon Spigelmeyer, spokesperson for the Manufacturers, used the table to illustrate the arbitrariness, subjectivity, and biases involved in job-evaluation methodologies. Practical duty nurses were scored higher than electricians in Wisconsin, Iowa, and Washington, but lower in Minnesota. Dental assistants were ranked higher than electricians in Wisconsin, and lower in the other three states. Telephone operators' scores ranged from 49 to 91 per cent of electricians' across the four states. Those of data entry operators ranged from 43 to 72 per cent. The Ontario Chamber of Commerce, the Canadian Newspaper Publishers Association, and the Canadian Manufacturers' Association copied this table from a document of the Wisconsin Association of

Manufacturing and Commerce,[73] and in 1986 presented it to the Ontario Consultation Panel holding hearings on pay equity.[74] Their arguments were similar to those of their American business counterparts regarding the subjectivity, arbitrariness, and biases involved in job-evaluation methodologies.[75] Other business associations, such as the National Federation of Independent Business and the Chamber of Commerce in the US, and the Canadian Federation of Independent Business, the Sudbury and District Chamber of Commerce, the Winnipeg Chamber of Commerce, the Retail Council of Canada, and the Automotive Parts Manufacturers Association in Canada, fell in line with this critique.[76] The Metropolitan Toronto Board of Trade argued that job evaluations could not detect the presence or absence of gender discrimination because of their inherently subjective nature, as reflected in the arbitrary assignment of weights to different factors and subfactors.[77] Management and personnel-officer associations within the new middle class, such as the American Society for Personnel Administrators and the Personnel Association of Ontario, reiterated the business arguments that pay equity had to be based primarily on objective market forces.[78]

TABLE 3.1
JOB WORTH POINTS AS A PERCENTAGE
OF POINTS ASSIGNED TO ELECTRICIANS

	Wisconsin	Iowa	Minnesota	Washington
Electrician	100	100	100	100
LPN 2 Nurse	150	124	79	108
Dental Assistant	108	77	50	73
Telephone Operator	91	64	49	60
Data Entry Operator 1	55	72	43	63

Not to be outdone, anti-feminist organizations also attacked the subjectivity of job-evaluation plans. Phyllis Schlafly of the anti-feminist Eagle Forum told a Congressional committee: 'Comparable worth evaluations must be recognized as a racket to get people with your own biases on the evaluation team or to saddle the evaluator with a contract that binds him [*sic*] to produce the results you predetermine.'[79] There was no essential difference between this opinion and those held by anti-feminist organizations in Canada. REAL Women argued that the job-evaluation process is inherently subjective ('the bias of the one doing the comparing'), raising the question 'how does one compare the value of the typist with that of a garbage collector?'[80] The National Citizens' Coalition rejected job evaluations on the grounds that they are inherently subjective and arbitrary, attempting to replace market-determined wages with the subjectivity of state evaluators. To back up its claim, it quoted several neo-conservative American opponents of comparable worth, such as June O'Neill and Charles Krauthammer, and Peter Germanis of the Heritage Foundation.[81]

(b) The labour-feminist response

Feminists have responded to such attacks on the objectivity of job evaluations by criticizing their crude and simplistic arguments. First, one cannot compare job evaluations *between states* (as the National Association of Manufacturers did in Table 3.1 above), since the job structures across state boundaries are different and not comparable. Second, one can compare job-worth scores only *within organizations*. Criticizing job-evaluation methodologies by comparing classification systems *between corporate establishments* is invalid because inter-corporate job structures are too varied to compare their relative composite scores. Third, it is not legitimate to compare *different job evaluation systems* (again, as the National Association of Manufacturers did in Table 3.1), as each system assigns *different weights* to effort, skill, responsibility, and working conditions.[82]

Many trade unions and feminist organizations strongly supported gender-neutral and objective job-evaluation methodologies despite the possibility of some minor flaws, which, they argued, should not hold up the granting of equal pay.[83] US labour organizations, wholly or partly in the public sector, that took this position included the American Federation of Government

Employees, the National Federation of Federal Employees, the National Treasury Employees Union, the Public Employees Department of the AFL-CIO, the Communications Workers of America, the American Federation of State, County and Municipal Employees, and the Service Employees International Union.[84] The same position was taken by such American feminist organizations as the National Organization of Women, the League of United Latin American Citizens (representing Hispanic women), and Federally Employed Women.[85]

The labour-feminist alliance in Canada also supported gender-neutral and objective job-evaluation plans, but added three additional demands. First, the Manitoba Association of Women and the Law wanted a further specification of the four criteria of skill, effort, responsibility, and working conditions.[86] Second, unions in Canada, taking account of the complexity of work situations, wanted a variety of job-evaluation methodologies to be used.[87] In 1980 the United Steelworkers recommended three separate job-evaluation plans: a production and maintenance plan using a point system weighted towards responsibility factors; an office and technical point system weighted more heavily towards skill and responsibility; and a supervisory plan weighted more heavily towards responsibility in the direction of others: 'Different factors and different weighting of the factors must be used since factors such as physical effort and hazards are of little value in office and technical jobs, while skills and mental effort are more important in such occupations and must be in greater proportion to the total weighting used in the plan for these jobs'.[88] Third, the unions suggested using a variety of mechanisms other than job evaluations as a means of achieving pay equity. With CUPE in the forefront, they suggested the following seven alternatives to be used separately or in combination with job-evaluation methodologies.

EQUALIZATION OF BASE OR STARTING RATES. In 1979 the British Columbia division of CUPE passed a resolution supporting the equalization of base or starting rates of pay between inside clerical workers (predominantly female) and outside manual workers (predominantly male) as one equal-pay strategy. Contract negotiations to achieve this end were started in municipal and school board locals in the lower British Columbia mainland.[89] Through negotiations, the Steelworkers also established equivalent base rates between the plant and the office in the steel industry.[90]

ACROSS-THE-BOARD DOLLAR INCREASES. At its 1981 convention, CUPE passed a resolution opposing percentage wage increases. Because these mean a greater absolute wage increase for higher-paid workers (who tend to be men) than lower-paid workers (who tend to be women), they discriminate against women.[91] Instead, as a way of implementing equal pay (at least partially), CUPE suggested the institution of either across-the-board dollar increases, so that everyone would receive the same absolute increase, or a percentage increase for low-paid workers and a sliding scale of lower percentage increases for higher-paid workers, as suggested by the Quebec CUPE locals.[92] The Manitoba Federation of Labour noted that, since 1970, it had been urging its affiliates 'to settle for straight dollar or dollar plus percentage settlements to raise the relative level of lower paid classifications, many of which have been "female dominated"'.[93] Between 1975 and 1985 the Manitoba Government Employees Association negotiated pay increases with the government that incorporated both 'flat dollars and percentage amounts', which had the effect of upgrading the lower classifications containing large numbers of women.[94]

REDUCING INCREMENT STEPS. CUPE argued that incremental systems are discriminatory because they are applied differentially to women and men. Women must often pass through a greater number of increment levels than men to achieve their negotiated level of pay. In most school boards clerical workers (female-predominant) must go through five increment levels, compared to one or two for maintenance workers (male-predominant). At Kenora Patricia Child and Family Services, there were six increment levels for social workers: women were hired at the lowest level, while men were hired at the upper levels, although both groups had the same training and experience. In Quebec hospitals, electricians had no incremental steps and were paid the full job rate almost immediately, while nurses had to work twelve years to reach their full job rate. Such differential application of incremental systems to women and men thus became a device used by employers to underpay women, despite the fact that they usually had sufficient experience and training to reach the full job rate at the top of the incremental steps. CUPE recommended that its locals negotiate the elimination or reduction of the incremental steps as a strategy for implementing equal pay.[95] The Steelworkers, rather than getting rid of increment levels, developed a plan through negotiations with management whereby increments occurred twice as fast in the female-predominant office, which had half as many job classifications as the male-predominant plan.[96]

INTEGRATION OF PAY LINES. As an alternative to job evaluation, CUPE also suggested integrating the pay lines of clerical and manual workers, so that no differential would exist between pay rates at different points along the scale from the lowest to the highest paid workers within each category.[97]

NEGOTIATION OF PAY-EQUITY ADJUSTMENTS. Some labour organizations, including the Manitoba Government Employees Union and the Ontario Federation of Labour, suggested that unions could also, as a pay-equity strategy, negotiate 'special pay adjustments for lower-paid classifications' through collective bargaining.[98] As a special strategy, the Ontario Public Service Employees Union (OPSEU) ran a linear regression line through the wages of female-and male-predominant public service jobs in Ontario. It found that for each 1 per cent increase of females in jobs, there was a $1.15 decrease in weekly wages, and arrived at a maxim: 'If you are a woman, the more women who do your kind of work, the less money you make; the more men who do your kind of work, the more you make.' OPSEU suggested a simple solution: employers should simply pay out the percentage gap shown by its linear-regression analysis based on the formula of 'percent female x $1.15'. For example, all females in a job class that is 78 per cent female would have 78 x $1.15 = $89.70 added to their weekly wages, or $4,664.40 a year. OPSEU felt that this simple, easily understandable method would avoid the expense of hiring the high-priced pay-equity consultants who, in its view, usually worked for branches of US multinational corporations.[99]

INCREASING MINIMUM-WAGE RATES. In its 1985-86 bargaining, CUPE's Ontario Council of Hospital Unions proposed a minimum entry-level rate; the wages of all positions below cleaner were to be brought up to the level of cleaner. This would establish a minimum wage rate of $10.00 per hour. Since most of the low-paid workers were women in clerical, housekeeping, laundry, and dietary positions, this was in effect an equal-pay proposal.[100]

POLICY-CAPTURING METHODOLOGY. In the mid-1980s, the Centre for Women in Government at the State University of New York at Albany developed this method as a radically new way of doing job evaluations for pay-equity purposes;[101] it was subsequently adapted by the Ontario Public Service Employees Union (OPSEU) and the Human Resources Secretariat in the Ontario Public Service.

In 1983, the Centre for Women in Government was asked by New York State and the Civil Service Employees Association to conduct a study of the content of all state employees' jobs for the purposes of pay equity. It decided to use a methodology in which an employer's implicit wage-setting policy is made explicit (i.e., 'captured') by identifying those factors that it compensates and those it does not. Determining the extent of discrimination based on gender and ethnic/racial minority-group membership, it consists of three stages.

First, by filling out closed-ended multiple-choice questionnaires, employees describe the characteristics of their own jobs. Between 30 November 1984 and 6 March 1985, 36,812 questionnaires were sent out to New York State employees; 27,394 were returned, for a response rate of 74 per cent. Analysis was conducted on 25,852 usable questionnaires covering 2,582 job titles. In 1989, OPSEU and the Human Resources Secretariat began their own policy-capturing study by sending out a preliminary questionnaire to a sample of employees in the Ontario Public Service. One or both of these two questionnaires included items measuring many of the factors and subfactors listed in Appendix B. For example, the 'skill' factor included formal education; reading, writing, and editing in one or more languages; math skills; use of computers; communications skills; memorization of facts; actual job experience; nurturing and comforting skills; and manual and physical skills. 'Effort' included intense concentration; careful attention to detail and accuracy; working under time pressure with pre-set quotas; and dealing on the telephone with people who are angry, threatening, or abusive. The 'responsibility' factor included working with confidential material, such as medical records or politically sensitive documents; time spent on co-ordinating projects; input in decisions affecting the public; guidance of work done by inmates; and responsibility for part-time staff, for money, and for finances. 'Working conditions' included the amount of physical mobility in the job; dust; lack of privacy; working under constant noise or with toxic chemicals; outdoor conditions; contact with dead or sick people; lifting people without the aid of mechanical devices; and the number of nights spent away from home.[102]

Second, an attempt is made to discover the common factors underlying the responses to the questionnaire items, and to identify which of these factors are compensated by the employer by statistically regressing wages and salaries on them. Statistical regression is a technique used to 'explain' or predict changes in something (e.g., salaries) on the basis of changes in something else (e.g., education and job experience). The New York study found that 15 job-content characteristics (consisting of 8 factors plus 7 other items and indexes) explained approximately 90 per cent of the variance in wages and salaries. The most important factors in compensation were education, job experience, management and supervision, and complexity in writing. Perhaps surprisingly, the study found that, independent of the 15 job characteristics, minority-group membership did not result in the undervaluing of jobs. However, also independent of these job characteristics, the proportion of women in a job *was* associated with lower pay—in other words, jobs disproportionately filled by women were found to be undervalued.

Third, policy-capturing methodology also makes it possible to determine which job characteristics are either not compensated or negatively rewarded. The New York study found that un-favourable working conditions (for 'those who work in unusual heat, cold, etc., or are involved in unusually strenuous physical effort') and 'communication with the public' were 'penalized rather than compensated'. Other job characteristics—such as 'contact with difficult clients and jobs involving stress', data entry, and computer programming—were found to be neither penalized nor rewarded. The authors of the study concluded that 'there may be bias in the current compensation model for New York State. For example, contact with difficult clients and data entry are content characteristics associated with disproportionately female and minority institutional and clerical jobs. They currently are not valuable job content characteristics for pay purposes.'[103]

Although policy-capturing methodology may be seen as the best way to achieve pay equity in large worksites with many employees spread across many diverse jobs, it has three major disadvantages. First, there is not the same collective involvement (e.g., as in pay-equity committees) of employees that occurs when some of the other methodologies are used. Second, because 'experts' use computers, statistical regression, and fixed-choice questionnaires, workers often find the whole procedure alienating and difficult to comprehend. Third, according to the authors of the New York State study, 'since existing wages are used as the basis for obtaining factors and weights, policy-capturing represents an essentially conservative approach to job evaluation. . . . it tends to preserve existing wage relationships among jobs and rationalize implicit pay policies.'[104] What is gained in statistical precision and scientific 'objectivity' and validity may be lost by failing to challenge an employer's implicit pay policy and missing an opportunity to create a collective solidarity among employees.

4. Hidden gender biases

Trade unions and feminists within the labour movement have worried about the possibility of biases in job-evaluation methodologies, particularly biases against women. These could take at least three different forms. A fourth kind of bias, against men, has been suggested by anti-feminist organizations.

(a) Inconsistency between pay rates and job evaluations

Historically, pay rates inconsistent with the evaluation points assigned to jobs were a significant form of discrimination against women. The United Electrical Workers in the US suggested that, during the Second World War (1939-45), General Electric and Westinghouse used job-evaluation schemes to *reinforce* pay discrimination against women. At the Westinghouse meter plant in Newark, New Jersey, even though they were put on the same evaluation scale as men's jobs, 'women's jobs were arbitrarily put into separate labour grades which pay rates 15 cents an hour less than the equivalent male rate with the same job content'. Similarly, at General Electric women and men were put on the same evaluation scale, but the pay rates for women's jobs were established arbitrarily at two-thirds the rates of male jobs.[105]

(b) Non-recognition of women's job skills

A more contemporary form of bias against women is to overlook or ignore skills specific to female-predominant jobs when assigning weights in job-evaluation scales. Connie Bryant, National Director of Public Workers within the Communications Workers of America, suggested that job-evaluation plans in the US public sector recognized lifting boxes and driving vans, but not typing or shorthand, as special skills. This works to the disadvantage of women, who are more likely to be doing the latter than lifting boxes or driving vans.[106] The Ontario Pay Equity Commission noted that women's job skills can be overlooked when doing studies of job content based on observations, interviews, and questionnaires. Men often overdescribe their job skills, while women often underdescribe theirs. 'For example, a male job class might be defined as involving "managing", while a similar function for a female job class might be described as "supervising."' In addition, skills that are seen as extensions of women's domestic responsibilities—such as nurturing and taking care of others—are often ignored, while 'physical strength', stereotypically associated with male job skills, is rarely overlooked.[107] OPSEU pointed out that the breadth of women's job descriptions may function to de-emphasize their skills:

> Women's work may be characterized under broad headings of 'clerk' or 'secretary', which fail to recognize substantial differences in the work and the skills required to perform it. In contrast, there may be an extensive, more individualized list of men's jobs such as maintenance plumber, maintenance electrician, electrical maintenance mechanic, mechanic 1 and mechanic 2.[108]

(c) Devaluation of women's job skills

The most common form of hidden gender bias against women in job evaluations is to assign low weights to skills important in female-predominant jobs. In 1985 the National Federation of Federal Employees in the US complained about these kinds of hidden gender biases in the Federal Government Factor Evaluation System, which had not been revised since 1923. It stated to Congress that the Factor Evaluation System assigns little value to contacts with co-workers and the public—important for nurses—but high value to contacts with 'high ranking officials'—more important to males in the authority hierarchy: 'The end result is that typically female jobs continue to be given lower grade status.'[109] Also in the US, the National Political Congress of Black Women, citing the work of Louise Howe, author of *Pink Collar Workers*, complained that in the federal government job evaluation, 'child care attendants, nursery school teachers, and home health aides were ranked at the bottom—at 878—lower than dog pound attendants—at 874—and marine mammal handlers—at 378—which were seen as more skilled.'[110] Even within the manual blue-collar sector, weightings may favour male-predominant jobs over female-predominant ones. For example, among semi-skilled manual workers, lifting may be given a greater weight than manual dexterity; women factory workers would thus rank lower than male factory workers on this factor.[111]

The Ontario Equal Pay Coalition recognized that past job evaluations often undervalued women's skills such as nurturing in child-care centres, or communications skills among receptionists and switchboard operators.[112] CUPE was concerned about gender biases that give men's jobs greater weight than women's. Group skills, such as co-operation and work-group communication, which are more important in some women's jobs, are often ranked (if at all) lower than the individual skills more important to male jobs. Similarly, the physical effort and danger involved in male jobs such as steel smelting are ranked higher than the working conditions important in women's office jobs, such as lack of privacy, eye strain, monotony, noise, and stress.[113]

(d) Anti-feminist concern with biases against men

Anti-feminist organizations have been mostly concerned with biases against men in job evaluations. Phyllis Schlafly of the anti-feminist Eagle Forum stated in 1985 that job evaluations had the potential of placing low weights on physical work—an important element in male blue-collar jobs. For instance, she suggested that combining the federal US white- and blue-collar job schemes would disadvantage men because the white-collar system placed only 5 per cent of total points on '"physical demands" and "working environment" combined'. She argued that the Willis evaluation scheme put men down by overweighting mental demands, thereby giving (female-predominant) nurses 122 points and (male-predominant) electricians and truck drivers only 30 and 10 points respectively.[114] In Canada, the National Citizens' Coalition summarized its view that pay equity was discrimination against men by changing the name of 'Pay Equity' to 'Pay Discrimination' in its 1986 brief to the Ontario government.[115]

OCCUPATIONAL MOBILITY

Two specialized questions regarding the mobility of women between occupations in the labour market have arisen in the pay-equity debates in both Canada and the US. First, has there been a trend towards the withering away of gendered occupational segregation, resulting in a narrowing of the wage gap that makes pay-equity legislation unnecessary or redundant? Second, would legislating pay equity raise the wages of women in traditional occupations, such as clerical and service work, thereby encouraging women to stay there and resulting in a strengthening of gendered occupational segregation? The disagreements between the business community and the labour-feminist alliance over each of these questions will be briefly outlined.

1. Does declining occupational segregation make pay-equity legislation unnecessary?

(a) The business answer

Business associations have suggested that, since women's situation in the labour market is already improving, there is no need to legislate equal pay for work of equal value. They have developed four closely related arguments.

EDUCATION. Business has argued that women are increasing their access to higher educational institutions in non-traditional areas at a faster rate than men. In 1985 the American Chamber of Commerce stated to a US Congressional subcommittee that, between 1971 and 1981, female enrolment had increased from 9 to 35 per cent in law schools, from 11 to 28 per cent in medical schools, and from 2 to 19 per cent in dental schools. It also noted increases in female enrolment in other non-traditional courses, such as engineering, business and management, communications, architecture and environmental design, physical science, and computer and information science.[116] Canadian business associations have made similar arguments.[117] The Metropolitan Toronto Board of Trade stated that between 1972 and 1982, 'the percentage of full-time women undergraduates increased 9%. Full-time graduates increased 12.5%. In the same years, the percentage of women receiving first degrees rose from 37.5% in 1972 to 51.9% in 1982. In Master's degrees from 23.7% to 40.4% and in Doctorates from 9.3% to 25.6%.'[118]

DECREASE IN OCCUPATIONAL SEGREGATION. Business associations have suggested that, on the basis of better education and training, women are already moving at an accelerated rate into non-traditional occupations, resulting in a decrease in gendered occupational segregation. In the US, both the National Association of Manufacturers and the Chamber of Commerce argued that occupational gender segregation was withering away.[119] As the Chamber of Commerce stated: 'More women are being employed as executives, administrators, managers, lawyers, doctors, dentists, engineers and highly skilled workers.'[120] In Canada, small businesses pointed out that women were setting up their own businesses in increasing numbers and at a faster rate than men. [121] A review of the American and Canadian literature, and research in Canada, by Bonnie Fox and John Fox, suggests that gender occupational segregation has been declining since the early 1960s, mostly because women have been entering occupations formerly dominated by men. Nevertheless, such segregation remains quite high: in Canada, 'over 60 per cent of men or women in the labour force in 1981 would have had to change occupational categories for the two genders to have had the same occupational distributions.'[122]

NARROWING OF THE WAGE GAP. As noted in Chapter 1, partly because of women's movement into non-traditional occupations, the gendered wage gap has been narrowing. Business groups have argued that this makes new pay-equity laws redundant. In 1985 the US Chamber of Commerce, using data from the Rand Corporation, suggested that between 1920 and 1980 the wage gap did not narrow, but that there was a substantial narrowing during the early 1980s, and that this would continue over the next twenty years.[123] Likewise, the National Association of Manufacturers noted that in 1970 a woman earned 59 cents of every dollar that a man earned, but that by the fourth quarter of 1984 this figure had climbed to 66 cents, and it would continue to improve in the future.[124] The Canadian Manufacturers' Association argued against equal-value legislation partly on the grounds that the wage gap was already narrowing in response to market and other non-governmental forces. In 1986 it told the Ontario Consultation Panel on Pay Equity: 'On an hourly basis, the earnings ratio between men and women in Canada has gone from 66 per cent in 1970 to 72 per cent in 1980 and finally to 78 per cent in 1982. These trends reflect long term changes in societal attitudes, job expectations and career choices.'[125] The Winnipeg Chamber of Commerce suggested that there was no need for the Manitoba Pay Equity Act because it 'is a very costly way to achieve something that is already happening on its own'. That is, the wage gap was disappearing in the public sector in Manitoba: between 1973 and 1984, the wage gap in the Manitoba civil service decreased by 28.8 per cent; in the same period, wages of females in the civil service rose by 364 per cent compared to 89 per cent for males.[126] The Metropolitan Toronto Board of Trade suggested that the wage 'gap will narrow naturally. . . . the gap problem is diminishing *in the absence of equal value legislation.*'[127]

YOUNG WOMEN. Business associations have suggested that the trend in the narrowing of the wage gap is already evident among young women entering the paid labour force. According to the US Chamber of Commerce, hourly-rated full-time women between the ages of 20 and 24 earn 89 per cent what men do, while in the general labour force, full-time women workers earn 64 per cent and hourly-rated women 72 per cent of what men do.[128]

In summary, the business community of North America has argued that gendered occupational segregation is decreasing because women are receiving a better and more specialized education than in the past. As a result, they are moving into the high-paying non-traditional occupations, and this is helping to narrow the gendered wage gap, thereby making redundant the legislation of equal pay for work of equal value.

(b) The feminist-labour answer

The labour-feminist alliance has offered four arguments rejecting the business position.

PERSISTENCE OF GENDERED OCCUPATIONAL SEGREGATION. As evidence that occupational segregation was persisting rather than withering away, in 1985 the American Federation of State, County and Municipal Employees contended that only 2 per cent of carpenters and auto mechanics and only 3 per cent of truck drivers were women. By 1981, women were still only 4 per cent of engineers, 14 per cent of judges and lawyers, and 15 per cent of doctors.[129] The National Organization of Women (NOW) noted that the employment of women in non-traditional occupations in the US federal government had worsened during the 1980s, and that gendered occupational segregation in the paid labour force was continuing.[130] In Canada, the United Food and Commercial Workers International Union (UFCW) noted the continuing gender segregation of jobs in retail grocery chains, despite attempts to reduce it through collective bargaining. The vast majority of cashiers, meat wrappers, and deli clerks were women, while the overwhelming majority of meat cutters, bakers, and grocery and produce clerks were men. The UFCW argued that the work of the women was equal to that of the men, yet women's jobs were undervalued by the employers and paid less. Even though the 'female' and 'male' labels of these jobs in the collective agreements

of the pre-1970s had been removed, this pattern of gender segregation has persisted into the 1980s.[131]

RACIAL OCCUPATIONAL SEGREGATION. The labour-feminist alliance has also argued that racial segregation is solidly integrated
with gendered occupational segregation, both of which reinforce
one another. These arguments have been made in the US by such
organizations as the Mexican-American Women's National Association (MANA) and NOW.[132] Gloria Barajas, vice-president for
program planning of MANA, told a subcommittee of the US Congress:

> Pay equity is a remedy for sex- and race-based wage discrimina-
> tion. Hispanic women are at the bottom of the wage gap between
> women and men. We remain there because of job segregation based
> on sex and race and/or ethnicity. Economic equity for Hispanic
> women will not occur until this job segregation is eliminated. Job
> segregation can only be eliminated through the establishment of
> comparable pay for work of equal value.[133]

WHY SHOULD WOMEN HAVE TO SWITCH JOBS? The labour-feminist
alliance has questioned why women should have to switch from
their traditional jobs, such as waiting on tables in restaurants or
typing in offices, to non-traditional jobs, such as carpentry or
welding, in order to achieve pay equity. In 1985 the American
Federation of State, County and Municipal Employees cited a
study indicating that 72 per cent of women would have to switch
jobs to achieve occupational equality with men; yet women have
had little success in entering traditional blue-collar jobs
dominated by men.[134] In Canada, the Federation of Women
Teachers' Association of Ontario argued that

> women should be able to choose other [non-traditional] occupa-
> tions. However, if women are in jobs which are undervalued, they
> should not have to change jobs in order to be adequately paid (or
> stay in the job until enough men enter the field and employers then
> re-evaluate the job). They should be paid properly for the work
> they now do, and move into other work only because they wish to
> do so.[135]

TIME REQUIRED TO CLOSE THE WAGE GAP. If there are signs of a
narrowing of the wage gap, according to the labour-feminist
alliance, the process has been extremely slow; it will take many
years for the gap to close without equal-value legislation. In the
US, NOW emphasized how little the wage gap had narrowed: in

1955, 'employers paid female workers less than 64 cents for every dollar paid to male workers, the same figure as in 1983'.[136] Jacob Mincer found that, in twelve industrialized countries, the wage gap fell from 38 per cent in 1960 to 29 per cent in 1980.[137] Extrapolating from his figures, if all factors remain in the same direction (which is an extremely risky assumption), the wage gap would narrow by an average of 0.45 per cent per year. Using this figure, it may be estimated that, other things being equal, the wage gap will not close completely until the year 2044, by which date very few women currently in the labour force will still be there. Neither the women's movement nor the labour movement is willing to wait that long.

2. Does pay-equity legislation increase occupational segregation?

(a) The business and anti-feminist answer

Business and neo-conservative anti-feminists have predicted that pay-equity legislation would increase occupational gender segregation by granting higher salaries to women in traditional jobs, thereby removing any incentive they might have had for moving into non-traditional employment, such as construction or engineering. In order to encourage women to move into non-traditional jobs, therefore, the state should not introduce equal pay for work of equal value. This argument was mounted by the Canadian Manufacturers' Association and the Metropolitan Toronto Board of Trade and, in the US, the National Association of Manufacturers. The latter argued that pay equity would introduce a 'separate but equal system' in which women might receive higher wages than at present, but would continue to be separated into gendered job ghettos.[138] Similarly, Phyllis Schlafly of the Eagle Forum told a US Congressional subcommittee: 'Women are already flooding the so-called traditional jobs by the millions. If the pay is raised for those jobs, even more women will seek those jobs and abandon plans to go into nontraditional lines of work.'[139]

(b) The labour-feminist answer

Rejecting the claim that pay-equity legislation would intensify gender-based job segregation, feminist and labour organizations argued that, on the contrary, it would break the barriers down. The Ontario Secondary School Teachers' Federation suggested that the positive relation between pay equity and job desegregation would help to open new possibilities for female students: 'equal pay legislation will go a long way in encouraging female students to choose non-traditional jobs.'[140] The Canadian Auto Workers Union, for its part, implied that pay equity would encourage men to apply for traditionally women's jobs. As its president, Bob White, told the Ontario government: 'Until the wage gap is closed we cannot hope to find more men in traditionally female jobs. No one would voluntarily take that kind of a pay cut.'[141]

ECONOMIC CONSEQUENCES

Both class and gender struggles have arisen over the possible economic consequences for the marketplace of legislating equal pay for work of equal value. These struggles have primarily focused on four points: potential costs; state deficits and taxes; inflation and consumer purchasing power; and the disruptive effects on companies and the competitiveness of capital. Business and its anti-feminist and neo-conservative allies have adopted the view that equal pay for work of equal value is too expensive; it would increase the state debt, taxes, and the inflation rate; and it would weaken the purchasing power of the consumer and the international competitive position of capital, leading to economic disruption and bankruptcies. The labour-feminist alliance has generally minimized the negative effects of the costs and economic disruptions, arguing that it is time business began to pay its women employees properly, after so many years of earning super-profits by underpaying them.

1. Costs of implementing pay equity

(a) The business position

Business associations in both Canada and the US have developed three main arguments to show that their corporations, the economy, and governments could not afford the astronomical costs of implementing equal pay for work of equal value.

SIZE OF COSTS. In 1985, Canadian business interests estimated that the public-sector Manitoba Pay Equity Act would cost $50 to $60 million over four years, and stated that they feared a repetition of what happened in the state of Washington, where initial costs escalated to over $1 billion because back-pay had been ordered by the courts.[142] In Ontario the Canadian Manufacturers' Association (CMA) estimated that if equal pay for work of equal value was extended to private industry and the wage gap closed over four to six years, the total cost to private industry would be between five and six billion dollars.[143] And this estimate covered only direct wage costs; it did not include indirect and related costs—for instance, the implementation and maintenance of a job-evaluation system ($500 per employee), government enforcement, and 'the "chain reaction" effect of wage increases demanded by other groups following the legislated adjustment affecting one group'.[144] The Kitchener Chamber of Commerce totalled the direct and indirect cost estimates to arrive at a figure of $11 billion.[145] However, a more 'reasonable' estimate by economist Morley Gunderson put the cost in a range between $1 and $3 billion to cover anywhere from 400,000 to 1 million persons, each of whom would receive a wage adjustment of from $2,000 to $3,000.[146] In the US the Chamber of Commerce, using estimates from economists, suggested that equal pay for work of equal value in the private sector would cost employers $320 billion.[147] If comparable worth was restricted to the federal-government sector, the Chamber estimated that it would cost $6.6 billion; the National Association of Manufacturers put the figure at anywhere from $4.46 billion to $7.4 billion.[148] At the local state level, the National Association of Manufacturers estimated that comparable-worth legislation would cost the state of Washington $800 million; the state of Minnesota $42 million, merely to cover 8,225 employees in 151 job classes; and the state of Iowa $30 to $50 million.[149] These costs, business argued, were exorbitant and should be reason enough to defeat pay equity. The Metropolitan Toronto Board of Trade thought it detected a hidden motive behind the size of these costs: 'Equal value law . . . would constitute a form of wealth distribution in the guise of anti-discrimination legislation.'[150] It was not entirely wrong.

COSTS TO SMALL BUSINESS. Small-business associations asked how their members could afford pay equity. The Canadian Federation of Independent Business and, in the US, the National Federation of Independent Business told their respective governments that because small businesses have neither personnel departments nor job-evaluation systems, the owners would have to either create these to satisfy the legislation, or perform all the extra tasks themselves. Pay equity would cost small businesses more per employee than large corporations.[151] The Canadian Federation of Independent Business argued that the Ontario government's estimate of $200 to $300 in administrative costs per employee to run a job-evaluation system was probably an under-estimate for small businesses:[152]

> many of the [state] regulations and forms, we are told, require the interpretation of an accountant or lawyer, and they all absorb the time and money of the owner-manager. This means valuable hours away from the direct business activities of the firm, and for many owner-managers it demands form-filling during evenings and weekends. Many resent the time dedicated to doing the 'government's work', such as collecting sales tax.[153]

PAYROLL COSTS. Most governments estimated that pay equity would cost no more than 1 per cent of payroll per year, or a maximum of 4 per cent over four years. Some business associations, such as the Ottawa-Carleton Board of Trade and the Ontario Chamber of Commerce, were willing to accept these costs as long as they did not go any higher.[154] Other business associations suggested that these estimates were unreasonably low. The Winnipeg Chamber of Commerce worried about the 4 per cent of payroll to implement the Manitoba public-sector Pay Equity Act. Looking south of the border, it argued that in the state of Minnesota an initial cost estimate of 4 per cent of payroll, or $40 million, had escalated to 10 per cent or $250 million (and this covered only half of the public-sector pay-equity program). The Chamber suggested that this would be particularly problematic in Manitoba because the province did not have a surplus, as Minnesota did, and the Manitoba plan included fringe benefits: 'It starts with an interpretation and a suggestion that a cost will be a certain number and then it mushrooms and it escalates and nobody knows where it's going to end. That's the concern.'[155] In a similar vein, the Automotive Parts Manufacturers' Association of Canada told the Ontario government:

> The estimates of a three-to-four percent overall increase in wages can be thrown out the window in the automotive sector. Our estimates indicate that long term costs associated with Equal Value legislation could amount to double, or even triple, of our basic wage bill. These additional costs include the costs of administra-tion, any direct wage increases, wage spiralling which will occur and the resultant increased costs from the pattern bargaining in the automotive sector.[156]

(b) The labour-feminist position

The labour-feminist alliance has made five arguments rebutting the business objections regarding the large costs of pay equity.

LARGE, PROFITABLE CORPORATIONS CAN PAY. Labourites and feminists have long suggested that large corporations with huge profits can well afford to pay women a wage equivalent to men's. At the end of the Second World War, the United Electrical Workers Union in the US pointed out that the electrical manufacturing industry had increased its profits before taxes by 380 per cent from 1936-39 to 1944 (a figure much higher than for US manufacturing as a whole). The electrical manufacturing industry was at the height of its financial strength at the end of the war, and would not suffer by having to pay women equal wages.[157] Similarly, the United Rubber Workers of America and the Congress of Industrial Organizations (CIO) suggested that American manufacturing industry, without having to raise prices, could well afford to pay equal wages to women, since in 1944 it had enjoyed record profits after taxes of $5.8 billion, which was projected to rise to $6.3 billion in 1946.[158] Forty years later, the Canadian Auto Workers Union developed an argument based not so much on profits as on corporate size as a criterion of ability to pay women equal wages. In the mid-1980s, female sewing-machine operators at General Motors had their pay pulled up to $14.00 per hour by the sheer predominance of men in the plant (92 per cent of GM workers are male). But women doing the same work at two small-parts manufacturing plants, Bendix Safety Restraints Ltd and TRW Canada Ltd, made only $9.00 an hour. Bob White, president of the Auto Workers, argued: 'The ability of the employer to pay higher rates is not at issue since both these small companies are subsidiaries of large multinationals.'[159] The argument about corporate profits or size was not taken too far, since the labour-feminist alliance also expected smaller companies, corporations in a sluggish economy, and not-so-profitable businesses to pay women equal wages. Michele Landsberg, a feminist writer for the *Toronto Star*, suggested that if employers cannot pay women decent and fair wages, they should 'get out of the plant'.[160]

WOMEN SUBSIDIZE THE SUPER-PROFITS OF BUSINESS. The labour-feminist alliance has also suggested that for too long women have been subsidizing employers. The amount that pay equity would cost, according to business, is precisely the amount by which women have been subsidizing employers—in other words, by which they have been underpaid. Clifford McAvoy, Washington representative of the United Electrical Workers Union, suggested a direct cause-and-effect relation between industry's super-exploitation of their underpaid women employees and the size of its profits. He pointed out that, at the beginning of the Second World War, the electric-lamps division of the electrical machinery industry in the US had a workforce consisting of 77 per cent women and a value-added (one measure of profit) per manufacturing worker of $5,259, whereas the generating, distribution, and industrial-apparatus division, with a workforce of only 19 per cent women, had a much lower value-added of $3,784 per manufacturing worker.[161] (Value-added is the selling price of manufactured goods minus the costs of electricity, fuel, and material used in production.) Canadian labourites and feminists also thought that employers were making profits out of underpaying their women employees. The Ontario Equal Pay Coalition told the province's Consultation Panel on Pay Equity in 1986: 'Women are already being very lenient with the business community which has profited for many years by paying women unfairly. Our back-pay demands are very modest considering the massive wage losses suffered by women over the years including the interest owing on back-pay adjustments.'[162] Using a 'liberal' estimate of a 30 per cent wage gap, the Congress of Canadian Women put these wage losses or the super-exploitation of women by businesses in Ontario, at $3 billion per year, or at the very least $10 billion between 1976 and 1986.[163]

HUMAN RIGHTS HAVE NO PRICE TAG. The labour-feminist alliance has also objected to the denial of a basic human right to women on the grounds that it might be 'too costly'. Human rights do not have a price-tag; it is inappropriate to argue against equal pay for work of equal value because it might be too 'costly' for employers. The Federation of Women Teachers' Associations of Ontario contended that 'no injustice can be permanently tolerated in a civilized society on the sole grounds that its correction would cost money'.[164] CUPE and the Equal Pay Coalition told the Ontario government that both Canadian and American courts have ruled that costs and administrative convenience are not valid grounds for justifying discrimination or alleged violation of human-rights codes.[165]

SIZE OF PAY-EQUITY FUNDS IN PAYROLLS. The labour-feminist

alliance has adopted two positions on the question of payrolls. One was to suggest that the pay gap would never be closed by limiting the proportion paid from payroll to a maximum of no more than 1 per cent per year. The Ontario Equal Pay Coalition, which saw this maximum as 'a technique to minimize the financial impact on employers', raised the possibility that large numbers of low-paid women in some private-sector firms would have to wait up to sixteen years before achieving equal pay, because in fact it would take 8 to 10 per cent of payroll to make up the difference.[166] The Canadian Association of Women Executives, on the other hand, perhaps reflecting its privileged class position, suggested 1 per cent per year for a combined equal-value and 'employment equity' program,[167] while the Manitoba Government Employees Association agreed with the '1 per cent per year over four years' set out in the 1985 Manitoba Pay Equity Act.[168] But many labourites and feminists were not satisfied with this position. Under the Act, once the 1 per cent per year for four consecutive years is spent, the employer has no further obligation to spend any more money on pay equity.[169] The Charter of Rights Coalition (Manitoba) and the Manitoba Association of Women and the Law saw this provision as particularly offensive because it would not be sufficient to close the wage gap.[170] The Charter of Rights Coalition found that the section seemed to legitimize spending less than 1 per cent in each twelve-month period. Moreover, the 1 per cent ceiling over one year and the 4 per cent ceiling over four years were too low: they were not based on realistic Manitoba figures on the size of the wage gap. The Coalition thus pushed for greater amounts of money to be set aside for pay equity.[171] The Ontario Federation of Labour, Organized Working Women, CUPE, and the Canadian Auto Workers Union suggested an *annual* ceiling of 3 per cent of payroll.[172] The Ontario Equal Pay Coalition wanted equal pay achieved within five years: at least 1 per cent of payroll during the first year, with the remaining adjustments to be paid out in four equal instalments over the next four years, and faster payouts made to the lowest-paid women.[173] The Ottawa Women's Lobby wanted all pay-equity adjustments to be made within a three-year period.[174]

The second suggestion made by the labour-feminist alliance was that corporations set up a special trusted pay-equity fund within the payroll, *separate from the funds drawn upon in collective bargaining*, which could be used to raise women's wages up to the level of men's. According to the Ontario Equal Pay Coalition, such a provision was needed for two reasons. First, there must be assurance 'that pay equity funds are not taken from the general wage package that union members are trying to secure. Without a separation of funds, the employers who intend to hold back general wage increases will be able to place enormous pressure on employees. This could lead to disruption in the workplace as male workers blame female co-workers for lost wages.' Second, the separation of pay-equity funds would assist the Pay Equity Commission in 'implementation monitoring. If the employer does not have to set aside a separate pay equity fund, the Commission will be left to weed through a maze of accounting and paperwork to establish whether or not women received pay equity adjustments and whether or not a pay equity plan has fulfilled the requirements of the Act.'[175]

GOVERNMENT SENSITIVITY TO THE BUSINESS POSITION. Finally, trade unions and feminist organizations have been critical of governments for being overly sensitive to the concerns of big business regarding the costs of pay equity. In 1982 a delegation of women representing women's-rights groups and trade unions presented a brief to Ontario Conservative Labour Minister Russell Ramsey, urging his government to introduce equal pay for work of equal value. When he replied that it would cost employers too much, Mary Cornish, one of the delegates, responded angrily: 'Sure there is a cost; but a cost to whom? There would be a cost to employers; but right now it is women who are bearing the costs.'[176] The same issue arose again in 1986 when the Ottawa Women's Lobby, the Ontario Equal Pay Coalition, OPSEU, the Service Employees International Union, and CUPE suggested that not only the Liberal government authors of the Ontario *Green Paper on Pay Equity*, but also the Government Consultation Panel on Pay Equity, headed by two men and one woman from the corporate business world, were more concerned with the costs of pay equity to employers than with the costs of unequal wages to women.[177]

2. State deficit and taxes

Business, together with anti-feminist and neo-conservatives, argued that equal pay for work of equal value would lead to unacceptable increases in state deficits and taxes. The National Association of Manufacturers in the US asked why the federal government was even contemplating comparable-worth legislation at a time when it was trying to reduce the federal deficit. It pointed to the example of San Jose, California, where the city had to increase taxes to pay for the 5 to 15 per cent pay-equity adjustments it granted its women employees in female-predominant jobs.[178] The American Farm Bureau Federation, representing commercial farm owners, warned that if the federal government were to introduce equal pay for work of equal value, 'the cost to the federal taxpayers would run into several billion dollars. The result would be an enormous increase in the already scandalous deficit or an increase in taxes, neither of which is acceptable to us.'[179] In Canada, REAL Women suggested that the 'already hard-pressed taxpayer' would have to bear the enormous cost of financing the government bureaucracy necessary to oversee a classification of occupational titles for equal-value legislation.[180] The Winnipeg Chamber of Commerce went one step further, arguing that 'women are provincial taxpayers and they will have to shoulder the burden of escalating provincial expenditures for increased wages' brought about by Manitoba's Pay Equity Act.[181]

Labourites and feminists have either denied that pay equity would increase state deficits and the tax load, or seen small tax increases as justified in view of the discrimination practised against women. Concern was also voiced over the areas in which big business was supporting increased state expenditures and where it was recommending cutbacks. In 1985 Mary Rose Oakar, the feminist chair of the Subcommittee on Compensation and Employee Benefits of the Committee on the Post Office and Civil Service in the US House of Representatives, criticized the National Association of Manufacturers for using the state deficit as an argument against comparable worth. Telling its spokesperson, Sharon Spigelmeyer, that the deficit was 'sure not caused by the way we treat women in the federal work force', she asked why the Manufacturers had not criticized the overcharging, fraud, and abuse in the huge cost overruns by military contractors.[182]

3. Inflation and consumer purchasing power

The labour-feminist alliance and those state officials supporting pay equity have argued that equal pay for work of equal value would put more money in the hands of underpaid women, thereby increasing their purchasing power and stimulating aggregate demand in the economy. This view was adopted in the US as early as 1945 by the United Electrical Workers Union, the United Rubber

Workers of America, and the Congress of Industrial Organizations.[183] Among US state officials in the same period, this argument was shared by the Honourable Lewis B. Schwellenbach,
Secretary of Labour, and Frieda Miller, Director of the Women's
Bureau in the Department of Labour.[184] In Ontario the Liberal
Minister Responsible for Women's Issues, Ian Scott, on introducing the *Green Paper on Pay Equity* in the provincial assembly in
1985, argued that pay equity would 'have a positive effect on
aggregate demand in the economy'.[185] In the *Green Paper*, the
government pointed out that one of the benefits of pay equity
would be greater aggregate demand on the basis of wage increases
in lower-income households.[186] Business and its allies within the
economics profession, however, rejected these arguments. In 1984
the US Chamber of Commerce argued that legislating comparable
worth would increase the inflation rate by 9.7 per cent, [187] and the
US National Association of Manufacturers suggested that some
pay-equity costs would be passed on to the consumer by raising
the price of goods and services.[188] The Canadian Manufacturers'
Association also rejected the argument that pay equity would
increase aggregate demand: 'While one could argue that the increased purchasing power rising from any adjustments would be
recirculated to increase demand within the economy, Ontario
consumers are free to purchase manufactured goods produced
outside of the province, the price of which would not reflect the
costs of equal value requirements.'[189] The Sudbury and District
Chamber of Commerce argued that pay equity 'will increase
consumer prices, as the costs must be passed along to the consumer, thus reducing the demand for consumer products'.[190]

4. Economic disruption and competitiveness of capital

Business, along with state officials sympathetic to its viewpoint,
has made two final arguments about the possible economic consequences of pay equity. First, it would impair the ability of
business to compete with firms in other states or countries that do
not have pay-equity laws. In the US during the 1930s and 1940s,
employers argued that they could not compete for markets against
firms located in other states that did not have pay-equity laws and
could thus pay their women employees lower wages.[191] In the
1980s in Canada, business associations such as the Kitchener
Chamber of Commerce, the Sudbury and District Chamber of
Commerce, and the Canadian Federation of Independent Busi-

ness, and anti-feminist organizations such as REAL Women, argued similarly that equal pay for work of equal value would impair the competitiveness of Canadian firms in international markets.[192] The Metropolitan Toronto Board of Trade warned:

> It is . . . important to consider our major trading pact partner, the United States. It would appear that the equal value (or comparable worth) doctrine is *not* going to take hold in that country on a national basis. The United States will, therefore, maintain the competitive edge, as Canada's major province [Ontario] attempts to enter into an extremely costly social scheme [pay equity]. Detrimental economic effects can only follow.[193]

As will be argued in Chapter 5, in the late 1980s business is using the same argument with reference to the Free Trade Agreement to beat back any further legislation of equal pay for work of equal value in Canada. In 1986 the Auto Parts Manufacturers' Association claimed that pay equity would reduce its competitive ability, since its members did not compete with jurisdictions, such as Minnesota and Manitoba, that have pay-equity legislation, but with Asian and South American countries without such laws.[194] The Retail Council of Canada offered a piece of advice to presumably male workers:

> Ontario workers are in a struggle for the maintenance of their livelihood competing with the vigorous new societies of the Pacific Rim and the mature, capable Republic to our south. . . . the proposal that wage rates be equalized exclusively by a levelling up rather than a levelling down is . . . unacceptable. Clearly, Ontario's ability to compete in world markets would suffer from a levelling process which would see rates go in only one direction.[195]

Referring to Ontario as the 'economic engine of Confederation', the National Citizens' Coalition predicted that enactment of the proposed Pay Equity Act would 'pour sugar in its gas tank'.[196] The Liberal government of David Peterson displayed great sensitivity to these views by raising questions about the possible effects of pay equity on 'competition from low-wage Third-World producers'.[197]

Second, business has argued that as a result of weakened competitiveness, pay equity would threaten the economic viability of some firms and push others into bankruptcy.[198] In an often-quoted statement, a US federal judge, in rejecting an unequal-pay suit by some Denver nurses, proclaimed graphically that 'the suit was pregnant with the possibility of disrupting the entire economic system of the United States of America'.[199] In Ontario the views of business and government officials converged on this point too. In 1982 the province's Conservative Labour Minister, Russell Ramsey, stated that 'when plants are on the verge, it [pay equity] could be another straw that would break the camel's back in some cases';[200] in 1986 the Canadian Federation of Independent Business echoed that view—in strikingly similar language: equal pay for work of equal value 'could possibly be the straw that breaks the camel's back, in many cases'.[201]

The labour-feminist alliance has replied to the economic doomsday predicted by business in three ways. First, it has denied that pay equity would weaken the competitiveness of firms or put any of them out of business.[202] Mary Rose Oakar of the US House of Representatives argued in 1985: 'Pay equity never put anyone out of business. As a matter of fact, in those States that have completed it . . . the State economies are doing a lot better. The corporations that have promoted it have done the same thing.'[203] Connie Bryant, national director of public workers in the Communications Workers of America, said that when her union bargained collectively for pay equity, 'we heard no protests from the employers. There were no claims that these special wage increases would cause bankruptcies, no threats that some delicate economic balance would be upturned. Why? Because it just was not so.'[204] A second argument was made as early as 1946, when the United Rubber Workers of America and some US government officials argued that the unfair competition between states through the use of cheap female labour could be eliminated by *introducing* pay equity in all regions of a country, or at the federal level, rather than blocking it.[205] Particularly significant was the insertion in the 1963 US Equal Pay Act of a justification for pay equity partly on the grounds that a wage differential based on sex 'constitutes an unfair method of competition'.[206] Finally, labour and women have pointed out that, in the past, business has used the same arguments about the injury to competitiveness and the possibility of bankruptcies whenever pro-labour or pro-women legislation—such as the minimum wage, health and safety, paid holidays, and pensions—was being considered.[207]

CONCLUSIONS

Business and its neo-conservative anti-feminist allies have held a completely different view of the marketplace than the labour-feminist alliance. They have seen the marketplace as simply obeying the laws of supply and demand; it therefore could not discriminate against women, and pay-equity legislation was not necessary. Conversely, the labour-feminist alliance has looked upon the marketplace as a place where employers, taking advantage of women as a cheap reserve army of labour, have used formal and informal stratagems to discriminate against them in order to keep their own profits high. To put an end to such discriminatory practices, state legislation in the form of equal pay for work of equal value and job evaluation plans was required.

The marketplace, however, cannot stand on its own. It needs household labour to prepare, or reproduce, workers for entry and re-entry into its sphere—the labour that wives perform when, for example, they cook meals for their wage-earning husbands so that the latter can return to work on a daily and weekly basis. The relationship between the household and the marketplace rests squarely on the public-private divide. The household deeply affects how women enter the paid labour market, but business, neo-conservatives, and anti-feminists have defined it as women's private sphere. Thus business has claimed that it cannot be held responsible for the way the household affects women's paid labour-force activity, that any influences emanating from the household on the inequality of women's wages are non-discriminatory and therefore cannot be the subject of pay-equity legislation. The labour-feminist alliance, on the other hand, has been more willing to challenge the separation of the private household and the public marketplace. It has argued that business profits from women's unpaid labour in the household, and that therefore the state must intervene in order to correct the negative domestic influences on women's pay, especially in instances where business takes advantage of the ways in which the household structures women's cheap reserve army of labour. It is to these topics that we turn in the next chapter.

Notes

[1] For examples of the large literature on this question, see Denton and Hunter, *Economic Sectors* (1984); Goyder, 'Income Differences' (1981); Ornstein, *Accounting for Gender Differentials* (1983); Edgecombe-Robb, 'Earnings Differentials' (1978); Randall K. Filer, 'Male-Female Wage Differences: The Importance of Compensat-

ing Differentials', *Industrial and Labor Relations Review* 38, no. 3 (April 1985), pp. 426-37; Gunderson, 'Male-Female Wage Differentials' (1975); 'Discrimination, Equal Pay' (1985); Holmes, 'Male-Female Earnings' (1976); Ronald Oaxaca, 'Male-Female Wage Differentials in Urban Labor Markets', *International Economic Review* 14, no. 3 (Oct. 1973), pp. 693-709; Shapiro and Stelcner, 'The Persistence of the Male-Female Earnings Gap' (1987); Miller, 'Gender Differences' (1987).

[2]Discrimination can also be hidden in the human-capital factors that make up the explained variance. For example, women may be discouraged from entering engineering courses because of discrimination in the educational institution. See Riddell, 'Work and Pay' (1985), p. 60. Discrimination can also operate in the educational system against women of colour. The Mexican-American Women's National Association in the US charged that 'elementary and secondary schools have promoted the acceptance of low job expectations by tracking Hispanic students into vocational rather than academic curricula' (US Congress, *Options* [1985], p. 641).

[3]US Congress, *Options* (1985), pp. 425, 472-3, 477, 687.

[4]Equal Pay Coalition, *Response* (1986), pp. 12-13.

[5]US Congress, *Options* (1985), pp. 244, 357, 434, 438.

[6]Ibid., pp. 399-400.

[7]Automotive Parts Manufacturers Association, *Statement* (1986), p. 2; Manitoba, *Oral Presentations* (1985), p. 16; National Citizens' Coalition, *Pay Discrimination* (1986), p. 13; and Block, 'Economic Intervention' (1981), p. 107.

[8]This is a quote from Dr June O'Neill, an opponent of comparable worth, in Board of Trade of Metropolitan Toronto, *Submission on Equal Pay* (1985), p. 4.

[9]US Congress, *Hearings* (1962), p. 71; *Options* (1985), pp. 313, 376, 384, 502, 589, and 601. See also REAL Women, *Green Paper* (1986), p. 4.

[10]Ontario Chamber of Commerce, *Submission to the Consultation Hearings Panel on the Green Paper on Pay Equity* (15 May 1986), p. 1.

[11]Riddell, 'Work and Pay' (1985), p. 60.

[12]REAL Women, *Green Paper* (1986), p. 4.

[13]US Congress, *Hearings* (1962), p. 71; *Options* (1985), pp. 314, 377, 537-8.

[14]Atlantic Provinces Chamber of Commerce, *Policy Resolutions, 1986-1987* (1986), p. 10.

[15]National Citizens' Coalition, *Pay Discrimination* (1986), p. 5.

[16]REAL Women, *Equal Pay for UNequal Work* (n.d.), pp. 2-3. For the views of the Fraser Institute, see Block, 'Economic Intervention' (1981), p. 108.

[17]Christian Labour Association of Canada, *Submission* (1986), pp. 4-5; see also *Letter on Equal Pay* (1985), p. 5.

[18]National Citizens' Coalition, *Pay Discrimination* (1986), p. 20. See also National Citizens' Coalition, 'NCC Backs 'Men and Women for a Fair Market Wage' Group', *News Release* (n.d.).

[19]National Citizens' Coalition, *Pay Discrimination* (1986), p. 17.

[20]Manitoba, *Oral Presentations* (1985), pp. 3-4.

[21]US Congress, *Options* (1985), pp. 394-5. A similar program was suggested by the Retail Council of Canada. See Manitoba, *Oral Presentations* (1985), p. 4.

[22]US Congress, *Options* (1985), p. 395.

[23]Canadian Manufacturers' Association, *Submission* (1986), p. 20.

[24]US Congress, *Options* (1985), p. 396.

[25] REAL Women, *Equal Pay for UNequal Work* (n.d.), p. 6; see also *Position Papers, Publication No. 3.* (n.d.), p. 5.

[26] US Congress, *Options* (1985), p. 326.

[27] For example, see National Citizens' Coalition, *Brief on Bill 154* (1987), pp. 2-3; REAL Women, *Equal Pay for UNequal Work* (n.d.), p. 5; Ottawa-Carleton Board of Trade, *Brief to the Consultation Panel* (1986), p. 5; Sudbury and District Chamber of Commerce, *Public Consultation* (1986), p. 3.

[28] National Citizens' Coalition, 'NCC Backs "Men and Women for a Fair Market Wage" Group', *News Release* (n.d.).

[29] For example, see McCallum, 'Does Equal Pay' (1985), p. 6.

[30] Buchele and Aldrich, 'How Much Difference' (1985).

[31] US Congress, *Options* (1985), p. 357. For a similar Canadian unionist argument, see the National Union of Provincial Government Employees, *Equal Value, Equal Pay: A Pay Equity Handbook for Unionists* (Researched and written by Carolyn Woloski; Ottawa, 1987).

[32] US Congress, *Options* (1985), pp. 235, 246.

[33] Congress of Canadian Women, *Submission* (1986), pp. 2-3.

[34] US Congress, *Hearings* (1962), p. 68; see also *Options* (1985), pp. 384-5.

[35] US Congress, *Options* (1985), p. 670.

[36] Carlson, *Mainstream Canada* (n.d.); Manitoba, *Oral Presentations* (1985), p. 17; Automotive Parts Manufacturers Association, *Statement* (1986), p. 2; Canadian Manufacturers' Association, *Submission* (1986), p. 19.

[37] Cited in North, 'The Feminine Mistake' (1971), p. 8.

[38] Ibid., p. 14.

[39] Ibid., p. 5.

[40] *Wall Street Journal*, 10 Aug. 1962, p.1.

[41] Canadian Manufacturers' Association, *Submission* (1986), p. 18. See also Kitchener Chamber of Commerce, *Green Paper* (1985), p. 2; Retail Council of Canada, *Submission* (1986), p. 5; Board of Trade of Metropolitan Toronto, *Submission on Equal Pay* (1985), pp. 15, 23-5.

[42] REAL Women, *Equal Pay for UNequal Work* (n.d.), p. 4; also see *Position Papers, Publication No. 3.* (n.d.), p. 5.

[43] National Citizens' Coalition, *Pay Discrimination* (1986), pp. 7-9. See also its *Brief* (1987), p. 3.

[44] Canadian Federation of Independent Business, *Equal Pay for Work of Equal Value* (1986), p. 9.

[45] Ibid., pp. 3, 20.

[46] Ibid., p. 8.

[47] National Citizens' Coalition, *Brief* (1987), p. 1; see also National Citizens' Coalition, 'NCC Backs "Men and Women' (n.d.); *Letter on Bill 154* (1987), pp. 1-2.

[48] US Congress, *Hearings* (1962), p. 73.

[49] *Wall Street Journal*, 10 Aug. 1962, p. 1.

[50] For the views of the Canadian Organization of Small Business, see McDougall, 'Here Comes Equal Pay' (1985), p. 35.

[51] Ibid., p. 33.

[52] National Citizens' Coalition, *Pay Discrimination* (1986), p. 20.

[53] Manitoba, *Oral Presentations* (1985), p. 7.

[54] McDougall, 'Here Comes Equal Pay' (1985), p. 38.

[55] US Congress, *Options* (1985), p. 691.

[56]Canadian Association of Women Executives, *Equal Pay, Equal Value* (1978), p. 9; *Submission* (1980), p. 4; see also Service Employees International Union, *Presentation* (1986), pp. 13-14.

[57]Congress of Canadian Women, *Submission* (1986), p. 2.

[58]Ontario Federation of Labour, *Brief* (1986), p. 20; see also National Union of Provincial Government Employees, *Equal Value, Equal Pay* (1987), p. 48.

[59]Federation of Women Teachers' Association of Ontario, *FWTAO Response* (1986), p. 24.

[60]Canadian Human Rights Commission, *Methodology and Principles for Applying Section 11 of the Canadian Human Rights Act* (Ottawa, 1982), p. 3.

[61]See Manitoba Pay Equity Bureau, *Job Evaluation* (Winnipeg, 1988), pp. 3-4; Ontario Pay Equity Commission, *How to Do Pay Equity Job Comparisons* (1989), pp. 22-6; Ontario Public Service Employees Union, *Equity at Work: A Pay Equity Manual for Practitioners* (Prepared by Sonja Greckol, Elizabeth Lennon, Pat McDermott, and Isla Peters; Toronto, 1987), pp. 72-3; Janice R. Bellace, 'Comparable Worth' (1984), pp. 672-4; Ontario, *Green Paper* (1985), p. 102.

[62]Bellace, 'Comparable Worth' (1984), p. 673.

[63]Ontario Pay Equity Commission, *How to Do Pay Equity Job Comparisons* (1989), pp. 23, 33.

[64]Ibid., p. 23.

[65]Bellace, 'Comparable Worth' (1984), p. 673, fn. 96.

[66]Ibid., pp. 673-4.

[67]Ontario Public Service Employees Union, *Equity at Work* (1987), pp. 73-5.

[68]Ontario Pay Equity Commission, *How To Do Pay Equity Job Comparisons* (1989), p. 35.

[69]Canadian Human Rights Commission, *Methodology and Principles* (1982), p. 3.

[70]For example, see Ontario Pay Equity Commission, *Determining Gender Predominance*, Pay Equity Implementation Series #7 (May 1988).

[71]US Congress, *Options* (1985), pp. 377-8.

[72]Ibid., p. 383.

[73]Wisconsin Association of Manufacturing & Commerce, *Comparable Worth: Questionable Theory and Faulty Process*, Special Report on Comparable Worth 2 (25 Jan. 1985).

[74]Ontario Chamber of Commerce, *Submission* (1986), p. 7; Canadian Manufacturers' Association, *Submission* (1986), pp. 9-10; Canadian Newspaper Publishers Association, *Submission to the [Ontario] Consultation Panel on Pay Equity* (Toronto, 15 May 1986), p. 4. At least one Canadian business association would have to disagree with this tactic since it argued that one cannot compare job values across different job-evaluation methodologies. See Board of Trade of Metropolitan Toronto, *Submission on Equal Pay* (1985), pp. 17-18; *Submission to the Consultation Panel* (1986), p. 12.

[75]Canadian Manufacturers' Association, *A CMA Discussion Paper on Equal Pay for Work of Equal Value* (Toronto, 1 Aug. 1985), p. 10; Ontario Chamber of Commerce, *Submission* (1986), pp. 6-8.

[76]US Congress, *Options* (1985), pp. 325, 539; Sudbury and District Chamber of Commerce, *Public Consultation* (1986), p. 4; Retail Council of Canada, *Submission* (1986), p. 11; Canadian Federation of Independent Business, *Equal Pay* (1986), p. 15; Manitoba, *Oral Presentations* (1985), p. 17; Automotive Parts Manufacturers Association, *Statement* (1986), p. 6.

[77] Board of Trade of Metropolitan Toronto, *Submission on Equal Pay* (1985), p. 19; *Submission to the Consultation Panel* (1986), p. 12.

[78] Personnel Association of Ontario, *Submission* (1986); US Congress, *Options* (1985), pp. 260, 265-8.

[79] US Congress, *Options* (1985) p. 454.

[80] REAL Women, *Equal Pay for UNequal Work* (n.d.), p. 4. See also *Position Papers* (n.d.), p. 4.

[81] National Citizens' Coalition, *Pay Discrimination* (1986), pp. 14-15. Similar arguments were made by the Christian Labour Assocation of Canada. See its *Submission* (1986), p. 5; and *Letter on Equal Pay* (1985), p. 11.

[82] See the critique of the National Association of Manufacturers by Mary Rose Oakar, Chair of the Subcommittee on Compensation and Employee Benefits of the Committee on the Post Office and Civil Service in the House of Representatives (US Congress, *Options* [1985], pp. 367-9). See also National Action Committee on the Status of Women, *Pay Equity in Ontario: We're Still Waiting* (Presentation before the Ontario Standing Committee on Justice hearing on Bill 154; Patricia McDermott and Isla Peters; 3 March 1987), p. 4.

[83] Some feminist labour organizations, such as Organized Working Women, openly admitted the subjective and non-scientific nature of job evaluations. See Organized Working Women and the Ottawa and District Labour Council, *Response* (1986), p. 10.

[84] US Congress, *Options* (1985), pp. 358, 421, 423, 468, 512-13, 545-6, 688, 690.

[85] Ibid., pp. 243, 442, 632.

[86] Manitoba, *Oral Presentations* (1985), p. 5.

[87] Equal Pay Coalition, *Equal Pay for Work of Equal Value: Media Release* (1985), p. 3; 'The Equal Pay Coalition's Media Release' (1985), p. 38; *Response* (1986), pp. 17-19; National Union of Provincial Government Employees, *Brief* (1986), p. 6.

[88] United Steelworkers of America, *Representation of the USWA Before the [Ontario] Select Committee on Bill 3—An Act to Amend the Employment Standards Act of 1974* (30 Jan. 1980), pp. 2-3.

[89] Canadian Union of Public Employees, *A Co-ordinated National Strategy* (1986), pp. 7-11; *Policy #3: Women's Economic Equality* (1985). See also Organized Working Women and Ottawa and District Labour Council, *Response* (1986), pp. 12-13.

[90] United Steelworkers of America, *Brief* (1986), pp. 15-16. For other organizations that supported the equalization of base entry rates, see Ontario Federation of Labour, *Brief* (1986), p. 14; Ontario Public Service Employees Union, *A Rose Is Not Enough* (1986), p. 7; and National Action Committee on the Status of Women, *Pay Equity in Ontario* (1987), pp. 2-3.

[91] Madeleine Parent, 'Equal Pay for Work of Equal Value Through Collective Bargaining', in Equal Pay Coalition, eds, *Equal Pay for Work of Equal Value* (Toronto, 1977), p. 9.

[92] Canadian Union of Public Employees, 'Workplace Inequality' (1985); *A Co-ordinated National Strategy* (1986), pp. 6-7.

[93] Manitoba Federation of Labour, *Response to the Law Amendments Committee* (1985), p. 1. The Ontario Federation of Labour also supported across-the-board increases as a pay-equity strategy. See Ontario Federation of Labour, *Brief* (1986), p. 14.

[94] Manitoba, *Oral Presentations* (1985), p. 12.

[95] Canadian Union of Public Employees, 'Workplace Inequality' (1985); *Response* (1986), pp. 16-17; *A Co-ordinated National Strategy* (1986), pp. 3-5. See also Ontario

Public Service Employees Union, *Submission to the Consultation Panel* (1986), pp. 13, 17.

[96] United Steelworkers of America, *Brief* (1986), pp. 15-16.

[97] Canadian Union of Public Employees, *A Co-ordinated National Strategy* (1986), pp. 11-14. See also Organized Working Women and Ottawa and District Labour Council, *Response* (1986), pp. 11-12; and National Action Committee on the Status of Women, *Pay Equity in Ontario* (1987), p. 3.

[98] Manitoba, *Oral Presentations* (1985), p. 12. See also Ontario Federation of Labour, *Brief* (1986), p. 14.

[99] Ontario Public Service Employees Union, *Meeting the Challenge* (1986), pp. 14-19. The findings of OPSEU are somewhat different from those for the Canadian economy as a whole. See Bonnie Fox and John Fox, 'Effects of Women's Employment on Wages', *Canadian Journal of Sociology* 8, no. 3, 1983, pp. 319-28; 'Women in the Labour Market, 1931-1981: Exclusion and Competition', *Canadian Review of Sociology and Anthropology* 23, no. 1 (1986), pp. 1-21. They found that the percentage of females in an occupation exerts a greater downward pressure on male wages than on female wages.

[100] Canadian Union of Public Employees, 'Workplace Inequality' (1985); 'Ontario Council of Hospital Employees—1985 Bargaining Demands on Equal Pay: Speakers' Notes on OCHU's Demand for a Minimum Hospital Workers Rate' (1985); *A Co-ordinated National Strategy* (1986), pp. 15-16. The OFL also supported increasing minimum-wage rates as a pay-equity strategy. See Ontario Federation of Labour, *Brief* (1986), p. 14.

[101] It is described in Ronnie J. Steinberg, Lois Haignere, Carol Possin, Cynthia H. Chertos, and Donald Treiman, *The New York State Pay Equity Study: A Research Report* (Albany, N.Y.: Center for Women in Government, State University of New York at Albany, 1986). See also Lewis, *Just Give Us the Money* (1988) pp. 82-3.

[102] Ronnie J. Steinberg, Carol C. Possin, Donald J. Treiman, *New York State Job Questionnaire* (Center for Women in Government, State University of New York at Albany, 1984); Ontario Public Service Employees Union and Human Resources Secretariat, *Pilot Test of the Pay Equity Survey* (Toronto, 16 Jan. 1989).

[103] Steinberg *et al.*, *New York State Pay Equity Study* (1986) pp. 159-60. Emphases in original.

[104] Ibid., p. 143.

[105] US Congress, *Hearings* (1946), pp. 162-3.

[106] US Congress, *Options* (1985), p. 433. See also East York Women Teachers' Association, *Response to the Green Paper on Pay Equity* (Presented by Lorraine Stewart; 27 March 1986), p. 8.

[107] Ontario Pay Equity Commission, *Gender-Neutral Job Comparison*, Implementation Series #9 (July 1988), p. 3. 'Overdescription' and 'underdescription' are terms that have spread throughout the literature, leaving little trace of their origins. On this, see Helen Remick, 'Strategies for Creating Sound, Bias-free Job Evaluation Plans' in *Job Evaluation and the EEO—The Emerging Issues* (I.R.C. Colloquium, University of Washington, Seattle, 1975, p. 4, cited in Manitoba, Pay Equity Bureau, *Pay Equity and Job Evaluation* (1968), p. 10.

[108] Ontario Public Service Employees Union, *Equity at Work* (1987), p. 44. See also Ontario Public Service Employees Union, *Submission* (1986), p. 11.

[109] US Congress, *Options* (1985), pp. 518-19.

[110] Ibid., p. 638.

[111] Bellace, 'Comparable Worth' (1984), p. 678.

[112] Equal Pay Coalition, *Response* (1986), p. 18.

[113] Canadian Union of Public Employees, *A Co-ordinated National Strategy* (1986), Appendix C, pp. 3-4. See also the Ontario Federation of Labour, *Making Up the Difference* (1984), p. 17.

[114] US Congress, *Options* (1985), p. 454.

[115] National Citizens' Coalition, *Pay Discrimination* (1986).

[116] US Congress, *Options* (1985), pp. 318, 319.

[117] See, for example, the statements made by the Winnipeg Chamber of Commerce in Manitoba, *Oral Presentations* (1985), p. 17.

[118] Board of Trade of Metropolitan Toronto, *Submission on Equal Pay* (1985), p. 9.

[119] US Congress, *Options* (1985), pp. 314, 340, 381.

[120] Ibid. (1985), p. 319.

[121] Carlson, *Mainstream Canada* (n.d.). See also *Globe and Mail*, 31 July 1984, p. 7.

[122] Bonnie Fox and John Fox, 'Occupational Gender Segregation of the Canadian Labour Force, 1931-81', *Canadian Review of Sociology and Anthropology* 24, no. 3 (1987), p. 390.

[123] US Congress, *Options* (1985), pp. 316-17.

[124] Ibid., p. 380.

[125] Canadian Manufacturers' Association, *Submission* (1986), pp. iii, 6.

[126] Manitoba, *Oral Presentations* (1985), p. 16; see also Sudbury and District Chamber of Commerce, *Public Consultation* (1986), pp. 3-4.

[127] Board of Trade of Metropolitan Toronto, *Submission on Equal Pay* (1985), pp. 9, 10; emphasis in original.

[128] US Congress, *Options* (1985), pp. 315-16.

[129] Ibid., pp. 475-6.

[130] Ibid., pp. 239-40, 242. See also National Action Committee on the Status of Women, *Brief* (1986), p. 2.

[131] United Food and Commercial Workers International Union, *Brief* (1986), pp. 3-6, and Tables 1 and 2.

[132] US Congress, *Options* (1985), pp. 239-40, 640.

[133] Ibid., p. 640.

[134] Ibid., p. 475.

[135] Federation of Women Teachers' Associations of Ontario, *FWTAO Response* (1986), pp. 24-5. See also Organized Working Women and Ottawa and District Labour Council, *Response* (1986), p. 3; National Union of Provincial Government Employees, *Equal Value, Equal Pay* (1987), pp. 48-9.

[136] US Congress, *Options* (1985), p. 239.

[137] Mincer, 'Intercountry Comparisons' (1985), pp. S1 to S2. The twelve countries were Australia, Britain, France, Germany, Israel, Italy, Japan, the Netherlands, Spain, Sweden, the United States, and the Soviet Union.

[138] See Canadian Manufacturers' Association, *Submission* (1986), pp. iii, 20; Board of Trade of Metropolitan Toronto, *Submission on Equal Pay* (1985), pp. 34-5; US Congress, *Options* (1985), p. 386.

[139] US Congress, *Options* (1985), p. 454.

[140] Ontario Secondary School Teachers' Federation, *Response* (1986), pp. 9-10.

[141] United Auto Workers Canada, *UAW Response* (1986), p. 6.

[142] Manitoba, *Oral Presentations* (1985), p. 20.

[143] Canadian Manufacturers' Association, *Submission* (1986), p. 17; McDougall,

'Here Comes Equal Pay' (1985), p. 33.

[144] Canadian Manufacturers' Association, *Submission* (1986), p. 17.

[145] Kitchener Chamber of Commerce, *Green Paper* (1985), p. 1. See also Board of Trade of Metropolitan Toronto, *Submission on Equal Pay* (1985), pp. 25-6.

[146] Morley Gunderson, *Costing Equal Value Legislation in Ontario* (A report to the Ontario Ministry of Labour; Toronto, 1985).

[147] Bureau of National Affairs, *Pay Equity and Comparable Worth* (Washington, D.C., 1984), p. 72.

[148] US Congress, *Options* (1985), pp. 333, 390.

[149] Ibid., pp. 389-90.

[150] Board of Trade of Metropolitan Toronto, *Submission on Equal Pay* (1985), p. 13; see also its *Submission to the Consultation Panel* (1986), p. 6.

[151] US Congress, *Options* (1985), p. 541; Canadian Federation of Independent Business, *Equal Pay* (1986).

[152] Canadian Federation of Independent Business, *Equal Pay* (1986), p. 12.

[153] Ibid., p. 9. Other business associations expressed similar concerns about the costs to small businesses. See Canadian Manufacturers' Association, *Submission* (1986), p. 10.

[154] Ottawa-Carleton Board of Trade. *Brief* (1986), p. 8; Ontario Chamber of Commerce, *Submission* (1986), p. 10.

[155] Manitoba, *Oral Presentations* (1985), pp. 18, 19. See also National Citizens' Coalition, *Brief* (1987), p. 2.

[156] Automotive Parts Manufacturers Association, *Statement* (1986), pp. 4, 8.

[157] US Congress, *Hearings* (1946), p. 166.

[158] Ibid., p. 172.

[159] United Auto Workers Canada, *UAW Response* (1986), p. 4.

[160] *Toronto Star*, 6 Feb. 1980, p. C3.

[161] US Congress, *Hearings* (1946), p. 166.

[162] Equal Pay Coalition, *Response* (1986), p. 28; see also National Union of Provincial Government Employees, *Brief* (1986), pp. 9-10.

[163] Congress of Canadian Women, *Submission* (1986), p. 2.

[164] Federation of Women Teachers' Associations of Ontario, *FWTAO Response* (1986), p. 23; see also Service Employees International Union, *Presentation* (1986), pp. 14-15.

[165] Equal Pay Coalition, *Response* (1986), pp. 38-9; Canadian Union of Public Employees, *Response* (1986), p. 31.

[166] Equal Pay Coalition, *Submission* (1987), p. 22.

[167] Canadian Association of Women Executives, *Response* (1986), pp. 5, 9.

[168] Manitoba, *Oral Presentations* (1985), p. 13.

[169] Manitoba, *The Pay Equity Act* (1985), sec. 7(3).

[170] Manitoba, *Oral Presentations* (1985), p. 5; Charter of Rights Coalition (Manitoba), *Submission* (1985), pp. 3-4.

[171] Charter of Rights Coalition (Manitoba), *Submission* (1985), pp. 3-4.

[172] Organized Working Women, *Brief to the Green Paper Hearings* (Toronto, 27 March 1986), p. 4; Ontario Federation of Labour, *Brief* (1986), p. 14; United Auto Workers Canada, *UAW Response* (1986); Canadian Union of Public Employees, *Response* (1986), p. 32.

[173] Equal Pay Coalition, *Submission* (1987), pp. 22-3; see also Ontario Coalition for Better Daycare, *Brief* (1986), p. 6.

[174] Ottawa Women's Lobby, *Submission* (1986), p. 20.

[175] Ontario Equal Pay Coalition, *Submission* (1987), pp. 33-4.

[176] *Globe and Mail*, 28 Aug. 1982, p. 1.

[177] Ottawa Women's Lobby, *Submission* (1986), p. 20; Service Employees International Union, *Presentation* (1986), p. 13; Equal Pay Coalition, *Response* (1986), p. 37; Canadian Union of Public Employees, *Response* (1986), p. 31; Ontario Public Service Employees Union, *Submission* (1986), pp. 22-3. The three corporate people heading the Consultation Panel were Charles David Clark, president and chief executive officer of Campbell Soup Co. Ltd, William Dimma, president and chief executive officer of Royal LePage Ltd, and Dr Gail Cook, executive vice-president of Bennecon Ltd., a Toronto management consulting firm (Kieran Simpson, ed., *Canadian Who's Who*, vol. 20 [Toronto: University of Toronto Press, 1985], pp. 219, 245, 319).

[178] US Congress, *Options* (1985), p. 391.

[179] Ibid., p. 670.

[180] REAL Women, *Position Papers, Publication No. 3* (n.d.), p. 5. See also National Citizens' Coalition, *Letter on Bill 154* (1987), p. 1; *Brief* (1987), p. 3.

[181] Manitoba, *Oral Presentations* (1985), p. 17; see also Board of Trade of Metropolitan Toronto, *Submission on Equal Pay* (1985), p. 21.

[182] US Congress, *Options* (1985), pp. 371-2. In her defence, Spigelmeyer replied that the Manufacturers did not support abuse or waste in government expenditures.

[183] US Congress, *Hearings* (1946), pp. 165, 172.

[184] Ibid., pp. 6, 16.

[185] Ontario, *Debates*, 19 Nov. 1985, p. 1594.

[186] Ontario, *Green Paper* (1985), p. 48; see also Ottawa Women's Lobby, *Submission* (1986), p. 21.

[187] Bureau of National Affairs, *Pay Equity and Comparable Worth* (1984), p. 72.

[188] US Congress, *Options* (1985), p. 391.

[189] Canadian Manufacturers' Association, *Submission* (1986), p. 18.

[190] Sudbury and District Chamber of Commerce, *Public Consultation* (1986), p. 2; see also Board of Trade of Metropolitan Toronto, *Submission on Equal Pay* (1985), pp. 25, 29, 34.

[191] US Congress, *Hearings* (1946), p. 172. Some employers, however, used this as an argument *in favour* of pay equity by suggesting that *all* states should introduce this measure.

[192] Kitchener Chamber of Commerce, *Green Paper* (1985), p. 1; Sudbury and District Chamber of Commerce, *Public Consultation* (1986), p. 2; Carlson, *Mainstream Canada* (n.d.), REAL Women, *Equal Pay for UNequal Work* (n.d.), p. 6. See also Atlantic Provinces Chamber of Commerce, *Policy Resolutions* (1986), p. 10.

[193] Board of Trade of Metropolitan Toronto, *Submission on Equal Pay* (1985), p. 30; emphasis in original.

[194] Auto Parts Manufacturers' Association of Canada, *Statement* (1986), p. 8.

[195] Retail Council of Canada, *Submission* (1986), pp. 6-7.

[196] National Citizens' Coalition, *Brief* (1987), p. 3.

[197] Ontario, *Green Paper* (1985), p. 47. See also Ontario, *Debates*, 19 Nov. 1985, p. 1596; Ontario Pay Equity Commission, *Report* (1989), pp. 68-9.

[198] This view was expressed in the US by the Chamber of Commerce and the American Retail Federation. See US Congress, *Options* (1985), p. 323; and, 'Equal Pay for Women Hits Retailers', *Business Week*, 29 Jan. 1972, p. 76.

[199] Cited in Board of Trade of Metropolitan Toronto, *Submission on Equal Pay* (1985), p. 27.

[200] Globe and Mail, 28 Aug. 1982, p. 1.

[201] Canadian Federation of Independent Business, *Equal Pay for Work of Equal Value* (1986), pp. 21-2.

[202] This view was expressed by Federally Employed Women in the United States in US Congress, *Options* (1985), p. 435.

[203] Ibid., pp. 510-11.

[204] Ibid., p. 430.

[205] US Congress, *Hearings* (1946), pp. 172, 173-4.

[206] US Congress, *Statutes at Large. Public Law 88-38 (1964), sec. 2 (a)*.

[207] This view was expressed by Mary Cornish, head of the Ontario Equal Pay Coalition, in the *Globe and Mail*, 28 Aug. 1982, p. 1, and by Bob White in United Auto Workers Canada, *UAW Response* (1986), p. 7.

4

The Household Workplace

With few exceptions, there has been a division of labour between business organizations and their 'front' coalitions in mounting arguments against projected pay-equity laws. As we have seen in the last chapter, business organizations such as the US and Ontario Chambers of Commerce and the Manufacturers' Associations in both countries have based much of their opposition to pay equity on marketplace issues. On the other hand, while not ignoring marketplace issues, their neo-conservative anti-feminist 'fronts', including in Canada the Fraser Institute, the National Citizens' Coalition, and REAL Women, have spent more time on the terrain of the household and the traditional nuclear family, the third area of political struggle over pay equity to be considered in this book. One notable exception to this division of labour was the Metropolitan Toronto Board of Trade: citing US opponents of pay equity, especially the US Commission on Civil Rights, it divided its time between the household, the marketplace, and the paid workplace in arguing against equal pay for work of equal value.[1]

It is worth noting a central contradiction in the position of the neo-conservative anti-feminists. According to their reasoning, the absence of pay-equity legislation means more jobs for women because they cost business less than men's, while one result of pay equity would be to drive many of those same women out of the work force and back into the home. Logically, then, if they really want to protect the patriarchal nuclear family they should support the equal-pay measures that would keep more women in the home. The convoluted logic of the forces opposing equal-pay legislation has nine interrelated aspects, which will be discussed in this chapter.

MARITAL STATUS: THE CAUSE OF UNEQUAL PAY?

In 1981 Vancouver's Fraser Institute suggested that marital status and women's domestic responsibilities were the most important reasons for the gendered wage gap. Walter Block, senior economist with the Institute, argued that 'the strongest determinant of the so-called male/female earnings "gap" is . . . marital status. . . marriage increases male earnings, and reduces female earnings.'[2] As evidence, Block cited a study analyzing the 1971 Census by Peter Kuch and Walter Haessel for Statistics Canada, purportedly showing that among the ever-married (presently married, widowed, divorced, or separated), women earned 33 cents for each dollar earned by men, but that among the never-married this ratio rose to 99 cents. Block concluded that this amounted to an insignificant absolute wage gap of $31.52 *per year* among the never-married.[3] Denton and Hunter, however, noted that Block ignored scientific evidence challenging his conclusions. On the basis of a reanalysis of the 1973 Canadian Mobility Study, they concluded that 'marital status is an inconsequential determinant of earnings for both men and women . . . As a result, the major argument in Block . . . is turned on its head.'[4]

Ignoring the Denton and Hunter critique, the National Citizens' Coalition cited the Fraser Institute in 1986 to argue that the wage gap was almost entirely due to marital status. Expanding on the 1971 Census study by Kuch and Haessel, it argued that among the never-married, women earned 83.1 per cent of what men did in 1981; among the single university-educated, this figure reached 91.3 per cent in 1982.[5]

Likewise, REAL Women suggested that the wage gap was caused, not by employer discrimination, but primarily by marital status. To back up this point, it also ignored the Denton-Hunter critique and cited the Fraser Institute's use of the Kuch and Haessel study, which allegedly showed that among never-married Canadians, women earned 99.2 per cent of what men did. '*In other words, salaries of never-married people are the same, regardless of sex.*' REAL Women concluded that 'MARITAL STATUS is the most important reason why there is a male/female income differential'. As an alternative to equal pay, the organization recommended changes in income-tax laws that would strengthen the financial security of women who decide to stay at home with their children rather than seek work outside.[6]

One business association that made similar arguments was the Metropolitan Toronto Board of Trade. Citing US authorities opposed to comparable worth, it suggested that 'the wage gap between single men who have never been married and single women who have never been married is small. . . . the wage gap between married men and married women is narrower at younger ages, but wider for those with children.'[7]

In response to these arguments that unequal pay is based on marital status, and thus is not the responsibility of employers and cannot not be corrected by pay-equity legislation, the women's and labour movements have either de-emphasized the role of marital status or wanted it ignored altogether in considering the causes of unequal pay. In the US, for example, the National Committee on Pay Equity (the national coalition of feminist and trade-union organizations advocating comparable-worth legislation) lobbied Congress to exclude marital status as a variable from a national study of unequal pay on the grounds that it was not directly job-related.[8] Of course, this was simply a strategic position intended to counter the opposition to comparable-worth legislation, since the women's movement has repeatedly argued that women are disadvantaged in the paid labour force because of their double day of labour in the household and the paid labour force.

THE DOUBLE DAY OF LABOUR AND UNEQUAL PAY

There was a curious convergence between feminist and anti-feminist and business organizations in the household explanations of women's unequal pay. According to both sides, one of the reasons why women earn less than men is their greater responsibility for child care and other domestic duties.[9] The Retail Council of Canada suggested that 'an unequal burden on women for the rearing of children . . . go[es] a considerable way in explaining the wage gap which currently exists'.[10] Women who work in the paid labour force must balance their wage work and domestic work; this leads many women to opt for part-time work that allows them greater flexibility in arranging their daily and weekly double-day-of-labour schedules. The fact that part-time work pays less than full-time work contributes to the gendered wage gap, since women are more likely than men to do part-time work. But feminist and anti-feminist organizations disagree on two questions.

OBLIGATION. Feminist organizations do not believe that women should be obliged to continue their double day of labour, especially when it means unequal pay. Such organizations see women's homework as onerous labour, whereas the neo-conservative anti-feminists regard it as a duty and responsibility to be faithfully executed for love of family.

SOLUTIONS. Feminists and anti-feminists also disagree on the domestic solution to women's unequal pay. Feminist organizations suggest either abandonment of the traditional nuclear family or a more equal distribution of domestic labour between women and men. The neo-conservative anti-feminists' answer entails a strengthening of the traditional nuclear family; they are more concerned with preserving the patriarchal nuclear family than with redressing women's unequal pay in the labour force.[11]

PAID LABOUR-FORCE INTERRUPTIONS

Neo-conservative anti-feminists and business interests argue that women, because of their greater commitment to their families and children, have a lower labour-force attachment than men and experience a greater number of labour-force interruptions. These interruptions occur for three reasons: (a) women leave the labour force for short maternity leaves or for longer periods to bear children; (b) they take part or whole days off work to care for sick husbands and children, or to attend to other pressing domestic responsibilities; (c) they quit their jobs to move when their husbands, with a primary commitment to their own careers, are relocated. Citing American sociologist Brigitte Berger, the Metropolitan Toronto Board of Trade told the Ontario government that family life is 'the single most meaningful' thing to 86 per cent of women, and paid work the most important to only 9 per cent.[12] Assuming the legitimacy of patriarchy, the anti-feminist neo-conservatives note, for example, that 'a woman's husband may decide to move out of the area; it is *his* decision, and his wife *must* follow'; they also consider it right and proper that a husband should quite a job for 'economic' reasons and a wife for 'family' reasons.[13] They conclude that because employers take a greater risk in hiring women, especially if they must invest in job-training, they should be compensated for that 'risk' by being allowed to pay women less than men: hence the gendered wage gap. In fact, however, the labour-feminist alliance has often denied that women interrupt their jobs more frequently than men. In the US, for instance, the League of United Latin American Citizens, representing Hispanic women, pointed to a Rand Corporation study showing that 'women do not quit their jobs at a greater rate than men. . . . of the full-time employees surveyed, 57 per cent of male workers had left their jobs within a year, compared to 55 per cent of female employees.'[14]

FREEDOM OF CHOICE AND INDIVIDUAL RESPONSIBILITY: BLAME THE VICTIM

1. The neo-conservative anti-feminist position

The anti-feminist neo-conservatives contend that full-time housewives make a free choice in emphasizing the family over a possible career. In addition, they suggest that women freely choose low-paying part-time work to provide them with flexibility in balancing domestic with paid job responsibilities. They conclude that pay-equity legislation can do nothing about wage inequities based on free will. This blame-the-victim rationalization of gender-based unequal pay was extended by the neo-conservative Fraser Institute into the area of women's supposed psychological fear of competition with men as grounds for telling women that they are responsible for their own low wages because they deliberately choose low-wage jobs. In his 1981 paper for the Institute, Block suggested that 'many women have great psychological and other personal difficulties in competing with men, and are thus, when married, more likely than men to *purposefully* keep their earnings below those of their spouses—with important implications for the low female/male earnings ratios for married people'.[15] For Block, these psychological difficulties manifest themselves when, at crucial points in their education, women choose marriage because they fear success in a career.[16] The arguments by REAL Women were not all that different: 'Women *choose* less demanding jobs—jobs that offer opportunities for part-time and flexible work schedules and permit easy exit and entry because of family responsibilities. They also choose to enter occupations which provide the smallest earning losses from anticipated absence from the labour force due to child bearing and rearing.' Citing an American study by Bohen and Viveros-Long, REAL Women argued that 'women characteristically had less demanding and absorbing jobs then men, even when they had comparable education and training . . . [since] they *choose* less demanding jobs because of their greater involvement in—and responsibility for—their children on a day-to-day basis.'[17] Similarly, the neo-conservative National Citizens' Coalition suggested that 'many women *pick* clean, safe, pleasant jobs which are easy to enter and exit in conformation with what they feel their child bearing and rearing responsibilities are'.[18] Not to be outdone, the Chamber of Commerce in the US and the Automotive Parts Manufacturers' Association of Canada emphasized that women wind up in low-paying jobs because they have freely chosen them in an open labour market.[19] In other words, female workers have to take personal responsibility for the jobs they get and the rates of pay they are given.

2. A feminist response

Feminist organizations have pointed to structural rather than individual factors to explain the low participation of women in higher-paying, traditionally male jobs. In the US the League of United Latin American Citizens pointed out that 'some women are blocked from entering traditional male jobs because of their limited education and training; some women may fear greater harassment in traditional male jobs, such as on construction sites and truck driving'.[20] Feminist groups such as the National Organization of Women in the US have rebelled against the idea that women have to take individual responsibility for their low wages and poor jobs.[21] But to translate their rebellion into concrete action, women have often had to face state laws that require them to fight individually, not collectively. This is the case with much human-rights and employment-standards legislation, which puts the burden on the individual woman employee to lodge a complaint against her employer; her powerless situation becomes absolute when reprisals are taken against her for doing so (including firing, demotion, loss in pay, and so on), even though such actions are illegal under much current legislation. This has been one of the chief complaints made by women's organizations against equal-pay legislation based solely on the complaints model, as noted in Chapter 2. In one case in Nova Scotia in 1969, in order to prevent male-female comparisons from being made, one employer removed all the women employees from their jobs.[22] As a solution to this kind of reprisal, the Canadian Association of Women Executives proposed to the Ontario Minister of Labour legislative changes that would allow (a) class action suits under equal-pay legislation, and (b) routine investigations of company policies to eliminate the need for individual complaints.[23]

FAMILY WAGE VS. WOMEN'S ECONOMIC SURVIVAL

The traditional household is one in which the husband/father alone earns the family wage and the wife/mother is a full-time labourer at home; the children and wife/mother are totally dependent on the father/husband for their cash income in order to meet their subsistence needs. The opposite patterns are those of the wife/mother working in a paid job outside the household to help to support the family and of the increasing numbers of single mothers who rely entirely on their own wages to support themselves and their children.

1. The neo-conservative anti-feminist position

The neo-conservatives argue that, with the winning of the family-wage concept in the industrial revolution, men were necessarily paid more than women because they had to support their wives and children. They contend that women do not have to be paid as much as men because they do not have the same burden of family support: women's wages, being at most supplemental to their husbands', should therefore be less then men's. In Great Britain, during the debate over equal pay in the late 1940s and early 1950s, the opponents of pay equity based their arguments partly on the assumption that 'a man with a family ought to take more money home than a single woman or a woman who is the second wage earner of a family'.[24] In the US, the anti-feminist neo-conservatives have argued that women should receive lower wages than men because part of their subsistence is paid for by their husbands' wages. Gary North, writing for the neo-conservative Foundation for Economic Education, suggested that a woman can accept 'menial wages' 'precisely because she enjoys the advantages of being a woman: she has a man who will help bear the financial burdens of her own upkeep. She is on the job in order to supplement his earnings, so she is willing to work for wages that are essentially supplemental in magnitude.' North dismisses the hardships of the single woman with the argument that similar suffering is experienced by the man with eight children who faces competition from 'bright, young, single college graduates who are willing to take over his job at the same pay, or perhaps sightly less pay'.[25] This attempt to justify the suffering of subordinated women with the misogynous argument that dominating men suffer, too, defies reason.

2. The labour-feminist position

The labour and women's movements have noted that, with the increasing participation of women in the paid labour force, the traditional nuclear family supported by a family wage is declining. They have made five closely related arguments.

WOMEN'S CONTRIBUTION TO FAMILY SUBSISTENCE. The historical increase in the cost of living has meant that women have had to contribute to their family's economic welfare in non-domestic ways by earning cash in paid jobs outside the household. Thus pay equity has become an economic necessity to raise the standard of living of entire families. This point has been made forcefully by the women's and labour movements in both Canada and the US. The National Organization of Women (NOW) argued before the 1985 US Congressional Subcommittee on Compensation and Employee Benefits that 'pay equity means economic survival for women and their families, and a reasonable chance to achieve a level of financial security necessary to provide for their own and children's futures'.[26] In Canada the United Steelworkers of America noted that 'many of our members' families concretely experience the impact of inequitable wage policies when their mothers, wives, or daughters receive less than the value which their work entitles them to'.[27] In a somewhat less patriarchal tone, the Amalgamated Clothing and Textile Workers Union argued: 'Discriminatory wage structures reflect an outdated notion that women needed less money then men because they were second-income earners. Women no longer work for money for extras; they work to buy the essentials of life.'[28]

SUBSISTENCE NEEDS OF SINGLE WOMEN. Many women must earn a living quite apart from the men they know, whether as husbands, fathers or lovers. Some are single without children. Others are single mothers, with added subsistence requirements. In both cases, pay equity is an economic necessity to raise the standard of living of women and their particular household formations. As early as 1946, the American labour movement used the economic needs of women living on their own as a rationale for pay-equity legislation. The United Electrical Workers noted that 25 per cent of women working in paid jobs before the Second World War were the chief earners for their families. Moreover, the war had left many women widows or with disabled husbands, thereby forcing more to become the chief wage earners. Clifford McAvoy,

Washington representative for the Electrical Workers, suggested that the layoff rates for women at the end of the war were much higher than for men, and rejected the argument that women worked for 'pin money'. Because women were working in paid jobs out of economic need, he supported the Pepper-Morse equal-pay-for-equal-work bill (which was defeated by Congress).[29] Similar positions were taken by the Congress of Industrial Organizations (CIO) and the United Rubber Workers of America.[30] The same arguments were still echoing through the halls of Congress in the 1980s during the debates over equal pay for work of equal value. The Women's Coalition of the National Federation of Federal Employees made the following statement to the 1985 Congressional Subcommittee on Compensation and Employee Benefits:

> What opponents of pay equity seem to disregard is the fact that women no longer work for 'pin money' but out of economic need. The number of single women who maintain families has risen 70 per cent in the last decade and their wages are crucial to support their families. . . . the American way of life has changed. A woman can no longer depend on a man to support her for the rest of her life. She, by definition, must be self-sufficient. But if the current wage system remains, she will be unable to support herself.[31]

THE FEMINIZATION OF POVERTY. Arguing that the unequal pay women receive for work of equal value is partly responsible for the fact that the majority of poor people are women and children, the feminist-labour alliance has suggested pay equity as a means to alleviate this situation. In the US, NOW has argued for a federal comparable-worth law partly on the same grounds: 'In 1983, seventy-five per cent of the nation's poor were women and children, and if the current trend continues, by the year 2000 one hundred per cent of the nation's poverty population will consist of women and children.'[32] Similar arguments were made by the National Treasury Employees Union.[33]

ELDERLY WOMEN. Feminist organizations and trade unions have suggested that the high rate of poverty among elderly women is the result of a lifelong experience of low and unequal wages. In the US, the National Committee on Pay Equity, a coalition of labour and feminist organizations, argued before the 1985 Congressional Subcommittee on Compensation and Employee Benefits: 'Twice as many women as men over the age of 65 live in poverty. Since pensions and social security benefits are based on prior earnings, low salaries mean less benefits and a great need for public assistance.'[34] Equal-value legislation would help to alleviate poverty among elderly women.

WOMEN OF COLOUR. No pay-equity law in the world is specifically designed to alleviate poverty among women of colour. Nevertheless, women of colour have suggested that such laws would go a long way toward this end. For example, in the US, the Mexican-American Women's National Association (MANA) lent strong support to a federal comparable-worth law on the grounds that the economic plight of Hispanic women was largely caused by racist and sexist discrimination by employers and educational institutions. Gloria Barajas, MANA's vice-president for program planning, told the 1985 Congressional Subcommittee on Compensation and Employee Benefits:

> More and more Hispanic women are falling into the category of single heads of household, and, as you know, more and more of them are slipping into the ranks of the poor. Pay-equity is a remedy for sex- and race-based wage discrimination.[35]

3. The state position

Some governments have enshrined the principle of the family's economic survival in their legislation as a rationale for pay equity. The 1963 US Equal Pay Act was justified partly on the grounds that the income differential based on sex 'depresses wages and living standards for the employees necessary for their health and efficiency'.[36] In 1982 the Canadian Human Rights Commission justified the inclusion of equal pay for work of equal value in the federal Human Rights Act partly on the basis of 1978 Statistics Canada reports: 'Although over 62% of working women support or help to support a family, 61% of women who work receive less then $6,000 a year, compared to 28% of men. Of sole support families headed by men, 8.5% have incomes below the poverty line; of sole support families with a woman head, 44.1% have incomes below the poverty line.'[37]

VALUE OF THE HOMEMAKER ROLE

Neo-conservative anti-feminist organizations have been concerned that pay-equity legislation might degrade the value of women's homemaker role, either by not providing for equal pay for domestic work or by attracting homemakers into the paid labour force with the higher wages resulting from the legislation. In 1986, seeing pay equity as a threat to the traditional family, the National Citizens' Coalition presented a long list of statistics from public-opinion polls, purportedly showing that women value the family and staying at home over pursuing a career outside.[38] It claimed that pay equity, like other state programs such as child care and affirmative action, 'either downgrades or rejects the crucial role most mothers now freely choose to play in their family's homes.'[39]

PRIVATIZATION: BACK-TO-THE-HOME

The anti-feminists have argued that pay equity would force women out of jobs or reduce their job opportunities, thereby forcing them back into the home on a more exclusive basis and decreasing the family's standard of living by making it dependent solely on the male earner's income. For example, the National Citizens' Coalition suggested that as a result of pay equity many women 'will lose their jobs to men who, because they will be the primary wage earners in their families (through a consensual husband/wife understanding), will have more stable long term employment prospects. Some of the women edged out of these jobs may return to work in the home, resulting in an [increase] of families with lower incomes and husbands as sole breadwinners.'[40]

Several observations about the Coalition's arguments are in order. First, as noted in Chapter 2, the prospect of women's losing jobs to men as a result of pay-equity legislation has never been scientifically verified. In raising it, the Coalition seemed to be parroting the views of its corporate backers rather than seriously considering the available economic studies and evidence. Second, the Coalition assumes that 'consensual understandings' between husband and wife lead men to become the primary wage earners in their families. Once again, had it consulted experts in women's studies or family studies, it would have discovered that men become primary wage earners largely through the combined historical strength of patriarchal and capitalist structures and the dominance of the male within the household. Third, the Coalition was playing on men's fears by suggesting that they would have 'more stable long term employment prospects' if they were to become the primary wage earners and many women were to leave the paid labour market. Finally, logic would seem to dictate that the Coalition should have supported rather than opposed pay equity, since according to its views such legislation would drive many women back into the home and strengthen the patriarchal nuclear family, even if it lowered the family's economic standard of living.

NATURAL SEX DIFFERENCES

Some anti-feminist neo-conservative groups have suggested that pay-equity legislation, by trying to equalize the jobs and wages of women and men, would violate their 'natural', biologically derived sex differences. Gwendolyn Landolt of REAL Women argued that 'the differences between men and women which are ascertained by biology and common sense should not be eliminated'.[41] The Christian Labour Association of Canada, on the right of the labour movement, while not advocating a too-rigid gendered division of labour, did state that 'certain jobs are more suited for men than for women, and vice versa. For example, while it is currently risky to suggest that women may be more apt to be secretaries than construction workers, there are nevertheless good reasons for making such a suggestion.'[42]

FAMILY AND SCHOOL SOCIALIZATION

Business and the anti-feminist neo-conservatives have argued that gendered occupational segregation and wage disparities are caused by years of gender socialization of young women in the family and schools rather than by employer discrimination in the capitalist workplace and marketplace. Young 'girls' have been taught to become nurses, not doctors; secretaries, not executives; waitresses, not restaurant owners. If women take those lower-paying positions, it is because of the way they are taught, not the way they are hired. For example, the National Association of Manufacturers in the US suggested in 1985 that women's low pay resulted partly from inappropriate socialization as to which jobs would be suitable for them; they pursued educational courses that were inappropriate for the higher-paying non-traditional jobs.[43] Pay-equity legislation would not remove wage disparities because it does not address the roots of the problem: the family and schools. The Retail Council of Canada noted that the 'stereotyping of women for certain jobs [which] begins at such an early age in the education process . . . go[es] a considerable way in explaining the wage gap which currently exists'.[44] The Metropolitan Toronto Board of Trade argued:

> Primarily, it is the educational system which has shown some discriminatory tendencies in directing boys and girls into various career streams. As a matter of principle, employers ought not be made liable for such discrimination. . . . Second, . . . whether or not child rearing and family orientation are in themselves desirable is a matter of opinion; the fact is that these factors are the cause of the wage gap. There is nothing in equal value which would alter these values.[45]

But at least one group supporting pay equity used the socialization model to its advantage. The Ontario Secondary School Teachers' Federation argued that pay equity should be introduced as quickly as possible so that female teachers, paid as male teachers and having access to the same positions, could provide more appropriate role models for their female students.[46]

CONCLUSIONS

The patriarchal capitalist state has usually structured the terms of reference for pay-equity struggles. In Canada this has been done through the use of Green Papers, which present a series of options that the state is considering in particular legislative areas; it then invites interested parties to comment on the options. One striking feature of almost all submissions to state agencies in the pay-equity struggle has been the way business associations, trade unions, and even feminist organizations have structured their briefs and critiques in terms of the agenda laid out by the state in the Green Paper. In causing this effect, whether consciously or unconsciously, the state engages in 'passive revolution' (see Chapter 5). It has co-opted feminist, union, and business groups by inducing them to discuss pay equity on its own terms rather than those laid down by the various groups'agendas.

However, there has been a curious discrepancy between the ideologies and the practices of feminists and neo-conservative anti-feminists in their arguments (or lack of them) over the role of households. Although feminists have developed sophisticated analyses of the household as a worksite and place of oppression for women, in the pay-equity issue it might appear that they have forfeited the ideological territory of the household to the neo-conservative anti-feminists. It is the latter who have kept raising the question of the family and the household in relation to pay equity. The pay-equity issue could have provided a golden opportunity for feminist groups to question the public-private divide on which all pay-equity legislation is constructed. They could have argued that pay-equity legislation has to address the isolation and oppression of women in the home in order for women's wages to be brought up to a level comparable to men's; they could have raised the question of women's child-care responsibilities in the home, and the effect of these on the channelling of women into low-paying jobs; they could have complained about women's domestic skills (such as household management), which are transportable to the paid labour market but are not compensated by employers. Yet, with few exceptions, feminist groups have not done so. Why? The reason appears to lie in a deliberate strategy by feminist organizations who did not wish to open up questions about the domestic or household roots of unequal pay out of fear that it would play into the hands of business and neo-conservative forces. The latter wanted to place the blame for unequal pay on the domestic sphere, and hence absolve themselves of any responsibility for it. This would have led to a direct sabotage of pay-equity legislation. It is this conscious strategizing, rather than any forfeiture of ideological territory to neo-conservative organizations, that explains the imbalance in discussions about the household by various groups in the pay-equity debates.

Notes

[1] Most of its arguments in the household area can be found in the Board of Trade of Metropolitan Toronto, *Submission on Equal Pay* (1985), especially pp. 3-8.

[2] Block, 'Economic Intervention' (1981), p. 108.

[3] Ibid., p. 112. See also Peter Kuch and Walter Haessel, *An Analysis of Earnings in Canada*, Catalogue 99-C758 (Ottawa: Statistics Canada, 1979), pp. 27-31, 113.

[4] Denton and Hunter, *Economic Sectors* (1984), pp. 23, 45.

[5] National Citizens' Coalition, *Pay Discrimination* (1986), p. 5.

[6] REAL Women, *Equal Pay for UNequal Work* (n.d.), pp. 2-3; *Green Paper* (1986), pp. 3, 10. Emphasis in original.

[7] Board of Trade of Metropolitan Toronto, *Submission on Equal Pay* (1985), pp. 5-6.

[8] US Congress, *Options* (1985), p. 290.

[9] For the conservative anti-feminsts, see Block, 'Economic Intervention' (1981), p.

108; Christian Labour Association of Canada, *Letter on Equal Pay* (1985), p. 5; *Submission on Equal Pay for Work of Equal Value to Consultation Panel on Pay Equity (Ontario)* (Toronto, 25 April 1986), p. 4. For the business attitude see, for example, the views of the US Chamber of Commerce in US Congress, *Options* (1985), p. 317.

[10] Retail Council of Canada, *Submission* (1986), p. 2.

[11] For example, see National Citizens' Coalition, 'Left-Wing Feminists Aim to Change Canadian Society', *Consensus* 11, no. 3 (June 1986); and, 'NCC Backs "Men and Women"' (n.d.).

[12] Board of Trade of Metropolitan Toronto, *Submission on Equal Pay* (1985), p. 6.

[13] See North, 'The Feminine Mistake' (1971), p. 7; emphasis added. See also Block, 'Economic Intervention' (1981), p. 108; Christian Labour Association of Canada, *Letter on Equal Pay* (1985), p. 5; *Submission* (1986), p. 4. Similar views were expressed by the business community. For the views of the US Chamber of Commerce, see US Congress, *Options* (1985), p. 317.

[14] US Congress, *Options* (1985), p. 630.

[15] Block, 'Economic Intervention' (1981), p. 246; emphasis added. See also Block on p. 108.

[16] Ibid., p. 244, fn. 11.

[17] REAL Women, *Green Paper* (1986), p. 2-3; emphasis in original.

[18] National Citizens' Coalition, *Pay Discrimination* (1986), p. 10; emphasis added.

[19] US Congress, *Options* (1985), p. 381; Automotive Parts Manufacturers Association, *Statement* (1986), p. 2-3. See also Ontario Mining Association, *Submission* (1986), p. 2; Board of Trade of Metropolitan Toronto, *Submission on Equal Pay* (1985), pp. 4-8.

[20] US Congress, *Options* (1985), p. 630.

[21] Ibid., p. 238.

[22] Canadian Association of Women Executives, *Equal Pay* (1978), p. 13.

[23] Ibid., pp. 5-6; *Submission* (1980), p. 5.

[24] Allen Potter, 'The Equal Pay Campaign Committee: A Case-Study of a Pressure Group', *Political Studies* 5, no. 1 (1957), p. 61.

[25] North, 'The Feminine Mistake' (1971), p. 5.

[26] US Congress, *Options* (1985), p. 233. A similar view was expressed by the American Federation of State, County and Municipal Employees on p. 472.

[27] United Steelworkers of America, *Brief* (1986), p. 1.

[28] Amalgamated Clothing and Textile Workers Union, *Implementing Pay Equity* (1986), pp. 11-12.

[29] US Congress, *Hearings* (1946), pp. 164-5.

[30] Ibid., p. 171.

[31] US Congress, *Options* (1985), pp. 524-5. See also London Status of Action Group, *Brief on 'Equal Pay for Work of Equal Value'* (Submitted to the Ontario Standing General Government Committee on Bill 3, Jan. 1980), p. 2.

[32] US Congress, *Options* (1985) p. 240.

[33] Ibid., p. 548.

[34] Ibid., p. 631.

[35] Ibid., p. 640.

[36] US Congress, *Statutes At Large, Public Law 88-38* (1964), sec. 2(a).

[37] Canadian Human Rights Commission, *Methodology and Principles* (1982), p. 1.

[38] National Citizens' Coalition, *Pay Discrimination* (1986), pp. 11-13.

[39] Ibid., p. 10.

[40] Ibid., p. 19.

[41] *Toronto Star*, 21 Feb. 1986, p. A22.

[42] Christian Labour Association of Canada, *Submission* (1986), p. 4.

[43] US Congress, *Options* (1985), p. 381.

[44] Retail Council of Canada, *Submission* (1986), p. 2.

[45] Board of Trade of Metropolitan Toronto, *Submission on Equal Pay* (1985), pp. 7-8; emphasis in original.

[46] Ontario Secondary School Teachers' Federation, *Response* (1986), pp. 5, 8-9; District 31 (Sudbury), *Response* (1986).

5

Passive Revolution

'To the Government: P.S. How Could You People Be Such Idiots!! No Vote For Liberals Next Election!!' This message was hand-scribbled at the end of a copy of a typed letter sent in 1987 to the Ontario Government by Colin M. Brown, Chair of the National Citizens' Coalition, protesting the proposed pay-equity bill (Bill 154). Copies of this letter without the message, dated 26 January 1987, had originally gone out to all Coalition supporters asking for donations for a media blitz against the bill.[1] The message seems to represent an admission that the Coalition had lost the fight to stop the legislation of equal pay for work of equal value, which was approved by the Ontario Legislature on 15 June 1987. Or had it?

In Chapter 1, I raised the question of how a patriarchal capitalist state could legislate equal pay for work of equal value when it appeared to run against the interests of male capitalists and in favour of women workers. Was such legislation—at the federal level in Canada, in the provinces of Prince Edward Island, Nova Scotia, Quebec, Ontario, and Manitoba, and in some US states—a victory for trade unionists and feminists against the interests of business and its neo-conservative and anti-feminist allies? Although I concluded that it was a *partial* victory for the labour-feminist alliance, I also suggested that it represented yet another instance of 'passive revolution', a concept popularized by Antonio Gramsci.

Gramsci used the term *passive revolution* to describe the 'revolution-restoration' cycle, or the situation in which a dominant group, faced with a threat to its position from a subordinate group, will attempt to absorb into itself the leading elements of the subordinate group in order to preserve its own power, even to the extent of making substantial modifications in the structure of the society.[2] These leading elements may be personnel, parts of social organizations, or ideas. The Ontario case can be used to illustrate one of the ways in which personnel from the labour and women's

movements can be absorbed into the state's bureaucratic structure. The Liberal government of David Peterson appointed the
following people to its newly-created Pay Equity Commission:
Wendy Cuthbertson, former member of the Canadian Auto
Workers, activist in the Fleck strike of 1978 and participant in the
Equal Pay Coalition, became Director of Information and Education Services at the Commission; Beth Symes, a feminist lawyer
and founder of the Women's Legal Education Action Fund (LEAF),
became Chair of the Pay Equity Hearings Tribunal; Janis Sarra, a
former Ontario Federation of Labour critic of the Ontario Consultation Panel on Pay Equity, became a vice-chair of the Hearings
Tribunal after serving a short stint with the Ontario Labour Relations Board; Geri Sheedy, former activist with the Retail,
Wholesale and Department Store Union in the Eaton's strike of
1984-85 and active member of the Equal Pay Coalition, became a
member of the Hearings Tribunal representing employees; Susan
George, former member of CUPE and the Ontario Federation of
Labour Women's Committee, also became a member of the Hearings Tribunal representing employees; finally, Brigid O'Reilly,
former executive board member of the National Action Committee on the Status of Women (NAC) and LEAF member, was appointed in the spring of 1989 to head the Pay Equity Commission,
replacing its former head, Dr George R. Podrebarac.[3]

A favourite technique of passive revolution is to sow dissension
in the ranks of the subordinate opposition, thereby weakening the
thrust of its revolutionary fervour. The revolution-in-the-making
becomes co-opted, and the old order is preserved, restored, or
reorganized. Besides the state absorption of trade-union and
feminist activists, passive revolution has occurred in three other
ways in the struggle for pay-equity. First, attempts have been
made by states and anti-feminist neo-conservative elements to
divide and conquer, or undermine the internal solidarity of the
labour-feminist alliance through the ideological manipulation of
sexism, racism, and classism. This strategy was more important at
the federal level in the United States than in Canada. Second,
where equal pay for work of equal value in its strong pro-active
version was actually passed, attempts were made to insert
loopholes, or what were termed in Chapter 2 *exemptions*, in the
legislation so that employers could avoid granting women wages
comparable to men's. Third, enough *weaknesses* and *defects* were
created in the equal-value legislation that many women would not

be able to qualify for pay-equity adjustments. These latter two passive revolutionary strategies were used in all jurisdictions, but particularly in Ontario.

In Ontario feminists and trade unionists seem to have been co-opted by state bureaucrats and politicians who, on one level, appeared to go against the wishes of the business community by establishing a pro-active version of equal pay for work of equal value but who, on another level, created so many loopholes and defects in the law that intelligent employers could avoid acting on it. Common vehicles for these loopholes have been the lists of exemptions and exceptions to pay equity, inserted in all acts, that have been extensively discussed throughout this book. In defence of these exceptions, governments have pointed to their gender-neutral application. But the Public Service Alliance of Canada, which has had considerable experience since the late 1970s in dealing with such exemptions under the guidelines of the Canadian Human Rights Act, recommended to the Ontario government in 1986 that it drop all such lists from its proposed act for two reasons: they 'can be used to justify disparate and discriminatory treatment'; and they are designed to 'appease employers', not women employees.[4]

One indication that business can adapt to equal pay for work of equal value, despite its initial opposition, is its acceptance of the Ontario Pay Equity Act after it was passed in 1987. In 1988 a majority of 200 companies surveyed in Ontario stated that 'pay equity "would not adversely affect their organization's ability to compete in the current business environment". More than 40 per cent of the respondents [companies] have conducted their pay-equity analysis, and 87 per cent said that the implementation timetables prescribed in the pay-equity legislation "are reasonable to achieve".[5] These findings run counter to the business arguments outlined particularly in Chapter 3. What happened in the meantime to change the minds of business? The answer may be sought in Gramsci's concept of passive revolution.

The fact that this concept is relevant to the pay-equity struggle does not mean that some women cannot win important pay-equity settlements. For example, in 1988 the Ontario Human Rights Commission awarded 350 mostly immigrant and part-time cleaners, members of CUPE at the Peel Board of Education, a pay increase of nearly 50 per cent to bring their wages more in line with those of full-time male custodians. While such victories represent genuine achievements to the women involved, they are also important to the viability and stability of the passive revolution: they mask the fact that most women will not achieve such victories, and thereby make the co-optation that much more effective. In the case of the cleaners, their wages were brought up to only \$9.94 per hour while the male custodians were making \$12.24.[6] To drive home the point, Paul Jordison, a national CUPE representative involved in the negotiations, emphasized: 'This settlement does not, I repeat, does not deal with equal pay for work of equal value.'[7]

The divide-and-conquer strategy used primarily by the neo-conservative anti-feminists in the United States will be discussed first. The next section will examine some of the weaknesses in equal-value legislation and how the loopholes and exemptions (for instance, in Manitoba, Ontario, and Prince Edward Island) can be manipulated by employers.

ATTACKING THE LABOUR-FEMINIST ALLIANCE: RACISM, SEXISM, CLASSISM

In 1984, when it appeared that the Pay Equity Bill sponsored by Congresswoman Mary Rose Oakar would pass in the US House of Representatives, James L. Byrne, Deputy Associate Director for Staffing in the government's Office of Personnel Management, wrote an internal memo to his Director, Donald J. Devine. He suggested that a job-evaluation study combining clerical and blue-collar occupations could be used to divide the white-collar and blue-collar unions against one another, especially since the blue-collar unions would lose out in such a study. Paper certificates, possessed by more white- than blue-collar union members, would receive greater weight than the physical effort that was more important in blue-collar jobs. Byrne further suggested:

the unions would be pitted against the radical feminist groups and would further divide this constituency of the left. Rather than allowing Oakar to manipulate the Administration on the gender issue, we could create disorder within the Democratic House pitting union against union and both against radical feminist groups.[8]

This memo illustrates the sort of tactics used in the attempt to defeat comparable worth. The forces pushing for equal pay for work of equal value, both in the US and in Canada, were a loose and fragile coalition of feminist organizations, trade unions, and minority racial-ethnic groups. Although this alliance was firmly rooted in the working class, there were latent divisions within it, which the opponents of comparable worth sought to exploit.

The anti-feminist neo-conservatives appeared to be particularly threatened by the connections they thought the labour-feminist alliance was making between the state, the capitalist workplace and the marketplace on the one hand, and the household workplace on the other. It was argued at the end of the last chapter that, from the point of view of feminism, feminist groups perhaps did not go far enough in questioning the public-private divide in their briefs on pay equity. Nevertheless, anti-feminist neo-conservatives seemed to be threatened by the labour-feminist argument that (a) the woman in the household needed a decent *individual*— not family—wage in her job in the capitalist workplace, but (b) because she was prevented from receiving one by employers in the labour market who discriminated against her, (c) the solution was state intervention in the form of mandatory job evaluations and pay-equity plans. Such intervention would give women the financial means to reduce their economic dependence on men, and help to liberate themselves from the constrictions of the household. In response, the neo-conservative anti-feminists attempted to weaken the labour-feminist coalition by dividing it along the lines where it seemed most vulnerable: class, sex/gender, and race/ethnicity. The ideological uses of these three factors to defeat opponents and buttress and mystify one's own position are known, respectively, as classism, sexism, and racism.

An attempt was made during the early 1980s by Republican President Ronald Reagan and Vice-President George Bush to use the symbolism of class, gender, and race to divide the labour-feminist alliance that was lobbying for comparable-worth legislation. The government agency selected to carry out this mission was the US Commission on Civil Rights, which had initially been set up by the Eisenhower administration to fight racial discrimination and support affirmative-action programs. After coming to power in 1980, however, Reagan and Bush turned the Commission into a vehicle to *oppose* race- and gender-based affirmative action, and equal pay for work of equal value. They fired the 'neutral' Commissioners and replaced them with people more ideologically compatible with their neo-conservative and anti-feminist views. To confuse the labour-feminist alliance, and especially women-of-colour organizations, two members of racial minorities were selected to lead the assault on comparable worth. These were Charles Pendleton, a male black director of the Great American First Savings Bank in San Diego, who was appointed the new Chair of the Civil Rights Commission, and a Hispanic woman, Linda Chavez, who was appointed Director of its staff.[9]

In 1984, two weeks after the re-election of Reagan and Bush, Pendleton and Chavez publicly declared their opposition to comparable worth—which they called 'Looney Tunes'.[10] In April 1985, by a vote of five to two, the US Commission on Civil Rights officially adopted a policy opposing comparable worth or equal pay for work of equal value.[11] Pendleton stated that 'comparable worth is to pay equity what the frontal lobotomy was to brain surgery in 1939'.[12] Using both classism and racism, he claimed that 'pay equity is a white, middle-class women's problem and . . . would hurt black women'. Pendleton argued that comparable worth would price black and Hispanic women, who have few skills, right out of the market, while benefitting the more highly skilled and educated white middle-class women.[13] Similarly, Phyllis Schlafly of the Eagle Forum used classism and racism by characterizing pay equity as a mechanism to force employers to raise the wages of 'some white- and pink-collar women above marketplace rates . . . while forcing the lower skilled women out of the job market altogether'.[14] Resorting to sexism, she described comparable worth and job evaluations as attacks on the blue-collar working-class male.[15] The neo-conservative and anti-feminist Foundation for Economic Education used classism in its attempt to divide the women's movement on pay equity. Gary North, writing for the Foundation, viewed the 'Women's Liberation Front' (WLF) as

> the advocate of a monopolistic, prestige competitive, high security employment system, one geared to all those women with impressive educational backgrounds and/or impressive physical proportions. The 'equal pay for equal work' scheme is essentially elitist. . . . the WLF members tend to be recruited from just these elitist segments of the nation's population. They are the girls with the college degrees and the affluent fathers who will be able to support them until they can find 'the right job' . . . . a group calling for the imposition of a government law [such as comparable worth] for the 'good of the masses' ultimately encourages a law which would benefit the elitist stratum from which it recruits its members.[16]

Neo-conservative anti-feminists in Canada seemed to take their cue from their American counterparts. Walter Block of the Fraser Institute tried to argue that an implicit pact had been struck between feminists pushing for equal pay for equal work and the racist leaders of South Africa's white-only trade unions:

> white racist labour union leaders . . . are actually on record expressing a willingness to have job reservation laws abolished—*provided* EPFEW *[equal pay for equal work] laws are substituted in their place.* With friends of EPFEW legislation such as Arrie Paulus, the head of the South African (whites only) Mine Workers Union, it surely needs no support of feminists.[17]

The Board of Trade of Metropolitan Toronto appeared to make an ideological use of racism when, quoting from Cornell University professor George Hildebrand, it suggested that because of pay-equity laws 'many of those who are displaced will be women who are black or from other minority groups whose earnings already place them at the poverty line or near to it'. Resorting to classism, it argued that 'equal value is based on elitest ideas to serve elitest purposes. At most, it will have the effect of shifting some wealth to those lower paid employees with the greatest needs.'[18] The National Citizens' Coalition employed sexism in suggesting that as women lodged complaints of unfair wages in relation to men, society would become more divided on a gender basis; in fact, it saw employment-equity legislation as having the general effect of pitting 'women . . . against men'.[19] REAL Women used both classism and sexism in suggesting that equal pay for work of equal value would benefit highly qualified and educated middle-class women by protecting their jobs and raising their salaries, while hurting the less qualified women in the working class who would lose their jobs to unskilled working-class men.[20]

The US Commission on Civil Rights and the American business community came together ideologically in their opposition to equal pay for work of equal value. The Chamber of Commerce warmly welcomed the Civil Rights Commission's 1985 vote to oppose comparable worth, and recommended acceptance of the Commission Report that accompanied the vote.[21] Not surprisingly, Pendleton, the black Chair of the Commission, and Chavez, its Hispanic staff director, took a position on pay equity identical to that of the business community and its neo-conservative and anti-feminist allies. Very briefly, they made the following points to the Subcommittee on Compensation and Employee Benefits of the Committee on the Post Office and Civil Service of the US House of Representatives: (a) legislating comparable worth would result in 'social and economic disaster'; (b) pay equity represents an unnatural intervention by the state in a free market; (c) there is a danger that, if comparable worth were set up in the federal government sector, pressures would build to extend it to the private sector; (d) there is no need to legislate comparable worth because the gender segregation of women in low-paying jobs is withering away, and the trend is towards a narrowing of the gendered pay gap; (e) job evaluations are subjective and biased rather than objective; (f) there is little discrimination against women, since their wages are determined by the objective laws of supply and demand in a free market; (g) because women have a primary commitment to the family and children, they voluntarily choose low-paying and part-time jobs so that they can interrupt their labour-force participation when family needs call; (h) comparable worth, like minimum wages, would hurt the poor, unskilled woman by pricing her out of the market, resulting in her unemployment as employers replaced her now more-expensive labour with labour-saving technology.[22]

Rejecting these attempts to divide it, the labour-feminist alliance developed four specific responses. First, it asserted the unity of working-class women and men, middle-class women, and racial- and ethnic-minority women and men. Second, as a concrete symbol of the solidarity between the women's and labour movements, the alliance suggested that a joint pay-equity committee, consisting of representatives of women's organizations, trade unions, minority organizations, and 'neutral' experts (but excluding business and the US Civil Rights Commission), be set up within the federal government to study pay equity. Third, through women-of-colour spokespersons the labour-feminist alliance pushed the issue of race to the centre of the pay-equity struggle to argue that ethnic- and racial-minority working-class women, rather than losing from pay equity, as the anti-feminists charged, would be among its greatest beneficiaries. Finally, the labour-feminist alliance directly criticized the US Commission on Civil Rights for failing, in its attacks on the rights of women and minorities, to fulfil its original mandate to eradicate discrimination.

In the US the business community, neo-conservatives, and anti-feminists were strong enough to defeat any attempt to create comprehensive legislation on pro-active equal pay for work of equal value in both the public and private sectors. In Canada, where neo-conservative and anti-feminist forces were weaker, equal pay for work of equal value has been institutionalized at the federal level and in some provincial jurisdictions. There is, however, considerable variation among these pieces of legislation. The strongest piece of legislation is in Ontario—it is pro-active and applies to both public and private sectors. The next strongest are those of Manitoba, Prince Edward Island, and Nova Scotia because they too are pro-active, though they apply only to parts of the public sector. The Quebec and federal-government laws are much weaker because, although applicable to both public and private sectors in their respective jurisdictions, they are complaint-based rather than pro-active. Several provinces, such as Saskatchewan, Alberta, and British Columbia, continue to resist pro-active equal pay for work of equal value.

MANIPULATING THE LOOPHOLES, EXEMPTIONS, AND WEAKNESSES

In 1987, the Equal Pay Coalition warned the Ontario government that the wording of its pay-equity bill (Bill 154) provided

> an incentive for some 'bad apple' employers to hire lawyers or consultants to advise on reorganizing their business to avoid Bill 154's requirements. For example:
> 1. Freezing or giving lesser wages to male target groups in order to reduce the ultimate payouts to their appropriate female comparison group.
> 2. Rearranging the occupancy of certain job classifications in order to ensure that those classifications do not qualify for pay equity adjustments.
> 3. Setting up artificially separate corporate entities to employ just under 100 workers so as to avoid having to prepare pay equity plans.[23]

Employers who are creative can live with the legislative distortion of equal pay for work of equal value because of the following loopholes, exemptions, and weaknesses in the law.

GENDER PREDOMINANCE. Under most legislation, only jobs with a vast majority of women (e.g., 60 to 70 per cent) can be compared with jobs in which the vast majority are men (e.g., 60 to 70 per cent) in order to establish the basis for pay-equity adjustments. However, employers can avoid paying their women workers equivalent wages simply by lowering the numbers of either women or men working in these particular jobs to just below their gender-predominance thresholds. Phyllis Schlafly gave a stark illustration of how this could be done by citing material from the Wisconsin Association of Manufacturing and Commerce:

> The Wisconsin Governor's task force study lists the job called Institution Aide as having a comparable worth gap of $5,132. But the employees in their position would not get a comparable worth raise because only 67 per cent of the 116 employees are women and Institution Aide cannot be designated a woman's job unless it meets the 70-per cent test. Now suppose that the State needs two more Institution Aides. If it hires two women, it will cross the 70 per cent threshold. The state will then give all Institution Aides a raise, and it will therefore cost the State $595,000 to hire two women. The personnel manager can easily manipulate the system, depending on whether he is pro-feminist or pro-budget cutting. Or, look at the position called Nursing Assistant 3. Because it has 70 per cent women, all 104 employees would be scheduled to get a raise of $3,626 to close the so-called comparable worth gap. If the personnel manager simply hires one male and fires two females, he can avoid comparable worth raises for all and save $377,136 in his budget.[24]

In the Ontario legislation an attempt was made to avoid this kind of manipulation through the use of *historical incumbency* and *gender stereotyping*. If the job is one that has traditionally been performed by men (such as shipping clerk), but the employer lowers the proportion of men in it below 70 per cent, the Ontario Act allows for the continued consideration of this job as male-predominant because its incumbents have historically been male. Similarily, if the current incumbents of industrial nursing positions are male, such jobs are still considered female-predominant, because that is the gender stereotype of 'nurse' in society.[25] But these two safeguards against manipulation by employers seem somewhat weak for three reasons. First, since the time frame for establishing historical incumbency and gender stereotyping is not clear it may be negotiated between labour and management—a process that employers in non-unionized workplaces (where most women work) can avoid. Or, it may have to form the basis of a later individual or group complaint after a pay-equity plan has been established. Second, the gender predominance of many jobs is so unstable that their historical incumbency and gender stereotyping cannot be established. The fact that they keep fluctuating above and below the gender-predominance threshold gives the employer a relatively free hand to manipulate the proportions of men and women to keep them below the threshold levels. Third, employers do not seem to be *required* by the Pay Equity Act to adhere to historical incumbency and gender stereotyping; rather, they appear to be given the *option* to use them or not. The Act only requires employers to '*regard*' historical incumbency and gender stereotyping,[26] and the Pay Equity Commission has weakened this provision even further by suggesting that the Act '*allows*' the use of historical incumbency and gender stereotyping, and that historical incumbency '*could*' be used.[27] Words like 'must' and 'obligated' are avoided entirely.

Gender predominance has other peculiar twists that are probably known to employers and their pay-equity consultants. A woman in a male-predominant job (e.g., welder) performing work comparable to that of the men in the same job but earning lower wages cannot qualify for a pay-equity adjustment, even if women in a female-predominant job (e.g., cleaner) successfully use the welder job class to win a pay-equity adjustment for themselves. In addition, a woman in a gender-neutral job class cannot compare her wages to those of a man in the same job class, even though her work may be equal or comparable.[28]

LABOUR-MARKET SHORTAGE. Under pay-equity legislation, employers could declare a labour-market shortage for the skills of certain high-paid male workers, such as carpenters, electricians, or welders. If they can prove such temporary shortages to pay-equity commissioners, women would not be allowed to compare their wages with the temporarily inflated wages of such positions for the purpose of obtaining pay-equity adjustments.[29] The Ontario Pay Equity Commission told employers how to take advantage of the labour-shortage exemption: 'Employers could . . . refer to outside data, such as labour market surveys, to demonstrate a skills shortage. A combination of market indicators and employer-specific recruitment history could also be used.' Once the shortage ends, the job rate ('highest rate of compensation') of the male job class may be used as a basis of comparison, even though its new and higher level results from a past shortage.[30]

CASUAL PART-TIME WORK. Throughout the pay-equity debates, business lobbied for the exclusion of part-time positions from equal-pay legislation, while the labour-feminist alliance feared this might happen and fought against it. Casual part-time work is included in the federal Canadian and US legislation, and in the public-sector pro-active laws of Prince Edward Island and Manitoba. However, it is excluded from the 1987 Ontario Act, with three exceptions. First, included is work 'performed for a least one-third of the normal work period that applies to similar full-time work'.[31] Using 1985 Canadian national statistics as a standard, women who worked full-time (30 hours or more per week) averaged 38.8 hours per week;[32] therefore one-third of normal full-time work would be 12.9 hours. Generalizing from Canada to Ontario, the Ontario Act includes women in part-time positions who work an average of 12.9 hours per week or more, but denies pay-equity to those who work less—yet they, in turn, are affected by the next two exceptions. Second, included in the Act is work 'performed on a seasonal basis in the same position for the same employer';[33] this would seem to cover, for example, women working in retail stores for six weeks during the annual Christmas rush. Third, also included in the Act is work 'performed on a regular and continuing basis, although for less than one-third of the normal work period that applies to similar full-time work.'[34] This seems to cover many women in the fast-food industry who may work only about 10 hours per week, but on a regular and continuing basis from one week to the next. Considering these three exceptions together, *excluded from the Act are non-seasonal, temporary, irregular, and discontinuous casual positions with hours less than one-third of normal full-time positions.* Since government statistical agencies have not created a category that matches this legal one, it is difficult to estimate how many casual positions and their female incumbents employers may exclude from pay-equity comparisons. In 1989, the Ontario Federation of Labour (OFL) and Equal Pay Coalition (EPC) claimed that the 1987 Ontario Act 'defines casual workers in a way that excludes 200,000 part-time workers', or approximately 10 per cent of the Ontario female labour force.[35] Using a year covered by both the Census and monthly labour force surveys, in 1985 Statistics Canada estimated that in Ontario there were 504,000 females in part-time positions defined as 'persons who usually work less than 30 hours per week' and did not consider themselves full-time.[36] Since this appears to include many part-time seasonal and permanent positions, it is too broad a category to be useful for interpreting the Act. In the

1986 Canada Census, Statistics Canada estimated that, in 1985, 515,495 women in Ontario worked 26 weeks or less and, of these, 250,685 worked 'mostly full-time'. Presumably the rest (264,810) worked 'mostly part-time' of 26 weeks or less.[37] This is much closer to the EPC/OFL figure, but presumably still includes many seasonal, regular, permanent and continuous positions and their incumbents. One feminist active in the Equal Pay Coalition has stated that most women in casual positions are covered by the Act. The safest conclusion is that there are a number of women in casual positions that employers may exclude from the Act, but the figure is probably lower than the 200,000 estimate offered by the Ontario Federation of Labour and the Equal Pay Coalition. Several pay-equity acts exclude positions similar to irregular casual work. For example, female students working on summer vacation are specifically excluded from the 1988 Prince Edward Island Act, and women paid by special fees or working on contracts are excluded from the 1985 Manitoba and 1988 Prince Edward Island Acts.

TEMPORARY TRAINING POSITIONS. Under guidelines to the Canadian Human Rights Act, employers are given the right to exclude from pay-equity comparisons and adjustments employees in a temporary training program 'that is equally available to male and female employees and leads to the career advancement of the employees who take part in the program.'[38] Their wages may be either higher (if they include training incentives) or lower than those of other persons normally in such positions. The pro-active 1987 Ontario and 1988 Nova Scotia Acts contain exemptions almost identical to the one in the Canadian Human Rights Commission Guidelines,[39] while none at all are found in the 1988 Prince Edward Island Act. The temporary training exemption is open to abuse by employers who run establishments with a high labour turnover of female workers, each of whom is placed on a probationary temporary training program before being given a permanent position; a 'revolving door' ensures that a sizeable portion of such female workers never qualify for pay equity.

TECHNOLOGY. Faced with the prospect of having to pay their cheaper women workers higher wages, employers have more incentive to cut back on their payouts by speeding up labour-saving automation and either firing the women or not replacing them when they quit or retire.

CONTRACTING OUT. If a company has a few high-paying male or low-paying female jobs that might be the focus of a pay-equity battle, it can simply contract them out to another private company whose employees are either all women or all men. Since pay-equity comparisons cannot be made between establishments, the company would thereby defeat any attempt by women employees to seek adjustments to their low wages.

RED-CIRCLING. Rather than contracting-out jobs, an employer can use the pretext of technological change to red-circle some of the high-paying male jobs, freeze their wages, and downgrade their 'official' qualifications. Under many pay-equity laws, women in an establishment could then not compare their wages to the higher wages of such positions, thereby reducing the size of any pay-equity settlement. The Ontario Chamber of Commerce was quite open in admitting that this was one of the ways employers could close the wage gap between women and men:

> The Ontario Chamber of Commerce does not agree with the Green Paper's suggestion that wages of an occupation should not ever be reduced in order to meet the requirement of equal pay for work of equal value. A male dominated job may be over-valued in the context of internal systems or external market forces and the economic viability of an operation may not allow for any further increase in the cost of labour. In these circumstances . . . one option would be the red circling of higher male rates until the female rates catch up. This concept would require that immediate resources available for wage increases be allocated to those employees who have been found to be disadvantaged in the past.[40]

Similarly, the Board of Trade of Metropolitan Toronto argued that 'by decreasing the costs of male dominated occupations, the impact of the equal value legislation will be somewhat minimized'.[41] Attitudes like these are particularly troubling to the labour movement because of their potential for dividing male and female union members.

It was perhaps in the passive-revolutionary spirit that, in 1989, the Ontario Pay Equity Commission sent out a newsletter informing employers and pay-equity consultants how, in the context of doing job evaluations, they could use red-circling to freeze or reduce the increases in the wages of highly-paid male workers. The Commission set up a fictitious Question and Answer exchange that deserves quoting at some length:

> Q: What are the circumstances under which a job class [can] be red-circled and how does the red-circling affect future wage increases?

A: The following examples illustrate under what circumstances a job class can be red-circled and the implications of red-circling on the job rate ['highest rate of compensation for a job class'] and on the incumbents' future pay increases:

Example 1

A new technology is introduced which eliminates the need for a job class. Five incumbents, as a result, are placed into a lower-level job and their salaries are red-circled.
A. For pay equity purposes, the job rate is the rate paid for the lower-level job. These five employees will retain their present wage. However, their salaries will either not increase *or* increase by smaller than normal increments until the lower-level job rate catches up to their rate of pay.

Example 2

After a gender-neutral job comparison, a job is found to be of a lower value, as noted below, and is red-circled.

	VALUE	SALARY RANGE OF MALE COMPARATOR JOB CLASS
Old	400 Points	$6.75 = $8.75
New	300 Points	$5.10 = $7.10

A. The lower job rate [$7.10] is used when the following is true:
1. The methodology that led to the red-circling is free of gender bias.
2. Future rate increases for those employees earning $7.10 or more are frozen or curtailed until the job's rate of pay ($5.10 to $7.10) equals or is greater than what the incumbents are currently earning.
3. A person newly hired for the red-circled job will be paid according to the new salary range.[42]

Four observations may be offered about these examples. First, the wages—rather than the job—are red-circled and so form the exemption. Second, in the second example above, red-circling and the lowering in the increases of male wages emerge directly out of a job comparison done to satisfy the requirements of the Pay Equity Act. This may confirm the fears of some male employees that the Act may lead to either freezing of their wages or reduced increases. Third, there is an apparent contradiction in the Commission's, on the one hand, stating that red-circling 'is not a means of avoiding the spirit and intent of the Act'[43], and on the other hand, through its Pay Equity Newsletter, informing employers how to use red-circling to freeze and reduce the increases in the wages of some male employees. The latter advice seems entirely in the spirit of the statement cited above from the Ontario Chamber of Commerce and the Board of Trade of Metropolitan Toronto. Is the Commission violating the spirit of the Act by using a pay-equity Newsletter to inform employers and consultants how to legitimately employ red-circling against employees? Fourth, as pointed out earlier, some former activists from the women's and labour movements—once critical of the loopholes in Bills 105 and 154—were appointed to positions on the Commission. On an individual level, what social psychological transformations have carried them from positions in the women's and labour movements from which they critiqued the bills for their pro-business exemptions (such as red-circling) to one of recommending how businesses might employ the exemptions *against* labour and women? On a societal level, what is the process whereby states co-opt critical social movements by absorbing many of their leading activists and exploiting their talents and experiences so that the position of the labour and women's movements is weakened and that of business strengthened?

JOB-EVALUATION METHODOLOGY. Employers, especially in non-unionized workplaces, may intentionally or unintentionally introduce pay-equity plans based on job-evaluation methodologies that implicitly mask gender biases against women so that they cannot qualify for higher wages. Although this is illegal under some pay-equity acts, such biases are often difficult to detect. For example, the working conditions of computer terminal operators—which may include back- and eye-strain—may be given a low weighting by a particular job-evaluation system, thereby minimizing the possibility of higher wages for the women suffering that strain. On the other hand, responsibility for giving directions can be given a high weighting by a job-evaluation system, thereby favouring men in management positions. When the two jobs are compared, the female-predominant computer-operator job may still score much lower than the male-predominant management job, thereby leaving untouched the low wages of the female operators.

COLLECTIVE BARGAINING. In their collective-bargaining sessions with unions, employers may simply deduct any pay-equity adjustments from the general wage increases granted to the male workers, even though most acts prohibit employers from reducing the wages and benefits of any employee in order to achieve pay equity. This prohibition can be sidestepped by the employer who simply becomes more recalcitrant in granting any general wage increases through the regular collective-bargaining process. This has the potential of driving a wedge between female and male workers unless they work out a strong strategy of solidarity before entering collective-bargaining sessions with management.

BURDEN OF LODGING COMPLAINTS. Most pay-equity acts are based, completely or in part, on the complaints model. This means that a woman is burdened with the individual responsibility of initially bringing a pay-equity complaint either to her steward in a unionized workplace or to her supervisor in a non-unionized establishment. If a settlement cannot be reached at this level, she can then try to get an investigator from the pay-equity bureau or commission, human-rights commission, or employment-standards branch of the government to look into her complaint, and if the investigator finds some legitimate grounds for it, she may be able to have a formal hearing. This process is time-consuming, and it places an enormous financial and emotional strain on the individual woman. In the process she may bear the wrath and possible retaliation of co-workers, union officials, and company management. It is therefore not surprising that many women, faced with such prospects, may decide in the end to live with their unequal pay.

PRIVATE SECTOR. Most comparable-worth acts, such as those at the state level in the US, and in Manitoba, Nova Scotia, and Prince Edward Island, do not extend to the private sector. Since most women in the paid labour force are in the private sector, the vast majority of women in those jurisdictions are excluded from coverage.

SIZE OF ESTABLISHMENT. Women in small workplaces in the private sector are usually not covered by pay-equity legislation. Under the 1985 Manitoba and 1987 Ontario Pay Equity Acts, for example, women in workplaces with fewer than ten employees do not qualify for adjustments. In 1989, the Ontario Pay Equity Commission claimed that this disqualified 217,883 women, or 10 per cent of the female labour force, from coverage by the Act.[44] The Equal Pay Coalition and Ontario Federation of Labour put this figure at 238,000, or 12 per cent of the total female labour force, or 15 per cent of the private-sector female labour force.[45] According to the Pay Equity Commission, this weakness in the Ontario Act is more serious for some sectors than others. The percentages of organizations in the public sector that it says are excluded from the Act because they have fewer than ten employees are as follows: child care, 53 per cent; health care, 19 per cent; community and social organizations, 41 per cent; public libraries, 64 per cent. In the private sector, the Commission claims that small size excludes the following percentages of organizations: apparel manufacturing, 34 per cent; other manufacturing, 39 per cent; retail, 74 per cent; personal service, 55 per cent; and tourism, 46 per cent. It is worth noting that the Commission suggests that these figures are low estimates.[46] In fact, they may be high estimates derived from the Commission's quantitative survey of about 100 employers and a number of large hospitals. Unfortunately, the questionnaires used in the survey elicited information about 'establishment' that could not be matched to its legal definition. In the Act, '"establishment" means all of the employees of an employer employed in a geographic division'. 'Geographic division', in turn, means 'a county, territorial district or regional municipality'. The Municipality of Metropolitan Toronto is considered a single geographic division; so are the combined Regional Municipality of Sudbury and Territorial District of Sudbury. Negotiations between management and union bargaining agents may alter this geographic definition by combining two or more geographic divisions of the same employer; where a union does not exist, the employer may decide on such a combination.[47] Therefore, several of an employer's small establishments, with fewer than 10 employees in one or more geographic divisions, may be combined, thereby creating one large establishment with 10 or more employees who are then covered by the Act. This seems to be the case for many of the Commission's figures cited above. For example, in the public sector, small 'day nurseries and private home day-care agencies and funded under agreements with municipalities under the *Day Nurseries Act*' within the same regional municipality, county or territorial district should be treated as a single establishment;[48] the same can be said for small public library branches or health care agencies or community and social organizations. In the private sector, there may be some cases in the Commission's figures in which some small retail outlets or tourist offices or personal service establishments (e.g., hair salons) may be combined with other establishments of the same employer within a geographic division to form a single and larger establishment covered by the Act. The conclusion is that a number of establishments in certain industries—especially in the private sector—may indeed have too few employees to be covered by the Act, but the correct percentages are probably considerably less than those cited above by the Commission.[49] Whatever the correct percentages, this exclusion from pay-equity coverage is a particularly heavy penalty for women, since they are more likely than men to be employed in small workplaces.

In addition, small employers in Ontario (10 to 99 employees) are not required to develop a pay-equity plan, although they are required to begin pay-equity adjustments by 1993 (50 to 99 employees) or 1994 (10 to 49 employees).[50] (Pay-equity adjustments in the absence of pay-equity plans are usually not based on comprehensive job evaluations.) This may make it difficult for their women employees to see how they might achieve wages comparable to men's. Since 98 per cent of the 265,000 private-sector firms in Ontario have fewer than 100 employees, practically none of them are obliged to create a pay-equity plan[51]—unless they are in the same geographic division and are owned by the same employer, in which case they constitute a single and larger establishment with perhaps more than 100 employees.

COMPARISONS WITHIN ESTABLISHMENTS. Under many pay-equity acts, comparisons between female-predominant and male-predominant jobs can be made only within establishments, not between them. This means that women in all- (or nearly-all-) female establishments can find no male positions with which to compare their job characteristics and wage rates, and so are disqualified from pay-equity adjustments. The Ontario Pay Equity Commission identified the following proportions of female-predominant jobs in the public sector for which it would be difficult to find male-predominant jobs to use as comparisons: child care, 93 per cent; health care, 80 per cent; community and social organizations, 77 per cent; and public libraries, 87 per cent.[52] However, my previous remarks regarding the accuracy of the Commission's figures on size of establishments seem to apply here as well. Women in small day-care centres could search for male comparator job classes throughout the day-care system in an entire county, regional municipality, or territorial district. The same is true for women in health care agencies or in community and social organizations or in public libraries. Even when such establishments in a geographic division are combined, the proportions making up male job and female job classes should change little, but the likelihood of finding a male comparator class seems to be greater. Moreover, since the funding for these establishments comes from either the provincial or municipal governments, there seems to be nothing preventing women from seeking male comparator job classes outside their own special agency or branch, although this does not appear to be the practice. For example, why can those female day-care workers who are subsidized by a municipality not compare their jobs with a male job class in a municipal road crew? The Commission's figures on all- or nearly-all female establishments, then, are probably high estimates of exclusions. In 1989 the Commission claimed that 867,000 of the 1.7 million women (50.6 per cent) who are supposed to be covered by the Pay Equity Act would be disqualified because of this single defect.[53] And this figure does not include the 485,000 women who are already excluded from the Ontario Act because they are covered by the weaker complaints-based provision of the Canadian Human Rights Act, or are in workplaces with fewer than 10 employees. Thus, using the Commission's high estimates, approximately 61 per cent of Ontario women are excluded from the Act because they are in (a) a federally regulated workplace (b) a workplace with fewer than 10 employees, or (c) a predominantly-female establishment that has no male job classes with which to make comparisons. The correct figure is probably considerably less. But even this would still be a low estimate of the numbers of women excluded from coverage. The Ontario Act defines 'establishment' on a geographic basis so that, for example, low-waged women retail employees in a grocery chain in one regional municipality could not compare their jobs to the high-paying male jobs in the chain's warehouse division in another regional municipality. As previously noted, there is a provision in the Act for employees and the employer to agree to override such geographic distinctions,[54] but most employers would probably refuse, since it is not in their interest to do so. This restrictive definition of 'establishment' thus excludes a further unknown number of women from qualifying for pay-equity adjustments under the Act.

EQUAL OR COMPARABLE VS. PROPORTIONAL VALUE. Under the Prince Edward Island, Nova Scotia, Manitoba, and Ontario Pay Equity Acts, women in female-predominant jobs can achieve pay-equity adjustments if their jobs are of 'equal or comparable value' to male-predominant jobs.[55] For example, in Ontario the job rate ('highest rate of compensation') for a female job class may be $10,000 and its value 100 points; the job rate for an equal or comparable male job class may be $15,000, its value also 100 points. Pay equity is achieved by granting $5,000 to the female job class. But how equal is 'equal'? How comparable is 'comparable'? Do the values of the female job class and male job class have to be identical? Or can they vary somewhat? None of the acts provide definitions. There is a provision in the Ontario and Nova Scotia Acts—but not in Prince Edward Island and Manitoba—for the absence of an equal or comparable male job class, in which case a comparison can be made between a female job class and a male job class with a value *lower* than that of the female job class *only if* the job rate (in Ontario) or pay rate (in Nova Scotia) of the male job class is *higher* than that of the female job class.[56] Using Ontario as an example, the job rate of a female job class may be $10,000, and its value 100 points; the job rate of a male job class may be $15,000, but now its value may be only 80 points. A pay-equity increase of $5,000 to the female job class is permitted. The difference in value between the two job classes appears to depart from 'equal' or 'comparable'. But what about the case in which both the value and the job rate for the male job class are higher than those for the female job class? For example, the value of the female job class may be 100 points, and its job rate $10,000; but the value of the male job class may now be 120 points, and its job rate $25,000. No pay-equity adjustment would be allowed in this case under any of the acts mentioned. The Ontario Federation of Labour and Equal Pay Coalition pointed out the problem with this restrictive language by using a fictitious example:

> Maria Espinola is a sewing machine operator at Ready-Wear Fashions. She earns $6.63 an hour after 16 years with the same non-union company. There *are* jobs done mainly by men at Ready-Wear [e.g., cutter]. But the manufacturer is adamant that the sewing machine operator's job is not equal in value to the cutter's job. . . .
> Because the law allows comparisons only between male and female jobs of *equal value*, Maria Espinola likely won't get one cent. Nor will hundreds of thousands of women working in offices, hospitals, factories, stores and other workplaces.[57]

In view of our previous discussion and the erroneous statement in this example that 'the law allows comparisons only . . . of *equal value'*, this passage makes sense only if the value of male-predominant cutters is greater than that of female-predominant sewing-machine operators—in which case a comparison between them cannot be made, and no pay-equity adjustment is forthcoming. Similarly, the Ontario Coalition for Better Daycare pointed out that the few males who do work in small community and privately operated day-care centres are probably in management positions. Since women day-care workers would, in all likelihood, not be performing work of equal value to that of male managers whose jobs have higher value (although this assumption should be critically examined), they could not compare their jobs with the few male jobs that do exist in day-care centres.[58] In 1986, citing the McDonald Royal Commission, the Retail Council of Canada predicted that the institutionalization of equal pay for work of equal value would lead to further political pressure to introduce proportional pay for work of proportional value.[59] Its prediction proved correct in 1989, when the Ontario Pay Equity Commission, recognizing the defect of the strict equal- or comparable-value and lower-value comparisons, recommended to the provincial Minister of Labour an amendment to the Pay Equity Act to allow comparisons of 'proportional value' through the use of 'wage lines' to make it 'possible to determine that the female job class is, for example, 50 percent of the value of the male job class and therefore should be paid 50 percent as much'.[60] No longer dependent on the NDP-Liberal accord, the Liberal government of David Peterson failed to act upon this and other recommendations for strengthening the Pay Equity Act.

CORRECTING THE SMALLEST WAGE GAP. In the 1987 Ontario Act, the 'salaries, wages, payments and benefits' of a 'job class' are called the 'job rate'; this is 'the *highest* rate of compensation for a job class'.[61] The Act was constructed in such a way that, where comparisons could be made with two or more male job classes, women would qualify for only the smallest possible wage adjustment.[62] In such a case, pay equity would be considered achieved when the job rate in the female job class 'is at least as great as the job rate for the male job class with the *lowest* job rate, if the work performed in both job classes is of equal or comparable value'. Since this would be the smallest difference for any possible comparison, it would give women the smallest possible pay-equity adjustment.[63] The difference between the female job rate and the lowest male job rate may, for example, be only $2,000, while the difference between the female job rate and a higher male job rate may be $6,000. The women would receive the lower $2,000 settlement rather than the higher $6,000. The Ontario Government chose to ignore the advice of the Ontario Coalition for Better Daycare, which in 1987 stated: 'where there are two male job classes with which comparisons are possible, the one with the highest wage rate should be used. Any other comparison only serves to undermine the true purpose of pay equity—paying male and female workers performing jobs which are of comparable value, equal wages.'[64] Similarly, the Confederation of Canadian Unions had warned the government in 1986 that the methodology of 'matching the minimum comparable male rate . . . would not only create a downward pressure on the higher-rated male classification but also deny women full equal pay for work of equal value'.[65] This defect in the Act seems to be in the interest of the employer. In the words of the Ontario Public Service Employees Union: 'It may be in their [employers'] interests to start with male job classes with the lowest job rates, hoping to find value matches for female job classes at the low end of the pay scale.'[66] In fact, the Board of Trade of Metropolitan Toronto expressed this interest when it told the Ontario government in 1986 that 'there can be no justification for adjusting female rates up to the average comparable male rate or the maximum comparable male rate'.[67] It recommended that 'the average female rate . . . be matched with the minimum comparable male rate'. The final legislation corresponded closely with the interests of the Board, with the exception that the highest rather than the average female rate was used. This defect also exists in the 1988 Nova Scotia Act[68], while the 1985 Manitoba and 1988 Prince Edward Island Acts were silent on the situation of two male job classes with a value equal or comparable to a female job class.

MONOCAUSAL EXPLANATION OF WAGE DISCRIMINATION. The use of gender predominance in many pay-equity acts seems to assume only one cause of wage discrimination against women: the crowding of women into occupational ghettos, which drives their wages down because of their 'oversupply'. This appears to be the rationale for the restriction of eligibility for pay-equity adjustments to women in positions with at least 60 per cent (Nova Scotia, Prince Edward Island, and Ontario) or 70 per cent women (Manitoba). There are many other sources of wage discrimination against women, such as the hiring and promotion practices of employers and personnel officers; educational institutions, the media, and the family; the unequal burden of household labour; penalties for time off work due to pregnancy or premenstrual syndrome; and the treatment of women as objects of male sexual pleasure. None of these sources of wage discrimination against women is directly recognized in any pay-equity act.

SENIORITY. This is usually based on length of service in an organization. Progression through the wage hierarchy, the granting of other benefits, and the timing of layoffs and recalls often depend, in part, on seniority. Almost all pay-equity laws allow employers to offer different wages to women and men on the basis of differences in their seniority—as long as the wage rate for the most senior position is equally attainable by both women and men and the seniority system does not discriminate against women (i.e., it is gender-neutral). In Ontario, the differences between the job rates of female and male job classes due to gender-neutral seniority are deducted before calculating pay-equity adjustments. 'For example, if the difference in compensation between two comparable job classes is found to be $1,000, but $300 of that difference can be demonstrated to be due to the higher seniority of the incumbents of the male job class, then the pay equity adjustments required for the female job class would be $700.'[69] But what is a 'gender-neutral seniority system'? No pay-equity act has been able to come up with a satisfactory definition. Consider the following three points. First, compared to men, women are often in job classes that have lower entry wage rates and have to go through a greater number of annual dollar increases to reach the maximum rate (the job rate in Ontario). Even though women often receive the same percentage increases as men, their lower base salary means that, in absolute terms, their annual increases are usually less. Is such a system discriminatory? A reasonable answer seems to be 'yes'. But in 1988 the Ontario Pay Equity Commission stated:

> If both the female job class and male comparator job class use a seniority system, the job rate is the maximum rate for each job class. Pay equity is achieved when the maximum salary of the female job class is equal to the maximum salary of the male comparator. However, *the minimum salaries and the number of steps in the scales may be* the same or *different* between the job classes.[70]

In other words, the Commission seems to consider seniority to be gender-neutral if the job rates of female and male job classes are equalized, even though, in the female job class, the entry-level wage rate may be lower and women may have to go through a greater number of smaller annual dollar increases to reach the maximum. Second, women have to suffer through more labour-force interruptions than men because of pregnancy leaves and other, briefer absences to care for sick family members. Some employers will place women back at the bottom of the seniority system when they return to work; others will freeze women's seniority level until they return to work; a few will continue to add weeks on to women's seniority, even though they are not at work. Pay-equity bureaus may consider the seniority system in all three of these cases gender-neutral because either the average or maximum wage rates between equal or comparable male and female job classes are the same. Yet this does not begin to tackle the way apparently gender-neutral seniority systems may be gender-biased by the structuring of the relationship between the domestic household sphere and the private marketplace: because of their reproductive household labour, women do not have the same ease of access as men to seniority systems. Third, women may not advance as quickly as men through seniority systems because they often switch jobs to get away from sexual harassers, forcing them to start all over again at the bottom of yet another seniority system. Once again, women do not have the same access as men to the seniority system—this time by the way power and control are structured into relations between women and men in paid work. The most reasonable conclusion to draw from this discussion is that so-called gender-neutral seniority systems that permit employers to pay women lower wages than men may in fact be gender-biased, and so contribute to the gendered wage gap.

MERIT AND JOB PERFORMANCE. Employers are permitted to exempt merit pay from pay-equity adjustments under legislation at the federal levels in Canada and the US, and in the provinces of Ontario, Prince Edward Island, and Nova Scotia—provided that three conditions are met: the merit is based on a formal performance rating; employees are aware of the rating system; and the system is gender-neutral, or merit pay is equally available to female and male employees.[71] The Ontario Pay Equity Commission explains how merit can be used as an exemption by describing a salary range with a reference point located somewhere between a maximum and minimum. Employees who perform the requirements of the job advance to the reference point, which may be the midpoint. For purposes of pay equity, this becomes the job rate. Employees who perform beyond the expectations of the job may advance from the job rate somewhere up to the maximum. The difference between the job rate (at the midpoint or reference point) and the maximum is the portion consisting of merit pay, and is exempted from use in pay-equity adjustments.[72] But is this portion gender-neutral? There are at least two considerations. First, men's lighter domestic workloads, and the reproduction of their labour-power by their spouses, help to provide them with the time and energy to become superior performers, who are then rewarded with merit pay. Conversely, women's double day of labour helps to rob them of time and energy, which interferes with their job performance, thereby helping to block their access to merit pay. Second, for men, superior performance resulting in merit pay is partly rooted in their gendered socialization as boys and their later streaming into specialized secondary and post-secondary education. Women are equally disadvantaged by the same patriarchal familial and educational socialization. Taking these two considerations into account, it seems difficult to argue that merit pay and performance levels can be completely gender-neutral.

LIMITS TO PAY-EQUITY SETTLEMENTS. Most pay-equity laws place a maximum limit, usually 1 per cent of payroll, on the size of any pay-equity settlement in any given year. This may force the most underpaid women to wait the longest to achieve wage parity with their male co-workers. For example, let's say that a heavily gender-segregated company that employs 250 women in female-predominant jobs and 50 men in male-predominant jobs has an annual payroll of $10 million. If it would take $5,000 on average to grant each of the 250 women a pay rate equivalent to that of the 50 men, the total size of the adjustment would be $1.25 million. But because of the 1 per cent ceiling, the company would have to pay out no more than $100,000 per year: hence it would take those women at least twelve and a half years before they achieved a pay rate comparable to that of their male co-workers, by which time a number of them would have quit or been fired. The quickest settlement would probably occur under the Nova Scotia legislation, since it requires that the total pay-equity adjustment be completed within four years, but does not put a cap on the amount of adjustment in any one year.[73] However, if the women were in Prince Edward Island, it would take them a long time to achieve their full pay-equity adjustments, since this province puts a maximum cap of 1 per cent of payroll per year on its public-sector employers.[74] Under the Manitoba legislation the women would never achieve the total adjustment, since it places a 1 per cent cap per year on adjustments over a maximum of four consecutive years.[75] In Ontario, these women would probably achieve full pay equity more quickly in the public than in the private sector. Employers in both sectors must pay out annually a *minimum* of 1 per cent of the previous year's payroll; if they wish, they can pay out more. In the public sector, full pay equity must be achieved by 31 December 1995. However, no such restriction is placed on private-sector employers—*except* small employers (with 10 to 99 employees) who choose *not* to post pay-equity plans: within this group, employers must achieve full pay equity by 1 January 1993, if they have 50 to 99 employees; they are given until 1 January 1994, if they have 10 to 49 employees. No such dates are imposed on them if they choose to establish a pay-equity plan. The weakness in the Ontario Act, then, is that large private-sector employers, and small private-sector ones (with 10 to 99 employees) who post pay-equity plans are given a longer time than public-sector employers to achieve full pay equity. The Ontario legislation is further restricted by the fact that the 1 per cent per year is calculated on a payroll defined as excluding benefits, while-pay equity adjustments include benefits. This reduces the absolute size of the 1 per cent, which would have been greater had it been calculated on the same basis as the pay-equity adjustments (that is, including benefits).[76]

GROUP OF JOBS: INTERNAL EQUITY OR INEQUITY? Under the 1987 Ontario Pay Equity Act, employers are not obliged to do a job comparison for every female job class if they can argue that some female job classes are located in a group of job classes that is at least 60 per cent female. Such groups can also be negotiated with the union, or be ordered by review officers from the Pay Equity Commission.[77] The group of job classes has 'a *progression of jobs* involving similar kinds of tasks and duties performed at *different levels* of skill, effort, responsibility, and working conditions' (an example might be 'clerk, senior clerk, clerk typist, intermediate clerk typist, and senior clerk typist').[78] The job class with the greatest number of employees is selected as the *representative* that is then compared to an equal or comparable male job class outside the group. The pay-equity adjustment in dollar terms based on the difference in the job rates (or 'highest rate of compensation for a job class') between the representative job class and the male job class is then granted to all job classes in the group.[79]

At least five weaknesses lurk beneath this method. (a) The representative job class does not have to be female-predominant (i.e., at least 60 per cent female). It may be a neutral job class, or even male-predominant (i.e., at least 70 per cent male). If the latter, then a male job class in the group is being compared to a male job class outside the group to determine equivalence of value and pay-equity adjustments. Paradoxically, two male job classes are being compared to determine whether women's work is under-valued. If the male job class in the group is found not to be undervalued, then the female job classes in the group do not receive any pay-equity adjustments—even though, had they been used in the comparison, they might have been found to be under-valued. (b) It is not clear why the most numerous job class should be considered representative of other job classes in the group. The 'representative' job class is not based on any actual representative sampling of all employees in the group. The other job classes are likely to diverge in several ways—for instance, in their values and job rates. (c) If the representative job class (whether female or male) has a higher job rate and value than the female job classes at the bottom of the group, the latter will, in all likelihood, receive a smaller pay-equity adjustment than they would have, had their own job classes been individually evaluated. (d) The requirement that all job classes receive the same dollar increase maintains past absolute differences among them. This is what the Commission calls 'internal equity'. From another perspective, it may be called 'income inequity' in the sense that the lower job classes can never hope to use the pay-equity legislation to catch up to the higher job classes (the legislation was not designed for this purpose). This is particularly serious when the male job classes are at the higher end of the group and the female job classes at the lower end: in this case, the Pay Equity Act can be used to *prevent* female job classes from closing the gendered wage gap within the group. (e) The Pay Equity Commission states that one advantage of the group method is that 'fewer job classes need to be evaluated'.[80] This may result in a cost saving to the employer. In passive-revolutionary fashion, the Commission also states that 'if an employer uses the group of jobs approach, all pay adjustments to each job class in the series will be pay equity adjustments that can be phased in under the one per cent of payroll per year.'[81] This statement is

puzzling for two reasons: first, the Commission seems to be suggesting that employers, using the group method, can fold all pay
adjustments negotiated outside the context of pay equity into the
pay-equity adjustments; second, it appears to suggest inadver-
tently that employers can violate the Act by granting pay-equity
adjustments less than 1 per cent of payroll (this is allowed only if
that is all it takes to achieve full pay equity). Perhaps the Commission did not intend to say these things, and the phrasing of its
statement is just awkward.

RELATIVE BARGAINING STRENGTH. In Ontario, after pay equity
has been achieved, the employer is permitted to maintain differences in compensation between male and female job classes if it can
be shown that such differences result from the relative bargaining
strength of the men's union.[82] It is a practical question how one
determines what portion of the job rate of a male job class results
from its superior bargaining strength. Most exemptions apply
during the process of attaining pay equity. The 'relative bargaining strength' exemption is different because it applies *after* pay
equity has been achieved, although such a point in time may be
difficult to determine because of changes in (among other things)
the nature of job duties, the gender composition of job classes, and
the applicability of other exemptions. The achievement of pay
equity during the 1990s does not mean that unequal pay for work
of equal value cannot be reintroduced by employers. Business
successfully lobbied the Ontario government to have 'relative
bargaining strength' inserted as an exemption to the 1987 Pay
Equity Act. This weighs particularly heavily on women, since men
are more likely both to be unionized and to belong to unions that
have, over a considerable number of years, won large wage increases for their members. Even after women attain equal pay,
therefore, they could lose ground as men in stronger bargaining
units move ahead again.[83]

COMPARISONS WITHIN BARGAINING UNITS. As noted in Chapter
2, many bargaining units are gender-predominant. Low-wage
cleaning women in a large corporation may be in one bargaining
unit while highly paid men on the shop floor may be in a different
one. It would be advantageous for the women cleaners to compare
their jobs with the men's. But some pay-equity acts, such as the
1987 Ontario Act, mandate comparisons initially *within* bargaining units. Only if male-predominant jobs cannot be found within
a woman's bargaining unit may comparisons be made with male-

predominant jobs in a different unit in the same establishment.[84] Because pay differences between bargaining units are often greater than those within the same unit, this provision reduces the total amount of compensation that women can hope to obtain. In addition, the pay rates for women who are not organized in bargaining units are normally lower than the rates for women and men in such units. For non-unionized women, the Ontario Act mandates an initial comparison only outside all bargaining units, so that they cannot compare their jobs with male-predominant jobs within bargaining units. Only if non-unionized jobs with at least 70 per cent men cannot be found can women begin to compare their jobs with male-predominant jobs in bargaining units. Again, such a provision reduces the size of the pay-equity adjustment by initially forcing women to compare their jobs with those of non-unionized men, who are likely to have lower wages than those who are unionized. The pro-active, public-sector laws of Manitoba and Nova Scotia do not include bargaining-unit restrictions to job comparisons, but rather mandate immediately comparisons between female- and male-predominant jobs throughout the entire establishment of the employer.[85]

MASKING DISCRIMINATION. Pay-equity plans are constructed on the basis of studies by economists and sociologists who have investigated the components of the gendered wage gap. But these researchers have been unable to explain anywhere from one-third to two-thirds of the gap. Unknown sources of gender discrimination, as well as other factors, lurk beneath the unexplained variance. It is difficult to understand why such studies never include measures of discriminatory practices by employers, managers, supervisors, and personnel officers in the hiring and promotion of women. In addition, it cannot be assumed that the explained variance does not contain hidden discriminatory factors. For instance, accounting for part of the wage gap by the differences in the amount and nature of education that women and men receive does not eliminate the possibility that gender discrimination may affect women's access to, and participation in, educational programs. In fact, education is a complicated social process that cannot be isolated from gender socialization in the home, in the media, and in educational institutions themselves, which may steer women away from choosing high-paying non-traditional careers.

THE DOUBLE DAY OF LABOUR. All pay-equity laws are inherently sexist and patriarchal in the sense that they are based on the distinction between the public sphere of the state and labour market and the private sphere of the household. The gender division of labour in the household and the double day of labour of women in part- or full-time paid jobs have a great impact on women's wages. Forced to seek out low-paying and part-time positions in order to balance a heavy workload at home, women often have to interrupt their paid careers in order to bear children and take care of them while they are young. Despite maternity leave, and some protection of seniority while on leave, women's wage progression through the ranks of corporate hierarchies is impeded. Yet there is no pay-equity act that attempts to address this problem.

PRIVATE PROPERTY RIGHTS. All pay-equity acts recognize the private prerogative of employers to set the wages of their employees. In non-unionized workplaces, this right is absolute and not shared with employees. Employers could introduce their own pay-equity plans, which in Ontario are checked only by the Pay Equity Commission. In large unionized workplaces, employers negotiate pay-equity plans with union representatives, but in practice the employer still has greater control over the shape and content of the plan. Since business interests have been so strongly opposed to equal pay for work of equal value, it would seem folly to entrust them with the final say over the shape of any pay-equity plan.

FREE TRADE. As a result of the Free Trade Agreement between Canada and the United States that went into effect in 1989, Canadian employers may increasingly argue that since most American states, as well as the US federal government, do not pay women equally for work of equal value, Canadian companies cannot compete on an equal footing.[86] This Canadian-American differential may be manipulated in three ways. First, Canadian businesses may lobby to weaken the application of equal pay for work of equal value in federally regulated industries under the Canadian Human Rights Act and in the private sectors of Ontario and Quebec, which are covered by the same legislation. Second, if their women employees demand equal pay for work of equal value, Canadian companies may threaten to shut down their Canadian operations and move their plants to the sunbelt of the US or to Third World countries where wage rates are much lower. Third, Canadian businesses may now lobby more strongly than ever against any move to implement pro-active equal pay for work of equal value in Saskatchewan, Alberta, and British Columbia, to prevent the extension of 'comparable worth' to the private sectors in all provinces outside Ontario, and to ensure that the Canadian Human Rights Act is not toughened to force the chartered banks and other federally regulated companies to introduce pro-active pay-equity plans.

CONCLUSIONS

Legislating equal pay for work of equal value has considerable potential for dividing and weakening the working class, the labour movement, and the women's movement in seven ways.

1. It solidifies gender divisions by institutionalizing comparisons between women's and men's jobs and wages. There is a hidden danger that male workers, believing their forgone income is being used to redress women's unequal wages, may blame women for their own failure to obtain greater wage increases in the future. Compensation consultants Sibson & Co., who did a 1989 survey of corporate organizations in Ontario contemplating pay-equity measures, reported that the 1987 Ontario Pay Equity Act 'is having a very strong impact . . . on attitudes in the male work force. We've found some situations where the organization may be dealing with 40 per cent of the male employees appealing results purely on the basis that they didn't get an increase and the women did.'[87]

2. Equal-value legislation weakens feminism by setting up a male standard against which women must compare themselves. Why use male wages as the standard against which women are to judge their wages? Would it not be preferable to construct a standard of worth based on the needs of women performing productive and reproductive labour (including child-bearing and -rearing) rather than on the needs of men performing productive labour only?

3. The legislative solution to equal pay for work of equal value has the potential to pit women against one another by qualifying some for pay-equity adjustments and disqualifying others merely because they are in different structural positions—such as jobs with fewer than 60 per cent women, or in workplaces that have no male-predominant job classes against which comparisons can be made, or in establishments with fewer than 10 employees.

4. Equal-value legislation ossifies job and wage hierarchies based on skill, effort, responsibility, and working conditions. The use of job-evaluation systems, points, and weights, while reducing gender differences, reinforces differences among workers rather than creating a sense of mutual solidarity and collectivism based on a levelling in the hierarchical division of labour.

5. The implementation of equal pay for work of equal value requires a mastery of complex technical and legal details in the legislation and in pay-equity plans and methodologies. Union officials, forced to master such details, become the 'experts', from whom rank-and-file women may become further alienated. The Ontario Public Service Employees Union seemed to recognize this potential danger when it argued that pay-equity legislation 'must be written in plain English so workers can understand it'.[88] In 1986, OPSEU president James Clancy condemned Bill 105, the proposed public-sector pay-equity bill, as 'a violation of our fundamental right to have laws written in clear and simple language. . . . This legislation is almost incomprehensible. . . . it will remain unintelligible to most of our members.'[89]

6. Because pay-equity laws do not deal with race and ethnicity, they may be interpreted as white legislation. They do not directly challenge the dominant position of the white majority. Women of colour may be helped by such legislation because of their low rates of pay, but pay equity does not deal directly with their double discrimination and oppression on cultural and gender bases.

7. Equal pay for work of equal value is classist, or contains class biases, in the sense that it does not challenge the unequal pay between workers and bosses (an issue raised in Chapter 1). What is the value of work put into a company by bosses, senior executives, and stock-market speculators compared to that of workers? Why do large investors who have put no work into a corporation receive thousands of dollars in dividends, while the working employees, who have contributed their hard labour, receive little in comparison? Is this unequal pay for unequal work of unequal value on a class basis? These questions have not been raised in the struggle for pay equity. Until they are raised and answered on a practical level, we will continue to obtain weak equal-value legislation, shot through with the defects, exemptions, and loopholes discussed throughout this book.

The class and gender struggles over pay equity pass through two major stages—a *pre-legislation* stage, and a *post-legislation* one.

The passage into law of a particular pay-equity bill marks the transition from the first to the second stage. Much of this book has been concerned with gender and class (and to some extent, ethnic/racial) struggles in the pre-legislation stage. Five characteristics distinguish these two stages.

First, the pre-legislation stage is marked by *group or sectoral lobbying* by the labour-feminist coalition and the alliances among business associations, neo-conservative groups, and anti-feminist organizations. The post-legislation stage focuses on *individual negotiations* between management and unions in separate paid workplaces or establishments, and *individual complaints* by them to pay-equity tribunals (e.g., that one or the other party is not negotiating in good faith to establish a pay-equity plan).

Second, the first stage is characterized by the *mobilization* of groups around pay-equity through inter-group alliances; the second stage, by their *demobilization* on this specific issue. Demobilization does not entail the complete disappearance of the alliances—often they continue, as shells of their former selves, carrying out 'moping-up' operations (such as lobbying to have amendments to the law passed). But the intensity of their activities is only a shadow of what it was in the first stage. However, there is a greater stability in business alliances than in labour-feminist alliances—and this carries over into the second stage.

Third, there are *open-ended* discussions and *exploration of alternatives* in the pre-legislation stage, although these are often bounded by state Green Papers, as noted at the end of Chapter 4. In the post-legislation stage, pay equity passes into rigid *institutionalization* and *legalization*: the open-ended discussions and exploration of alternatives end, to be replaced by efforts to interpret and apply the various sections of the law.

Fourth, the second stage represents the *continuation in other forms of the first stage's class and gender struggles*. Often the same issues central to the labour-feminist and neo-conservative, anti-feminist business alliances during the first stage re-emerge in the second stage, either in negotiations around pay-equity in the paid workplace, or in pay-equity tribunal hearings into complaints by corporations, unions, and individuals. One case in point was the 1989 complaint before the Ontario Pay Equity Hearings Tribunal by the Ontario Nurses Association (ONA) against the Regional Municipality of Haldimand-Norfolk, with the Haldimand-Norfolk Regional Board of Commissioners of Police having intervenor status. The ONA was searching for male comparators in a broader definition of its members' employer's establishment (the Regional Municipality). It argued that the Police Commission (which has the male job classes of 'constables, sargeant, staff sargeant, court administrator, assistant court administrator, inspector, superintendent, administrator, identification technician and transfer guard') was part of that establishment partly on the grounds that the Regional Municipality controls its budget. The Regional Municipality and the Police Commission, once they realized the implications of using police male comparators in a broader definition of the employer's establishment, argued that their two establishments were separate on the grounds that the Board of Commission of Police is an 'employer in its own right'.[90] This particular dispute was foreshadowed by the labour-feminist and business struggle in the pre-legislation stage over the definition of establishment discussed in Chapter 2.

Finally, in each stage the *statization* of the gender and class struggles (i.e., the struggles through specific state institutions) is different: in the pre-legislation stage, the struggles occur through the state legislature and executive; in the post-legislation stage, the struggles shift to specialized state bureaucracies, usually called pay-equity bureaus or commissions, whose specialized function is to administer the act and hear complaints within specialized hearings tribunals. Class and gender structures are integrated into the internal organization of the tribunal. The bureau or commission and its hearings tribunal become partial 'femocracies' (in which feminists are state bureaucrats), though a few men are members as well. The tribunal is structured to reflect equal representation from employers and employees, much as state labour boards are. Each of the tribunal panels (which hear the complaints) consists of three persons—a chair representing the state or 'public interest' (however that concept is defined), one member representing employees, and one representing employers or management. Its decisions often reflect the location of its three members in the class and gender structures of society. For example, in the ONA case just discussed, the tribunal panel consisted of Janis Sarra as vice-chair representing the state, Geri Sheedy representing employees, and Sharon Laing representing employers and management. The decision was a 2-to-1 split vote, with Sarra and Sheedy forming the majority in favour of the ONA, and Laing forming the dissenting minority favouring the Regional Municipality and Police Commission.

Throughout this book there has been considerable discussion of discrimination—both gender and, to a lesser extent, racial/ethnic. It can be individual or systemic. *Individual discrimination* tends to place responsibility and blame for actions on individual persons, often in positions of power, such as men over women, or employers over employees. *Systemic discrimination* traces gender and ethnic/racial biases to the way institutions and organizations have been structured in the past, so that individuals who happen to be members of certain categories (e.g., women and visible minorities) suffer as a result. There have been recent moves to dismiss the importance of individual discrimination and focus instead on systemic discrimination. This is a healthy development in terms of tracing the structural roots of discrimination. However, it ignores the reality of discrimination—it is both systemic *and* individual. Throughout this book the perceptive reader may have noticed that women and employees, and their feminist and union representatives, tend to discuss both individual and systemic discrimination, while the more powerful (such as business and management) tend to view discrimination as systemic rather than individual. This is a demonstration of one ideological feature of the pay-equity debate: the more powerful favour a systemic approach as a way of avoiding responsibility for their actions in an attempt to shift blame elsewhere; the family and the educational institution have been favourite targets. The less powerful favour a combined focus on both as a way of placing responsibility on the more powerful—men, employers, managers, and supervisors— while at the same time recognizing the structural roots of discrimination. The contrast in these ideological uses of discrimination was evident in a fascinating exchange between Mary Cornish, who represented the ONA, and the Ontario Pay Equity Hearings Tribunal in the 1989 case mentioned above. Combining the individual and the systemic, Cornish 'urged the Tribunal to adopt a systemic approach to the [Pay Equity] Act. . . [she] suggested that the persons that have historically been responsible for setting the discriminatory wage practices are the appropriate persons to redress the discrimination. She urged the Tribunal to adopt the test that whoever controls the purse strings is the employer for the purposes of pay equity.'[91] On the other hand, Janis Sarra and Geri Sheedy, who formed the majority on the femocratic tribunal panel, were in the contradictory position

of trying to reconcile their roots in the women's and labour movements with their structural location in a patriarchal capitalist state
that represents primarily the interests of men and the business
class and only secondarily those of women and the working class.
They responded to Cornish by adopting the business, neo-conservative, and anti-feminist emphasis on systemic over individual
discrimination in order to argue *in favour* of the feminist-labour
position on the employer's establishment:

> The [Pay Equity] law is a recognition of the systemic nature of wage
> discrimination. . . . The Act addresses wage discrimination which
> has developed over time through systems and practices of compen-
> sation. This is not necessarily the result of individual practices, but
> in large measure is due to institutional practices which have
> resulted in wage discrimination. The legislation was designed not
> to punish or lay blame for inequitable wage practices, but to
> provide an affirmative action plan to identify and redress the
> discrimination. Just as the Act does not require wage discrimina-
> tion to be proven as intentional, so too it does not hold those
> responsible for creating wage inequities as 'guilty'. In that respect
> we do not adopt the submission by the Applicant [Cornish] that
> one of the tests the Tribunal should apply is 'whoever is responsible
> for the wage discrimination should be made to pay'.[92]

Passive revolution entails the absorption of radical principles of
social movements that in certain eras are perceived as threatening
to state, business, and neo-conservative interests. In the case of
pay equity, many states have absorbed the women's movement's
principle of 'equal pay for work of equal value'. And in the course
of that absorption, the principle undergoes, in Gramsci's terms,
'transformism' or 'molecular' change, towards de-radicalization;
in other words, it becomes less threatening to dominant groups in
society. Thus 'equal pay for work of equal value' becomes 'pay
equity', which, though holding out the promise of pay adjustments for some women, contains legal loopholes that effectively
exclude many others. Rather than closing the wage gap completely, the state—by its own admission—promises that this measure
will close only about one-quarter to one-third of it. (The rest of the
gap will have to be closed through affirmative action, universal
public child care, non-gendered domestic labour, gender-neutral
socialization in households and schools, and stronger legislation
against sexual harassment and pornography that degrade
women.) 'Equal pay for work of equal value', which once served

to organize the women's movement, now becomes a state legal practice for its disorganization and immobilization.

In passive revolutions, state bureaucracies also absorb some personnel from social movements—in the pay-equity case, from the women's and labour movements—and this has a double-edged effect. On the one hand, absorption tends to de-radicalize the people who move into the state: former activists who once critiqued and organized against defective pay-equity laws must now defend and implement them, and as a result, social movements lose some of their critical activists. As a minor example, Susan George (former member of the Canadian Union of Public Employees and the Ontario Federation of Labour Women's Committee, who moved into the Ontario Pay Equity Tribunal as a member representing employees) was placed in the position of partaking in a decision that denied a request from the Ontario Public Service Employees Union (that it be given the names of the non-unionized employees of Cybermedix Health Services outside of its own bargaining unit for the purposes of negotiating a pay-equity plan with Cybermedix).[93] Obviously, such names would have been useful in any future organizing drive. On the other hand, earning a living can be difficult in the insecure, often voluntary positions within social movements, and the new state bureaucracies do offer some measure of job and income security. The absorbed personnel, as individuals, are committed to the genuine state reforms (as opposed to token reformism) for which they have fought, and do not want to see them mitigated by a state filling its pay-equity bureaus with their opponents. An excellent example of this was the 1989 decision by the Ontario Pay Equity Hearings Tribunal on the criteria to be used in defining an employer's establishment (see page 34 in Chapter 2). This decision was tremendously important for the labour-feminist alliance because it allowed the Ontario Nurses Association (ONA) to use as comparators the male job classes in the Police Commission of Haldimand-Norfolk Regional Municipality. As mentioned previously, the person on the Tribunal opposing this decision was Sharon Laing who represented employers. The decision favouring the ONA was carried only because Janis Sarra and Geri Sheedy formed a two-thirds majority. As noted earlier in this chapter (on page 154), both Sheedy and Sarra came out of the labour-feminist alliance. The decision might have gone the other way had neo-conservative business representatives taken their place on the panel.

There is considerable tension between working for progressive reforms 'within the system' and fending off co-optation by that 'system'.

Passive revolutions often occur when there are crises of legitimacy in the practices of dominant classes and states. The women's movement has accused employers of using discriminatory wage policies and the state of aiding and abetting them in this by refusing to act against them. In the paid workplace, such policies have unwittingly helped some women, who have sought organizational support in bringing about changes, to organize into trade unions. Employers have been anxious to counter this trend through moderate legislative solutions. Politicians have awakened, reluctantly, to the increased radicalization of women who, performing a double day of labour inside and outside the home, have refused to continue suffering discriminatory wage practices and have threatened to translate their dissatisfaction into votes for opposing electoral candidates and parties. Faced with opposition to equal pay for work of equal value from business, but strong support from labour and feminist communities, politicians have tried to increase their legitimacy by passing watered-down pay-equity laws, which are pleasing to some within these communities but not to others. In this way they have helped to undermine charges of doing nothing about gender discrimination, while at the same time offering ways in which the business class can live with the new legal reality. In the process, popular movements and their radical agendas have become somewhat attenuated and dominant classes and groups stronger. The women's and labour movements are now forced to work with the new legislation while developing alternative ways of organizing in coalition politics to push for an equal-pay-for-work-or-equal-value law closer to their original principles.

Notes

[1]National Citizens' Coalition, *Letter on Bill 154* (1987), p. 4.

[2]See Antonio Gramsci, *Selections from the Prison Notebooks*, edited and translated by Quintin Hoare and Geoffrey Nowell Smith (New York: International Publishers, 1971), pp. 58-9, 105-20; Anne Showstock Sassoon, 'Passive Revolution and the Politics of Reform', pp. 127-48 in her edited *Approaches to Gramsci* (London: Writers and Readers Publishing Cooperative Society, 1982); Christine Buci-Gluck-

smann, 'State, Transition and Passive Revolution', pp. 207-36 in Chantal Mouffe, ed. *Gramsi and Marxist Theory* (London: Routledge and Kegan Paul, 1979).

[3] Ontario Pay Equity Commission, *Newsletter* 1, no. 1 (March 1988), p. 3; 1, no. 2 (July 1988), p. 4; 1, no. 4 (May 1989), p. 3.

[4] Public Service Alliance of Canada, *Submission* (1986), pp. 3-4.

[5] Ontario Pay Equity Commission, *Newsletter* 1, no. 3 (Jan. 1989), p. 8.

[6] *Toronto Star*, 3 Dec. 1988, pp. A1, A19; *Globe and Mail*, 3 Dec. 1988, p. A8; 5 Dec. 1988, p. A15; *Hamilton Spectator*, 2 Dec. 1988, p. A1; 3 Dec. 1988, p. A9.

[7] *Globe and Mail*, 5 Dec. 1988, p. A15.

[8] Bureau of National Affairs, *Pay Equity and Comparable Worth* (1984), p. 138.

[9] US Congress, *Options* (1985), p. 167.

[10] Ibid., p. 446.

[11] Ibid., p. 588.

[12] Ibid., p. 155.

[13] Ibid., pp. 170, 504.

[14] Ibid., pp. 453, 504.

[15] Ibid., p. 454.

[16] North, 'The Feminine Mistake' (1971), pp. 12-13.

[17] Block, 'Economic Intervention' (1981), p. 106; emphasis in original.

[18] Board of Trade of Metropolitan Toronto, *Submission on Equal Pay* (1985), pp. 28, 35-6.

[19] National Citizens' Coalition, *Pay Discrimination* (1986), p. 21.

[20] REAL Women, *Equal Pay for UNequal Work* (n.d.), p. 5; *Position Papers, Publication No. 3.* (n.d.), p. 5; *Green Paper* (1986), pp. 7-8; *Globe and Mail*, 17 Sept. 1986, p. A6.

[21] US Congress, *Options* (1985), pp. 323-4.

[22] Ibid., pp. 159, 161, 163-6, 174-6, 565, 570-2, 574-8, 581. A similar attitude to comparable worth was expressed by the United States Office of Personnel Management, *Comparable Worth For Federal Jobs: A Wrong Turn Off the Road Toward Pay Equity and Women's Career Advancement* (Document 149-40-3; Washington, D.C., Sept. 1987).

[23] Equal Pay Coalition, *Submission* (1987), p. 41.

[24] US Congress, *Options* (1985), pp. 454-5. Similarly, the Ontario Public Service Employees Union argued that, with respect to the 60 per cent cut-off level for female predominance in the Ontario legislation, 'employers attempting to circumvent the law could hire just enough males into a job to "beat" the cut-off percentage' (Ontario Public Service Employees Union, *Submission* [1986], p. 10); for an identical argument, see Confederation of Canadian Unions, *A Brief* (1986), p. 6.

[25] Ontario Pay Equity Commission, *Determining Gender Predominance*, Implementation Series #7 (May 1988). See also Prince Edward Island, Pay Equity Act (1988), sec. 2(4).

[26] Ontario, *Pay Equity Act, 1987* (1988), sec. 1(5).

[27] Ontario Pay Equity Commission, *Determining Gender Predominance*, Implementation Series # 7 (May 1988), p. 3.

[28] Ontario Pay Equity Commission, *Introduction to Pay Equity*, Implementation Series #1 (March 1988), pp. 4-5.

[29] In the legal terminology of the 1987 Ontario Act, women would not be able to compare the job rate ('the highest rate of compensation') of female job classes to

that part of the job rate of male job classes temporarily inflated by labour-market shortages (Ontario, *Pay Equity Act, 1987.* [1988], secs. 1[1], 6, 8(1)[e]). In the 1988 Nova Scotia legislation, women would not be able to compare the 'pay rate' ('range of pay') of 'female-dominated classes' with that part of the pay rate of 'male-dominated classes' temporarily inflated by shortages (Nova Scotia, *An Act to Provide Pay Equity* [1988], secs. 13 [4][d], 17). In the 1988 Prince Edward Island Act, women in 'female-dominated classes' would not be able to compare their 'average range of pay' with that part of the wages of 'male-dominated classes' temporarily inflated by shortages (Prince Edward Island, *Pay Equity Act* [1988], secs. 7 [2] and 8 [1][c]).

30 Ontario Pay Equity Commission, *Permissible Differences in Compensation,* Implementation Series #13 (Nov. 1988), p. 5.

31 Ontario, *Pay Equity Act, 1987* (1988), sec. 8(4)(a).

32 Statistics Canada, *The Labour Force, December, 1985,* Catalogue 71-001 (January, 1986), p. 113.

33 Ontario, *Pay Equity Act, 1987* (1988), sec. 8(4)(b).

34 Ibid., sec. 8(4)(c). Irregular casual positions are excluded from the 1988 Pay Equity Act in Nova Scotia (sec. 3[f]).

35 Equal Pay Coalition and Ontario Federation of Labour, *Ontario Pay Equity Law: One Million Denied* (Toronto, 1989).

36 Statistics Canada, *The Labour Force, December, 1985* (1986), p. 114.

37 Statistics Canada, *1986 Canada Census,* Catalogue 93-112 (March 1989), Table 2, p. 100.

38 Canadian Human Rights Commission, *Equal Pay for Work of Equal Value Interpretation Guide* (1984), p. 3.

39 Nova Scotia, *An Act to Provide for Pay Equity* (1988), sec. 13(4)(b); Ontario, *Pay Equity Act, 1987* (1988), sec. 8(1)(b).

40 Ontario Chamber of Commerce, *Submission* (1986), pp. 9-10.

41 Board of Trade of Metropolitan Toronto, *Submission on Equal Pay* (1985), p. 33.

42 Ontario Pay Equity Commission, *Newsletter,* 1, no. 5 (June 1989), p. 4. I thank Pat McDermott for pointing this out to me.

43 Ibid., p. 4.

44 Ontario Pay Equity Commission, *Report* (1989), p. 166.

45 Equal Pay Coalition and Ontario Federation of Labour, *Ontario Pay Equity Law* (1989); Equal Pay Coalition, *Submission* (1987), pp. 7-8, Appendix B.

46 Ontario Pay Equity Commission, *Report* (1989), pp. 50-2.

47 Ontario, *Pay Equity Act, 1987* (1988), secs. 1(1), 14(3)(a), 15(2)(a).

48 Ibid., Appendix.

49 I thank Pat McDermott for bringing this to my attention.

50 Ontario Pay Equity Commission, *Gender-Neutral Job Comparison,* Implementation Series #9 (July 1988), p. 1; *Calculating the Number of Employees in the Private Sector,* Implementation Series #3 (March 1988), p. 2; *Pay Equity Adjustments,* Implementation Series #14 (Nov. 1988), p. 3.

51 Ontario Pay Equity Commission, *Report* (1989), p. 95.

52 Ibid., p. 55.

53 Ibid., p. 5; *Globe and Mail,* 17 Jan. 1989, p. A1; *Toronto Star,* 17 Jan. 1989, p. A9.

54 Ontario, *Pay Equity Act, 1987* (1988), sec. 1(1), 14(3)(a), 15(3)(a); Ontario Pay Equity Commission, *Definition of Establishment,* Implementation Series #4 (March 1988), p. 1.

[55] Prince Edward Island, *Pay Equity Act* (1988), secs. 1(j), 2(3)(4), 7(2); Nova Scotia, *An Act to Provide Pay Equity* (1988), sec. 17(a); Ontario, *Pay Equity Act, 1987* (1988), sec. 6(1); Manitoba, *Pay Equity Act*, (1985), sec. 6(2).

[56] Ontario Equal Pay Coalition and Ontario Federation of Labour, *Ontario Pay Equity Law* (1989); for an identical argument, see Ontario Nurses Association, *Submission* (1986), p. 19.

[57] Ontario, *Pay Equity Act, 1987* (1988), sec. 6(2); Nova Scotia *An Act to Provide for Pay Equity* (1988), sec. 17(a).

[58] Ontario Coalition for Better Daycare, *Day Care Brief* (1986), p. 3.

[59] Retail Council of Canada, *Submission* (1986), p. 14.

[60] Ontario Pay Equity Commission, *Report* (1989), pp. 76-80.

[61] Ontario, *Pay Equity Act, 1987* (1988), sec. 1(1); emphasis added.

[62] For this interpretation, see Ontario Public Service Employees Union, *Meeting the Challenge* (1986), pp. 9-10.

[63] Ontario, *Pay Equity Act, 1987* (1988), sec. 6(3a); emphases added. Ontario Pay Equity Commission, *Which Job Classes to Compare*, Implementation Series #10 (July 1988).

[64] Ontario Coalition for Better Daycare, *Brief to the Standing Committee* (1987), p. 5; an identical position was adopted by the Equal Pay Coalition, *Submission* (1987), pp. 13-14.

[65] Confederation of Canadian Unions, *A Brief* (1986), p. 4.

[66] Ontario Public Service Employees Union, *Equity at Work* (1987), p. 104.

[67] Board of Trade of Metropolitan Toronto, *Submission to the Consultation Panel* (1986), pp. 17, 18.

[68] Nova Scotia, *An Act to Provide for Pay Equity* (1988), sec. 17(b).

[69] Ontario Pay Equity Commission. *Permissible Differences in Compensation* Implementation Series #13 (Nov. 1988), p. 2.

[70] Ontario Pay Equity Commission, *Determining Job Rate—Salaries/Wages/Payments*, Implementation Series #11 (August 1988), p. 6.

[71] See n. 99 in Chapter 2.

[72] Ontario Pay Equity Commission, *Determining Job Rate—Salaries/Wages/Payments*, Implementation Series #11 (August 1988).

[73] Nova Scotia, *An Act to Provide for Pay Equity* (1988), sec. 14(1).

[74] Prince Edward Island, *Pay Equity Act* (1988), sec. 11.

[75] Manitoba, *The Pay Equity Act* (1985), sec. 7(3).

[76] Ontario, *Pay Equity Act, 1987* (1988), sec. 13(4)-(6); Ontario Pay Equity Commission, *Pay Equity Adjustments*, Implementation Series #14 (Nov. 1988), pp. 3-4.

[77] Ontario, *Pay Equity Act, 1987* (1988), sec. 6(6)-(10).

[78] Ontario Pay Equity Commission, *Using the 'Group of Jobs' Approach*, Implementation Series #6 (May 1988), p. 1. Emphases in original.

[79] Ibid., pp. 2-4.

[80] Ibid., p. 3.

[81] Ibid., p. 4.

[82] Ontario, *Pay Equity Act, 1987* (1988), sec. 8(2).

[83] Equal Pay Coalition, *Submission* (1987), p. 30.

[84] Ontario Pay Equity Commission, *Definition of Establishment*, Implementation Series #4 (March 1988), p. 6; Ontario, *Pay Equity Act, 1987* (1988), sec. 6(4), 6(5).

[85] Manitoba, *Pay Equity Act* (1985), secs. 9(1) and 14(1); Nova Scotia, *An Act to Provide for Pay Equity* (1988), sec. 13(3).

[86] For example, this argument was made by John Doddridge, president of Hayes-Dana Inc., manufacturer of truck parts for the auto companies. See *Globe and Mail*, 23 March 1989, pp. B1-B2.

[87] *Globe and Mail*, 5 Oct. 1989, p. B10.

[88] Ontario Public Service Employees Union, *A Rose Is Not Enough* (1986), p. 4.

[89] Ontario Public Service Employees Union, *Meeting the Challenge* (1986), pp. 6, 13.

[90] Ontario Pay Equity Commission, *Decisions of the Pay Equity Hearings Tribunal*, File No. 0001-89 (30 June 1989).

[91] Ibid., paragraph 29.

[92] Ibid., paragraphs 40, 44.

[93] Ibid., File No. 0003-89 (6 July 1989). The other members of this hearings panel were Beth Symes, Chair, and Donald Dudar, representing employers. This panel granted the other requests of OPSEU.

Appendix A:
Theoretical Definitions

The concepts of patriarchy, class, and state may not be familiar to all readers, and even among those familiar with them, their definitions and meanings are subject to debate. Although other writers have analyzed their various meanings more thoroughly, a brief discussion of how they have been used in this book may help to clarify the text.

PATRIARCHY

One of the most central yet controversial concepts in women's studies is 'patriarchy.' There is little agreement among feminist writers as to its meaning,[1] and some, especially socialist feminists, have debated whether it should be used at all. Yet it continues to enjoy wide popularity, and has increasingly appeared outside women's studies in the general social-science literature. For the purposes of this book 'patriarchy' has been treated as a historical materialist concept—one rooted in concrete social existence that changes over time rather than in abstract ideas that remain timeless. The following are some salient features.

MALE CONTROL. Men exercise control over women. This control is of two types: a personal power exercised informally in face-to-face encounters between women and men, as in families or social clubs; and an impersonal domination exercised formally through positions in organizations—the kind of power held by managers or supervisors in corporate business organizations or the state. It goes without saying that there is considerable variation in the degree to which different men exercise control over different women.

IDEOLOGY. 'Ideology' has many meanings. In this book, it means the set of social practices—including, but not restricted to, individual acts, social acts, social relations, ideas, beliefs, customs, opinions, and attitudes—that legitimize an activity or institution by masking or mystifying certain aspects of it. Patriarchy is ideological in the sense that it consists of social practices that legitimize male control by masking or mystifying its nature, causes, functions, and consequences. The phrase 'housework is not work' is perhaps one of the most powerful examples of patriarchal ideology.

MATERIALISM. The 'ultimate' or 'final' materialist basis of patriarchy is labour, or the concrete activity that people engage in as they produce and reproduce life and the means of their livelihood. This includes unpaid labour both in the household and in the informal economy, as well as paid labour in the household and the 'official' labour force. Any adequate theory of feminism cannot accept the separation between paid labour in the public sphere of the marketplace and unpaid labour in the private sphere of the household:[2] both are 'economic' activities and hence form part of the 'economy'. In feminism, the value of labour is not defined by its payment; in patriarchy, it is. One of the roots of patriarchy is male control of woman's labour, both in the official labour force and in the household. Even sexual activity, whether for pleasure or to produce babies, is labour; thus part of man's control over woman's labour is his control over her sexual activity.

The central materialist relation between women and men is the extraction of surplus, or unpaid, labour by men from women.[3] This occurs in the household under the family-wage system, in which the full-time wife/mother does not receive an adequate portion of the wage to provide her own means of subsistence, but must expend much of her portion on the rest of the household. A dramatic example of this is the worldwide custom of the wife/mother skipping her meal or eating the leftovers so that her husband and children may eat better. Despite such sacrifices, her own labour is not lessened. The unpaid surplus labour extracted in the household takes the form outside the household of surplus value. This is appropriated most often by the business*man* as he exploits both female and male employees in his enterprise.

SOCIAL STRUCTURE. Patriarchy does not emerge out of the isolated acts of individuals cut off from the rest of society. It emerges out of, and is fully integrated with, the social relations among individuals, groups, and social organizations.

BIOLOGICAL NON-REDUCTIONISM. Patriarchy cannot be reduced to biological matter that remains fixed throughout history; it does not depend on the natural differences between females or males, such as the ability of females to menstruate or of males to produce sperm. Thus it is a mistake to confuse sex with gender, biological females with feminism, or biological males with patriarchy.[4] The support for patriarchy shown by Margaret Thatcher, Prime Minister of England, and the support for feminism shown by Henry Morgentaler, a Canadian doctor who advocates reproductive choice for women, are two cases in point. The variations in support for feminism among females and for patriarchy among males—and vice versa—are empirical questions to be determined in each concrete situation. Empirically, biological females support feminism more than biological males do; the latter support patriarchy more than the former. Theoretically, some feminists have suggested that the support for patriarchy among some biological females is a form of false consciousness: patriarchal ideology is so overpowering that it pushes biological females in directions that contradict their 'true objective interests'. All of these considerations are distinct from the question of socio-historical reproductive biological labour: its ideological denial is a hallmark of patriarchy; its affirmation is a central feature of feminism.

PSYCHOLOGICAL NON-REDUCTIONISM. Patriarchy cannot be reduced to psychological causes. It does not emerge out of the deep recesses of the unconscious or subconscious, nor from electrical impulses of the brain, nor from the libidinal urgings of the male, nor from any innate desire on the part of men to control women.

INTERDEPENDENCE AND SOLIDARITY AMONG MEN. Men support one another—in different degrees—in controlling women, their labour, and their bodies. This occurs in four ways. First, there is *direct* support when one man assists another man in the subordination of a woman—as in the movie *The Accused*, where male spectators in a bar cheered on the gang rape of a woman on a pin-ball machine. Second, there is *indirect* support when men not only do not protest against the subordination of women, but benefit from it. For example, men who do not rape women nevertheless give indirect support to men who do by not working to prevent it. They benefit indirectly from the fear this produces among women, whose behaviour is thereby constrained.[5] For instance, women may be afraid to take high-paying night-shift jobs out of fear of being raped going to or coming home from work; this fear reduces the competition for such jobs and leaves more of them to men. Third, men support each other in their *social relations* with one another in male clubs, male bars, male sports, and the military, all of which may at times encourage some element of physical or psychological degradation of women. In 1986, for example, a newspaper story described an upper-class strip club in Dearborn, Michigan, where accountants, lawyers, managers, businessmen, and executives gathered every Thursday evening with fake sub-machine guns to shoot water at 'slithering' women on a stage in G-strings and T-shirts. As one of the women remarked: '"The guys just love squirting you in the crotch. . . . You're like a target for these guys; it gives them a feeling of overpowering you."' Here the gun becomes a phallic symbol that allows the men to act out their aggression against women.[6] Fourth, men support one another in terms of *ideology* by denying their subordination of women. For example, male advertising executives will incorporate the liberated 'you've-come-a-long-way-baby' theme in their ads but still ask their secretaries to fetch their coffee and buy Valentine presents for them to give their wives.

HIERARCHY AMONG MEN. All men do not benefit equally from the subordination of women, nor do all men depend directly on one another in their mutual support of patriarchy; there is little evidence of a conscious conspiracy to subordinate women. Men are divided among themselves in terms of a number of characteristics, the most important being class, race/ethnicity, age, and position within corporate hierarchies, whether in the public or the private sector of the economy. The white bourgeois man who employs 300 immigrant women at below-minimum wages in his garment factory derives infinitely greater benefits from patriarchy than the working-class man whose wife fetches his slippers and serves his meals.

HIERARCHY AMONG WOMEN. All women are not equally subordinated or oppressed or exploited by men. Women are divided by the same characteristics that divide men: class, race/ethnicity, age, and position within corporate hierarchies. However, the divisions among women are not as great as among men. For example, there are very few women among the ranks of the economic élite, or in senior executive positions in national and multinational corporations. Parts of the women's movement have always been sensitive to class differences among women;[7] there is a vast difference between the corporate woman executive and the woman cleaner who polishes the executive suite at night. There is also a vast difference between the white wife of a corporate executive and the

Jamaican maid she employs. During the 1980s the women's movement in Great Britain, Canada, and the US became sensitized to racial and ethnic differences among women, and to the issue of racism.[8] The term 'women of colour' is an explicit acknowledgement of the diversity in the cultural backgrounds of women. It is not only corporate white men who exploit and subordinate working-class women and men of different racial and ethnic groups; some corporate white women do too, but there are far fewer of them. Despite these hierarchical differences, women display greater solidarity with one another than do men who tend to be more competitive with one another (though this is not to deny that women compete with one another as well).

MULTIPLICITY OF INSTITUTIONS AND ORGANIZATIONS. Because of women's role in biological production, many feminists have focused on the family as the primary patriarchal institution, or the root of patriarchy in society. But patriarchy varies across time and between societies, and the family is by no means the only institution in society that is constructed on it. Among the institutions and organizations in which patriarchy plays a dominant role are the state (including the civil service, parliament or legislatures, the judicial system, education, hospitals, armed forces, prisons, and police), religion, the economy, corporations, trade unions, the media, social clubs, sports, voluntary associations, entertainment, the arts, science, technology, and the professions. Patriarchy is not a constant throughout all these institutions and organizations, however; there are tremendous variations in how patriarchy is structured into each of them.

RELATIONS BETWEEN PATRIARCHY AND CAPTIALISM. Capitalism is a system based on nine factors: (a) the constant conversion of things and activities into commodities to be bought and sold in the marketplace; (b) the use of money as the medium of exchange; (c) private ownership and control of the means of production (such as tools and machinery); (d) the separation of workers from these means of production; (e) the conversion of workers into wage-labourers; (f) the buying and selling of labour-power (the capacity to labour); (g) exploitation of wage-labourers by those who own and control the means of production; (h) private appropriation of the proceeds of this exploitation (surplus value); and (i) the expanded accumulation of capital on the basis of this appropriation. Patriarchy both supports capitalism and contradicts it. One of the significant ways in which it supports capitalism is the fact that a woman's unpaid domestic labour produces children who become future labourers in capitalism, and reproduces her husband's labour power so that he can return daily to his wage-work in which he is exploited by those who own and control the means of production and who thereby earn a surplus value (profit);[9] another is the fact that the owners and controllers of the means of production earn a super-profit from the wages they pay women workers below the value of what it costs them to reproduce their labour-power (unequal pay for work of equal value).[10] But patriarchy and capitalism are also contradictory in that the demand for cheap labour by the owners and controllers of the means of production attracts full-time housewives into the paid labour force, thereby undermining the authority of the man in the patriarchal nuclear family based on the family wage.[11] Moreover, some owners and controllers of the means of production have converted sexuality into a commodity by selling fetishized women's bodies in pornographic magazines and videos and in advertising for other commodities, such as clothes, beer, and cars. Although this practice obviously has several patriarchal aspects, it also suggests an image of the woman as liberated sexually, which contradicts the notion that her sexual body is controlled by her husband.

NON-SYSTEM. A human body is an organism consisting of many parts (e.g., heart, brain, legs, arms) connected to one another in various ways (e.g., by blood vessels and muscle tissue). It is called a system because those interrelated parts work together in set patterns, as when the heart pumps blood to the brain so that it can direct the arms and legs when the person decides to walk. Each adult human body is physically independent of other human bodies. Some feminists regard patriarchy as an independent system made up of interrelated parts—much as we have described the human body—that is interdependent with capitalism. For example, parents teach their daughters to cook and their sons to fix cars—patterns that are reinforced by schools and television: all of this is useful to capitalism when, for example, wives of car mechanics cook for their husbands and so reproduce their labour-power, thereby saving the husbands' employers from having to pay them higher wages to buy their meals. This is called the 'dual systems theory'. Other feminists reject this view; they look upon patriarchy neither as a system, nor as interdependent with capitalism, but as *integrated* with it, even though there may be contradictions between them. This is the view adopted in this book. Thus we speak of 'patriarchal capitalism,' or 'the patriarchal capitalist state', rather than simply 'patriarchy' in the absence of either capitalism or the capitalist state.

LEVELS OF ABSTRACTION. Social reality can be described at different levels of abstraction. At a low level, focusing on a particular, concrete case, one might say that 'Ontario legislated equal value in 1987 partly because of the 1985 NDP-Liberal Accord'; at a high level, one might make a more general statement, such as 'equal pay for work of equal value is likely to be legislated in those countries with strong women's movements'. Marxists distinguish three levels of abstraction within capitalism:[12] (a) at a very high level of abstraction, a capitalist *mode of production* consisting of relationships among a worker, a business person or capitalist, and the means of production (such as tools and machinery), which may be common to many societies; (b) at a lower level of abstraction, a capitalist *social formation* or society within a specific era, such as post-World War Two Canada between 1946 and 1990; and (c) at the lowest level of abstraction, a capitalist *conjuncture*, or a society at one particular point in time, such as Canada in the year 1990. Feminists have often debated whether patriarchy has universal features common to many societies, as in the capitalist mode of production, or is different in each specific society, as in the capitalist conjuncture. Even though there are no levels of abstraction in patriarchy comparable to those in capitalism, nevertheless this book takes the view that it is possible to discuss patriarchy at each of capitalism's three levels, pointing out its compatibility and contradictions with the capitalist mode of production, social formation, and conjuncture.[13] For example:

(a) At the level of the capitalist *mode of production*: a man, because of his control of the means of production (e.g., factories) or reproduction (e.g., the family house), may control the labour power of one or more women. This may be common to all capitalist societies.

(b) At the level of the capitalist *social formation*: in the post-World War Two US between 1946 and the present, one of the mainstays of patriarchy has been male bourgeois control and ownership of the television industry—a phenomenon peculiar to this era. By displaying female sexuality in ways pleasing to men, this may have become an efficient means of reinforcing patriarchal notions in women.

(c) At the level of a particular capitalist *conjuncture*: in Quebec, a distinct society within Canada, the Liberal government instituted a budget in 1988 that gave parents a $500 cash bonus for each of their first two children and a $3,000 cash bonus for each additional child. Although the intent was to reverse the province's declining fertility rate, its effect appears to be to confine women to domestic labour in child-bearing and child-rearing. Only a few Western societies, such as France, have instituted this patriarchal practice.[14]

AGENCY. Although patriarchy is a social structure that has taken on the appearance of a predetermined fortress constraining the actions of individuals, groups, and organizations, human agents do have some latitude to act within its constraints. To adapt a phrase from Marx: Women make their own history, but they do not make it just as they please; they do not make it under feminist circumstances chosen by themselves, but under patriarchal circumstances directly encountered, given and transmitted from the past.[15] Conceiving of feminists as agents of change, albeit within the constraints of patriarchal structures, combats the image, popular among some radical feminists, of women as passive victims. Breaches in patriarchy created by its contradictions with capitalism, such as those mentioned above, provide opportunities for feminists as agents to recreate history in a less patriarchal fashion.

REPRODUCTION. Patriarchy does not feed off itself, like some self-regenerating hydra-like organism; in order to survive, it must be created, recreated, maintained, enforced, reinforced, instilled, and nurtured by human agents. This 'reproduction' occurs daily, weekly, monthly, yearly, from generation to generation. All the institutions and organizations in society listed above participate in this process in varying degrees. The mother in the family institution instils patriarchal values in her children when she encourages her daughter to play house and her son to play with his dad's tools. Teachers in educational institutions socialize their students into patriarchal attitudes when they direct male students into courses leading to engineering institutes and female students into courses leading to nursing schools. Religious institutions reinforce patriarchal attitudes by insisting on a male deity. Drill-sergeants in military institutions instil patriarchal aggression towards women (misogyny) by training their recruits to treat their weapons like phalluses and their enemies like women: as one US Marine put it, 'Don't get screwed first'.[16]

CLASS

A second major concept used throughout the book is 'class'. One of the major concepts in marxian sociology, it has been the subject of considerable debate and revision among both neo-marxists[17] and feminists.[18] Here, however, I will only indicate some of the major aspects of class as the term has been used in this book.

BUSINESS (BOURGEOISIE). The business class, or bourgeoisie, consists of people who own and/or control the means of production (factories, offices, tools, equipment, technology, natural resources, etc.). Control of these means in contemporary Canada typically takes the form of control over corporations (the powerful executive managers) and/or ownership of significant blocks of shares that allow the exercise of a considerable amount of control over these corporations. Such ownership and control permit members of the business class to 'work for themselves' rather than for others. They do not exchange their labour-power for a wage or salary in the labour market; rather, they purchase, for a wage, the labour-power of workers from whom they extract surplus labour. If they are in the industrial sector, they exploit wage-workers by extracting surplus value from them.[19] This forms the basis of their extended accumulation of capital. The business class also includes medium- and small-business people, but its commanding heights are controlled by the large executive players and finance capitalists.[20] This has been the main class opposing equal pay for work of equal value.

WORKING CLASS. The working class consists of people who work not for themselves but for others, typically those who own and/or control the corporations of society or those who control the state. These people sell their labour-power, or capacity to work, in exchange for a wage, which they and their families use to survive economically. Wage-workers in the industrial sector are exploited by members of the business class; their unpaid labour forms the basis of the latter's wealth. Workers do not own and/or control the means of production or significant blocks of corporate assets, although a few may own some shares in corporations. In alliance with the women's movement, the organized working class in trade unions has supported equal pay for work of equal value.

PETTY BOURGEOISIE. This class consists of those who own and control their own businesses, work in them, and hire no or little wage-labour to help. Found more frequently among farmers than among urban dwellers, it has been declining in most Western capitalist societies, although recently it has displayed some signs of resurgence.[21]

NEW MIDDLE CLASS. The new middle class (sometimes called the new petty bourgeoisie) consists of managers, supervisors, executives, and professionals who have some partial control over the way in which the means of production are put into operation, over the labour of members of the working class, and over their own work. Similar in one respect to members of the working class, they sell their labour-power in exchange for a salary. Ideologically, the upper echelons of this class are allied with the bourgeoisie,[22] taking an ancillary role in controlling the labour of the working class and erecting barriers to equal pay, union certification, and free collective bargaining. Some sections of this class have joined the labour-feminist alliance to support equal-value legislation, while others have joined business to oppose it.

FEMINIZATION OF CLASS. Women are under-represented in the business, petty bourgeois, and new middle classes, but over-represented in the working class; men are over-represented in the business and new middle classes, and to some extent in the petty bourgeoisie.[23] Only recently has there been an increasing trend for women to set up their own small businesses. There is a convergence between class power and patriarchal power in corporations to the extent that executives, managers, and supervisors are usually men, and non-supervisory workers are women. This is one of the many ways in which capitalism and patriarchy are thoroughly integrated.

With the significant exception of Frederick Engels, Marxist thinkers in general have failed to recognize the existence of classes in households.[24] Instead, they exclude full-time housewives from classes, or assign them the class of their husbands. Can this practice be modified? To the extent that full-time housewives and mothers (a) do not own and control the means of non-household production or the means of household production and reproduction (their own bodies, refrigerators, vacuum cleaners, sewing machines, cars), and (b) labour at producing products (e.g., meals) for consumption in the household or commodities (e.g., husband's and children's labour power) for sale in the labour market outside the household, are they workers and full-fledged members of the working class, even though they may not directly exchange their own labour power for a wage and may not be directly exploited by the business class? To the extent that working-class men own and control the household means of production and reproduction, are they in a contradictory class position? Are they members of the working class because they do not own and control the means of production outside the household and must sell their labour power for a wage in order to survive? But can they be full-fledged members of the working class when they own and control the means of household production and reproduction? Under this revised notion of class, are the most consistently working-class (a) full-time housewives who do not own and control any means of production or reproduction, and who labour in the household without any paid help, and (b) women who perform a double day of labour in unpaid work in the household and paid work outside the household, and who do not own or control any means of production or reproduction?

STATE

Four issues must be clarified to have an adequate understanding of the way 'state' has been used in this book.

1. Institutional vs. functional definition

According to the institutional perspective, the state is a complex of institutions that interact within a system. Ralph Miliband, a British Marxist political scientist, suggests the parts of this system: the government (or executive, which speaks and acts on behalf of the state); the administration (including the civil service, central bank, public corporations, and various regulatory bodies); the military (police forces and paramilitary, security, and secret intelligence services); judges and the entire judicial system; the subcentral government (provincial and local levels of the state, which may have institutions parallel to those of the central state); and representative assemblies (the House of Commons in England and Canada, or the Senate and House of Representatives in the US Congress). Excluded from the state system under this definition, even though they may wield considerable political power, are the mass media, political parties, pressure groups, churches, education, the health-care system, and giant corporations.[25]

A different way of defining the state focuses on the functions that various 'state apparatuses' perform in reproducing, or maintaining through time, capitalist forces of production (such as machinery and labour power) and capitalist relations of production (such as social classes). Louis Althusser identifies two kinds: (a) repressive state apparatuses, which function ultimately by violence, including the government, administration, prisons, police, courts, and the army; (b) ideological state apparatuses, which function primarily through ideology, encompassing religion, education, the family, law, the political system (including political parties), trade unions, communications ('press, radio and television'), and culture ('Literature, the Arts, sports, etc.'). As Althusser points out, the repressive apparatuses have secondary ideological features and the ideological apparatuses have secondary repressive features. The repressive apparatuses are more unified and controlled by the business class than the ideological apparatuses. Hence there is more room for class struggle in the ideological apparatuses.[26]

The definition of 'state' used in this book lies between Miliband's and Althusser's for two reasons. First, Althusser includes too many apparatuses, such as the family, trade unions, and religion, within the state, while Miliband excludes too many institutions, such as the mass media, education, and the health-care system.[27] The institutions considered within the state in this book are the central and regional governments (federal, provincial, and municipal or local); the administration in its broadest sense; parliamentary assemblies; the armed forces and police (but not security guards working for private corporations); intelligence and security services (MI-5 in England, CSIS in Canada and the CIA in the US); all the different levels of the judicial and court system; prisons, reform institutions, and asylums; law (excluding the rules of private associations); education and the schools (except for private schools); the health-care system (but not private nursing homes); parts of the mass media in some countries (the BBC in England and CBC in Canada, but not ABC, NBC, or CBS in the US); and Crown corporations (but not private corporations). The boundary between state and non-state organizations varies from one country to the next and from one time period to another. Three general criteria that determine the location of this boundary are the appointment of an organization's directors and its control and financing by the government, administration, or legislature. The state institutions that play the most prominent role in this book are the government, the civil service, legislatures, and the law.

There is also a second reason for the way 'state' is used in this book. Althusser's picture of the 'functional state' does not make sufficient allowance for the dysfunctional state. In fact, state institutions or apparatuses do not always reproduce the forces and relations of production: at times they do the opposite. For example, the central government and the department of finance may run up huge deficits; these may fuel inflation, which may force small companies out of business. Does this mean that the central government and the finance department should no longer be considered part of the state system? Hardly. Although reproducing the forces and relations of production is one of the capitalist state's central activities, it should not be made the central criterion of its definition. Miliband suggests four state functions—the repressive, economic, ideological-cultural, and international—but does not make them the criteria for defining where the state begins and ends.[28] In this sense, the conception of the state used in this book is closer to Miliband's than Althusser's.

2. Independence of the state from class

Does the capitalist state simply reflect the interests of the business class? Does business directly manipulate the capitalist state? Does the state further some of the interests of the working class? Or is the capitalist state independent of classes? In the debates on these questions there are three broad positions.

One position holds that the capitalist state is manipulated, directly or indirectly, by the business class, so that its policies are those of this class. This manipulation takes place through business personnel who may either sit on the councils of the state or, from their position outside the state, apply direct pressure on state personnel to achieve their goals. This view of the state is somewhat crudely known as *instrumentalism* because it assumes that the bourgeoisie wields the state as its own 'instrument';[29] in other words, the state acts *at the behest* of the business class.[30] Needless to say, in this view the state is not independent of class.

According to another view, the capitalist state is a matrix of three structural levels within the capitalist mode of production—economic, political, and ideological—on each of which are inscribed the class contradictions of the capitalist society or social formation. The predominance of the business class over the working class in society and their mutual struggle are built into the internal structures of the state. The laws and policies of the state therefore reflect, in the long term, business interests. However, since the power of business over the working class is not absolute, some state laws and policies do reflect the short-term interests of the working class. The function of the state is to maintain cohesion, or prevent open warfare, among the classes in the society. This essentially means that the state functions to control competition among the different parts of the business class, and maintains the dominance of this class over the working class by disorganizing the latter. State labour-relations acts appear to be in the interests of the working class, since they allow members of this class to form legal bargaining units and negotiate contracts binding on the employer. However, these units and contracts introduce an element of stability and control in the paid workplace that favours employers. Members of the bargaining unit cannot legally strike during the length of a contract. It is the duty of the union steward and business agent to ensure that an illegal or wildcat strike does not occur, and in this sense the union agent disciplines the workers on behalf of management.[31] This ensures some predictability in employers' production plans. In addition, the bargaining units within the same workplace are often divided into office workers and shop-floor workers, and then subdivided into full-time and part-time workers. This division introduces an element of tension among workers and helps to disorganize the union within the workplace. In this view of the state, known as *structuralism*,[32] the state appears neither completely dependent on nor completely independent of class; it is 'relatively autonomous' because the internal competition within the business class and its contradictions with the working class give the state some room to manoeuvre. In the structuralist view, the personal intervention of the business class is not required in order to ensure the implementation of its interests in state policies and laws. In Miliband's words, the state acts *on behalf*, not at the behest, of the bourgeoisie.

In a third view, the state is completely independent of classes. State policies and laws are created by legislators, bureaucrats, and officials in their own interests—for instance, in order to get re-elected, or to increase the power of a particular department. To the extent that class impinges in any way on these policies and laws, it is in the form of a more or less equal competition among the classes for the ear of the politician or state official. The state is therefore viewed as neutral; it is an impartial umpire adjudicating the contending claims of competing classes and interest groups.

But the politicians and officials make the final decisions according to their own interests and logic, not those of the different classes in society.[33]

The contrasts and apparent irreconcilability among these three theories of the state have been overdrawn for philosophical, ideological, and theoretical reasons. In practice, the most appropriate theory of the state depends on the specific state policies and organization under consideration. The decision to introduce, say, mining-depletion allowances may best be interpreted from the instrumentalist perspective; the state's fiscal and social welfare policies may best be understood within the structuralist theory; the Canada-United States Free Trade Agreement may best be explained by a combination of structuralism and instrumentalism; the decision to create an inner super-cabinet may be better comprehended through the independence view of the state. But the choice of theories to explain a given state policy or organization is not random. Specific state policies that strike at the particular short-term interests of one fraction or part of a class are subject to intense lobbying from that class fraction (instrumentalism). State policies that bear on the more fundamental relations of production, property ownership, and labour markets seem more understandable within structuralism. Policies that address the reorganization of state departments, or depend on the local interests of constituencies and politicians, are perhaps partially understandable within the independence view. Nevertheless, all state policies in the Western industrial countries are ultimately located in the context of a capitalist society and to some degree are constrained by the contradictions of that society. In this sense, therefore, it seems that the instrumentalist and independence views of the state must be regarded as contained within the framework described by the structuralist view.

3. State as agency vs. structure

There has been intense debate between those who conceive of the state as a structure embedded within the mode of production and those who conceive of it as constituted, at least in part, by acting and willing human subjects who direct its course.[34] The former view summarizes the structuralist position just outlined, while the latter tends to be adopted by both the instrumentalists and those who see the state as completely independent of classes. For the purposes of this book, the capitalist state has been treated as a structure embedded within the capitalist mode of production, but one that also includes human agents who, from their locations in its various positions, attempt to direct its course within the constraints imposed by this structure and mode of production.

4. Feminist critiques of the genderless patriarchal state

The feminist approach to the state assumed in this book touches on seven interrelated issues.

PATRIARCHAL IDEOLOGY OF POLITICAL THEORY. Feminists have critiqued the sexism, or the elevation of man and denigration of woman, that is evident in much political theorizing.[35] Much of their critique has centred on the rigid dichotomy between the public sphere of the state (and the marketplace), and the private sphere of the household and personal life. In much political theory and philosophy, man equals the public, the public is the political, and therefore man is political; woman, on the other hand, equals the private, the private is nonpolitical, and therefore woman is nonpolitical.[36] The male, public sphere of the state became the rational, the cultural, the superior; the female, private sphere of the domestic became the irrational, the natural, the inferior. Since woman and the domestic sphere were non- or a-political, they were not appropriate topics for study in political science and political sociology. Political man became the universal, genderless 'man', within which woman was included as the unknown default. In this way, political theory operated as patriarchal ideology: it denied its patriarchal assumptions by refusing to acknowledge that there was 'an issue'; it denied that its exclusion of women from the political and public sphere constituted subordination with the argument that the political and public were genderless. One of the greatest acknowledgements of women was in empirical political science: gender was added as a 'control variable' in statistical analyses of voting patterns without any acknowledgement of how well that word 'control' fitted the patriarchal ideology behind such studies. Women were viewed as more conservative than their husbands because they were located in the non-political domestic sphere, and thus not capable of independent political thought and action.

THE POLITICAL WORKPLACE. In the 1960s feminists began to recognize the state as a special political workplace for women. On the one hand, the expansion of the state in that period was seen as a golden opportunity for women, who, shut out of private industry, would have an opportunity for advancement in the more 'humane' state. On the other hand, it was also clear that the state represented a strict division of labour along gender lines: state bureaucrats and managers were men; clerical staff and cleaners were women.[37] In campaigns for public office, men were the official candidates, fundraisers, and paid campaign managers; women were the unpaid volunteer canvassers, backroom clerical workers, and servers of coffee and lunch.[38] This led, during the 1970s and 1980s, to demands for affirmative action so that women could advance to more senior positions within the civil service and party bureaucracies, and be elected to parliamentary assemblies.[39]

MALE INSTRUMENTALISM. In an analysis that recalls the instrumentalist view and its emphasis on individual wills and networks, some feminists began to look upon the state as an instrument that, in the hands of men, was wielded to advance male interests. In this view—bordering on a conspiracy theory—men in other institutions, such as the economy, used their influence through networking and manipulation of the 'backroom boys' to maintain the state as a bastion of male power. Women who wanted to advance into the state had to break into the male clique.[40]

REFORMISM. Liberal feminists, displaying a faith in individual rationality, the eradication of patriarchy through non-sexist education, and progressive changes in state laws through lobbying and electioneering, did not challenge the public/private divide. They simply wanted to increase the mobility of women back and forth between the private household and the public marketplace and state. In their view, since capitalism did not inherently oppress women, it did not have to be overthrown. Liberal feminists wanted to create a more level playing field so that women could compete more equally with men in capitalism: they should be given access to all occupations, regardless of hazardous working conditions or the physical difficulties of the job. Accordingly, liberal feminists targeted sex discrimination in agitating for such reforms as equal pay for work of equal value, publicly funded day-care centres, and the prohibition of sexual harassment in the paid workplace. Most important, paid maternity leave was to be instituted so that women could be supported economically and have their job seniority protected while they left the paid labour force to have babies.[41]

PATRIARCHAL STRUCTURALISM. Radical feminists place primary emphasis on sex and gender rather than class in explaining the oppression of women; although different opinions are held, some make naturalistic assumptions about the superiority and 'goodness' of women, the inferiority and 'evilness' of men, and the role of biological reproduction and sexuality in the family as the root of woman's subordination to man. In an analysis that bears striking similarities to structuralism, in the 1970s they began to locate the structure of the state in the more general structure of patriarchy in society. Male subordination of women in and through the state was simply a reflection of male subordination of women in society. The state functioned to oppress women in society and to maintain male rule. For example, the state was seen as protecting the rapist, not his victim.[42] Women were to be liberated by the overthrow of patriarchy without the overthrow of capitalism.

CAPITALIST STATE OPPRESSION OF WOMEN. Socialist feminists, integrating features of marxism and radical feminism, trace women's oppression and subordination to both sex/gender and class. Women as workers are subordinated and exploited by the business class; women as women are oppressed by men. To liberate themselves, women have to take into account both sex/gender (or patriarchy) and class (or capitalism). Borrowing from marxist structuralism, in the 1970s socialist feminists came to view the capitalist state as functioning to reproduce the capitalist relations of production *in a gendered way*. The state oppresses working-class women *on behalf*, though not at the behest, of the bourgeoisie by maintaining the patriarchal family wage that ensures women's subordination to men and their availability as a cheap reserve army of labour to be drawn out of the household when needed by capitalist companies. In this view, state welfare policies largely support the patriarchal family wage and women's role in the reserve army of labour.[43] Thus women cannot hope for liberation by simply overthrowing patriarchy; it is the capitalist patriarchal corporation and the capitalist patriarchal state that have to be overthrown to achieve full equality with men.

PATRIARCHAL CAPITALIST PASSIVE REVOLUTION. In 1983 the Canadian Advisory Council on the Status of Women—a 25-member government-appointed body that, according to criteria laid down earlier in this appendix, is part of the federal state—contracted Julie White, an independent researcher, to produce a book on women and the economy. In 1986, in collaboration with Patty

Deline and Barbara Cameron, White submitted a 400-page, six-teen-chapter manuscript. When it was published by the Council in the fall of 1987, it had been reduced to 190 pages and had nine chapters missing. Two Council members had charged that the original manuscript was too biased towards labour and unions. The contents had been altered—without the permission of the authors—to reflect the more pro-business and pro-free-trade stance of the Council members appointed since Progressive Conservative Prime Minister Brian Mulroney came to power in 1984.[44] This example illustrates the double-edged experience of working through the state. On the one hand, the Advisory Council on the Status of Women had been set up in 1973 by the federal state to promote the advancement of women in society; on the other hand, this same state seemed unwilling to have women advance 'too far' or threaten fundamental patriarchal interests. As this example shows, advances in the cause of women have been circumscribed by the capitalist nature of the state.

Such attempts on the part of the state to steer the direction of social change into 'safe channels' did not suddenly arise with the growth of feminism and the women's movement. As long ago as 1929, the Italian marxist Antonio Gramsci used the term *passive revolution* to describe the tendency of a dominant group, faced with a threat to its position, to attempt to co-opt the revolution-in-the-making and deflect it from its course. (This concept is outlined more fully in Chapter 5 above).

Does Gramsci's scenario describe the relationship of the state to feminism and the women's movement? With the rise of second-wave feminism in the latter 1960s and the 1970s, the state faced three kinds of challenges: feminist critiques of its structures and departments for largely excluding women from policy-making positions; claims that state policies and laws overtly or covertly condoned sex and gender discrimination in practically all areas of social life; and the increasing participation of women voters in the paid labour force, which intensified feminist consciousness and was bound to have implications for politicians seeking re-election. Politicians and state bureaucrats reacted to these challenges in six ways: (a) studies and commissions were set up to investigate the 'status of women' in order to recommend improvements; (b) women's bureaus and ministries responsible for the status of women were established; (c) voluntary affirmative-action programs for women were instituted within many departments of the state; (d) women were encouraged to become candidates for parliamentary assemblies, and of those elected a few were given token cabinet positions; (e) attempts were made either to amend old laws to remove sex discrimination, or to introduce entirely new laws to equalize the opportunities for women with those for men in the paid labour force; and (f) the state helped to finance feminist group projects, such as shelters for abused women and rape crisis centres. Have these six responses been 'genuine', or have they decapitated the women's movement in order to preserve patriarchal capitalism?[45] For example, by funding and sponsoring feminist groups, programs, and projects, the patriarchal capitalist state established a degree of control over the direction of the women's movement. Women's groups that applied to the state for funding had to meet criteria determined by the state. This often distorted the groups' agendas and turned them in a different, more liberal direction. In Canada, for instance, the Women's Program in the department of the Secretary of State was set up in order to fund women's groups dedicated to advancing the equality of women. But the battle between the National Action Committee on the Status of Women (NAC) and the anti-feminist REAL Women for state funding gave the media an avenue to depict women as internally divided,[46] and in 1989 the federal government, under the guise of promoting women's equality, began funding REAL Women while slashing the budget of NAC. By the late 1980s, the praxis of feminism has left women's organizations with a significant problem: liberal feminists recognize that even some of the limited goals they asked the state to reach, such as an equal number of women and men in the House of Commons by 1994, will not be attainable for a very long time; radical feminists ask whether it is even possible to use a patriarchal state to advance feminist interests; and socialist feminists ask whether there is not a contradiction in trying to use a patriarchal capitalist state to accomplish socialist feminist aims.[47] These contradictions lie at the heart of this book. Labour-relations acts, human-rights legislation on sexual harassment in the paid workplace, and new laws on equal pay for work of equal value seem to help women equalize the conditions of their labour with those of men. Yet there is still a gnawing sense that they have fostered a false sense of security, as their implementation has left many women still far from the goal of equality.

Notes

[1]See, for example, the collection of articles in Lydia Sargent, ed., *Women and Revolution: A Discussion of the Unhappy Marriage of Marxism and Feminism* (Boston: South End Press, 1981). See also Veronica Beechey, 'On Patriarchy', *Feminist Review* 3 (1979), pp. 66-82; Zillah R. Eisenstein, ed., *Capitalist Patriarchy and the Case for Socialist Feminism* (New York: Monthly Review Press, 1979); Michele Barrett, *Women's Oppression Today: Problems in Marxist Feminist Analysis* (London: Verso, 1980); Zillah Eisenstein, *Feminism and Sexual Equality: the Crisis in Liberal America* (New York: Monthly Review Press, 1984); Bonnie Fox, 'Conceptualizing "Patriarchy"', *Canadian Review of Sociology and Anthrolpology* 25, no. 2 (May 1988), pp. 163-82.

[2]See Janet Siltanen and Michelle Stanworth, 'The Politics of Private Woman and Public Man', pp. 185-208 in their edited book, *Women and the Public Sphere: A Critique of Sociology and Politics* (London: Hutchinson, 1984); and Carole Pateman, 'Feminist Critiques of the Public/Private Dichotomy', pp. 281-303 in S.I. Benn and G.F. Gaus, eds, *Public and Private in Social Life* (London: Croom Helm, 1983).

[3]For this view see, for example, Christine Delphy, *Close to Home: A Materialist Analysis of Women's Oppression*, trans. and ed. by Diana Leonard (London: Hutchinson in association with The Explorations in Feminism Collective, 1984), especially pp. 57-77; and Varda Burstyn, 'Masculine Dominance and the State', pp. 45-89 in Ralph Miliband and John Saville, eds, *The Socialist Register, 1983* (London: Merlin Press, 1983).

[4]This is different from saying that biological sex and social gender are inextricably connected. See, for example, Pat and Hugh Armstrong, 'Bodies in History', pp. 25-32 in Pat Armstrong, Hugh Armstrong, Patricia Connelly, and Angela Miles, *Feminist Marxism or Marxist Feminism: A Debate* (Toronto: Garamond, 1985).

[5]Susan Brownmiller, *Against Our Will: Men, Women and Rape* (New York: Bantam Books, 1975).

[6]Dorothy Lipovenko, 'Gun Gimmick Packs Them in At B.T.'s', *Globe and Mail*, 12 Nov. 1986, pp. B1, B2.

[7]For example, see Dorothy Smith, 'Women's Inequality and the Family', pp. 156-95 in Allan Moscovitch and Glenn Drover, eds, *Inequality: Essays on the Political Economy of Welfare* (Toronto: University of Toronto Press, 1981); Dorothy Smith, 'Women, The Family and the Productive Process', pp. 312-44 in J. Paul Grayson, ed., *Introduction to Sociology: An Alternative Approach* (Toronto: Gage, 1983); and Dorothy Smith, 'Women, Class, Family', in Varda Burstyn and Dorothy Smith, *Women, Class, Family and the State* (Toronto: Garamond, 1985).

[8]For Canada see, for example, Makeda Silvera, *Silenced* (Toronto: Williams-Walker, 1983); Winnie Ng, 'Immigrant Women: The Silent Partners of the Women's Movement', *Canadian Woman Studies* 4, no. 2 (Winter 1982), pp. 87-8; Nancy Adamson, Linda Briskin, and Margaret McPhail, *Feminist Organizing For Change* (Toronto: Oxford University Press, 1988), pp. 293-5; Lisa Rochon, 'Race Issue Splits Women's Press', *Globe and Mail*, 8 Aug. 1988, p. C5; *Broadside* 9, no. 8 (June 1988), p. 5; 10, no. 3 (Dec. 1988-Jan. 1989), pp. 2, 4, 7; and Women's Press, *Everywoman's Almanac 1989* (Toronto, 1988).

For the US see, for example, Angela Y. Davis, *Women, Race and Class* (New York: Random House, 1981); Gloria I. Joseph and Jill Lewis, eds, *Common Differences:*

Conflicts in Black and White Feminist Perspectives (Boston: South End Press, 1981); Bell Hooks, *Ain't I A Woman: Black Women and Feminism* (Boston: South End Press, 1981); Bell Hooks, *Feminist Theory: From Margin to Center* (Boston: South End Press, 1984); Bonnie Thornton Dill, 'Race, Class, and Gender: Prospects for an All-Inclusive Sisterhood', *Feminist Studies* 9, no. 1 (Spring 1983), pp. 131-50; and Phyllis Marynick Palmer, 'White Women/Black Women: The Dualism of Female Identity and Experience in the United States', *Feminist Studies* 9, no. 1 (Spring 1983), pp. 151-70.

For England see, for example, Valerie Amos and Pratibha Parmar, 'Challenging Imperial Feminism', *Feminist Review* 17 (July 1984), pp. 3-19; Amina Mama, 'Black Women, the Economic Crisis and the British State', *Feminist Review* 17 (July 1984), pp. 21-35; Parita Trivedi, 'To Deny Our Fullness: Asian Women in the Making of History', *Feminist Review* 17 (July 1984), pp. 37-51; Floya Anthias and Nira Yuval-Davis, 'Contextualizing Feminism—Gender, Ethnic and Class Divisions', *Feminist Review* 17 (July 1984), pp. 62-75; Michele Barrett and Mary McIntosh, 'Ethnocentrism and Socialist-Feminist Theory', *Feminist Review* 20 (Summer 1985), pp. 23-47; and Kum-Kum Bhavnani and Margaret Coulson, 'Transforming Socialist-Feminism: The Challenge of Racism', *Feminist Review* 23 (June 1986), pp. 81-92.

[9] During the 1970s, there was an extended debate among some socialist feminists about the function of women's domestic labour for capitalism. For a partial selection see Eli Zaretsky, 'Capitalism, The Family, and Personal Life', *Socialist Revolution* 13-14 (1973), pp. 69-125; 15 (1973), pp. 19-71; Wally Seccombe, 'The Housewife and Her Labour Under Capitalism', *New Left Review* 83 (Jan.-Feb. 1973), pp. 3-24; Jean Gardiner, 'Women's Domestic Labour', *New Left Review* 89 (Jan.-Feb. 1975), pp. 47-58; Margaret Coulson, Branka Magas, and Hilary Wainwright, '"The Housewife and her Labour Under Capitalism"—A Critique', *New Left Review* 89 (Jan.-Feb. 1975), pp. 59-71; Wally Seccombe, 'Domestic Labour— Reply to Critics', *New Left Review* 94 (Nov.-Dec. 1975), pp. 85-96; Bonnie Fox, *Hidden in the Household: Women's Domestic Labour Under Capitalism* (Toronto: Women's Press, 1980); Meg Luxton, *More Than a Labour of Love: Three Generations of Women's Work in the Home* (Toronto: Women's Press, 1980). Much of the critique of this debate concerned four points: its economistic nature and inattention to questions of ideology; the tendency to picture the housewife as a passive rather than an active agent of change; the emphasis on the functions rather then the dysfunctions of domestic labour for capitalism; and the inability of participants in the debate to answer the question of why it was specifically women who performed domestic labour.

[10] Veronica Beechey, 'Some Notes on Female Wage Labour in Capitalist Production', *Capital and Class* 3 (Autumn 1977), pp. 45-66; and Floya Anthias, 'Women and the Reserve Army of Labour: A Critique of Veronica Beechey', *Capital and Class* 10 (Spring 1980), pp. 50-63.

[11] The strength of patriarchal ideology is suggested in the fact that women in full-time paid work outside the household do a double day of labour and have husbands who increase their domestic labour only minimally. This often is also the case for women whose husbands are unemployed or on strike.

[12] Etienne Balibar, 'On the Basic Concepts of Historical Materialism', Part III in Louis Althusser and Etienne Balibar, *Reading Capital* (London: NLB, 1970); Nicos Poulantzas, *Political Power and Social Classes* (London: NLB, 1973), pp. 11-33; and

Erik Olin Wright, *Classes* (London: Verso, 1985), pp. 10-12, 109-14.

[13] This issue was debated among Armstrong, Armstrong, Connelly, and Miles in their *Feminist Marxism or Marxist Feminism*.

[14] Benoit Aubin, 'Quebec Budget "A Revolution", Family Activist Says', *Globe and Mail*, 18 May 1988, p. A4.

[15] Marx's original statement was: 'Men make their own history, but they do not make it just as they please; they do not make it under circumstances chosen by themselves, but under circumstances directly encountered, given and transmitted from the past' (Karl Marx, *The 18th Brumaire of Louis Bonaparte* [New York: International Publishers, 1963 (1852)], p. 15).

[16] See the film by Gwynne Dyer, *Anybody's Son Will Do. The War Series*. National Film Board, 1983.

[17] See Nicos Poulantzas, *Classes in Contemporary Capitalism* (London: NLB, 1975); Erik Olin Wright, 'The Class Structure of Advanced Capitalist Societies', pp. 30-110 in his *Class, Crisis and the State* (London: NLB, 1978); Erik Olin Wright, *Classes* (London: Verso, 1985); Guglielmo Carchedi, *On the Economic Identification of Social Classes* (London: Routledge and Kegan Paul, 1977); Guglielmo Carchedi, 'Two Models of Class Analysis', *Capital and Class* 29 (Summer 1986), pp. 195-215, which is reprinted in his *Class Analysis and Social Research* (Oxford: Basil Blackwell, 1987); Erik Olin Wright, ed., *The Debate on Classes* (London: Verso, 1989).

[18] See, for example, Bonnie Fox, 'The Feminist Challenge: A Reconsideration of Social Inequality and Economic Development', in Robert J. Brym with Bonnie Fox, *From Culture to Power: The Sociology of English Canada* (Toronto: Oxford University Press, 1989).

[19] For empirical data on this, see Carl J. Cuneo. 'Class Exploitation in Canada', *Canadian Review of Sociology and Anthropology* 15, no. 3 (1978), pp. 284-300; and Cuneo, 'Class Struggle and Measurement of the Rate of Surplus Value', *Canadian Review of Sociology and Anthropology* 19, no. 3 (Aug. 1982), pp. 377-425.

[20] For analyses of this class in Canada, see John Porter, The *Vertical Mosaic* (Toronto: University of Toronto Press, 1965); Wallace Clement, *The Canadian Corporate Elite* (Toronto: McClelland and Stewart, 1975); Clement, *Continental Corporate Power* (Toronto: McClelland and Stewart, 1978); Jorge Niosi, *The Economy of Canada: Who Controls It?* (Montreal: Black Rose, 1978); Niosi, *Canadian Capitalism: A Study of Power in the Canadian Business Establishment* (Toronto: James Lorimer, 1981); Niosi, *Canadian Multinationals* (Toronto: Between the Lines, 1985); William K. Carroll, *Corporate Power and Canadian Capitalism* (Vancouver: University of British Columbia Press, 1986); Diane Francis, *Controlling Interest: Who Controls Canada?* (Toronto: Macmillan, 1986); Linda McQuaig, *Behind Closed Doors: How the Rich Won Control of Canada's Tax System . . . And Ended Up Richer* (Markham, Ont.: Penguin, 1987); and Ann Finlayson, *Whose Money Is It Anyway? The Showdown on Pensions* (Markham, Ont.: Penguin, 1988).

[21] Carl J. Cuneo, 'Has the Traditional Petite Bourgeoisie Persisted?', *Canadian Journal of Sociology* 9, no. 3 (1984), pp. 36-82.

[22] For example, see the data on Sweden and the US in Wright, *Classes*, pp. 259-80.

[23] Carl J. Cuneo, 'Have Women Become More Proletarianized than Men?', *Canadian Review of Sociology and Anthropology* 22, no. 4 (Nov. 1985), pp. 465-95.

[24] Engels wrote in part: 'The first class antagonism which appears in history coincides with the development of the antagonism between man and woman in

monogamian marriage, and the first class oppression with that of the female sex by the male. . . . In the family, he [the man] is the bourgeois; the wife represents the proletariat.' See Frederick Engels, *The Origin of the Family, Private Property, and the State* (New York: Pathfinder Press, 1972 [1884]), pp. 75, 81-2. See also Janet Sayers, Mary Evans, and Nannecke Redclift, eds, *Engels Revisited: New Feminist Essays* (London: Tavistock Publications, 1987).

[25]Ralph Miliband, *The State in Capitalist Society: The Analysis of the Western System of Power* (London: Quartet Books, 1973 [1969]), pp. 46-51.

[26]Louis Althusser, 'Ideology and Ideological State Apparatuses (Notes Toward an Investigation)', pp. 121-73 in his *Lenin and Philosophy and Other Essays*, translated from the French by Ben Brewster (London: NLB, 1971).

[27]Miliband does, however, analyze religion, the mass media, and education as parts of the system of political power.

[28]Ralph Miliband, *Marxism and Politics* (Oxford: Oxford University Press, 1977), pp. 90-106.

[29]Miliband calls this Marx's 'primary view of the state'. See his 'Marx and the State', in Miliband and Saville, eds, *Socialist Register*, (1965) p. 283; see also David A. Gold, Clarence Y.H. Lo, and Erik Olin Wright, 'Recent Developments in Marxist Theories of the Capitalist State', *Monthly Review* 27, no. 5 (Oct. 1975), pp. 32-5.

[30]Miliband suggests that 'while the state does act, in Marxist terms, *on behalf* of the "ruling class", it does not for the most part act *at its behest*' (*Marxism and Politics*, p. 74).

[31]Richard Hyman, *Marxism and the Sociology of Trade Unionism* (London: Pluto Press, 1971), pp. 20-1.

[32]The clearest and most sustained articulation of this view is by Poulantzas, especially in his *Political Power and Social Classes* (1973) and *State, Power, Socialism* (London: NLB, 1978), although between these two books his views show considerable modification and development. For an interpretation of these changes, see Bob Jessop, *Nicos Poulantzas: Marxist Theory and Political Strategy* (London: Macmillan, 1985). For a Canadian application of structuralism, see Rianne Mahon, 'Canadian Public Policy: The Unequal Structure of Representation', pp. 165-98 in Leo Panitch, ed., *The Canadian State: Political Economy and Political Power* (Toronto: University of Toronto Press, 1977).

[33]For example, see Theda Skocpol, 'Bringing the State Back In: Strategies of Analysis in Current Research', pp. 3-37 in Peter B. Evans, Dietrich Rueschemeyer, and Theda Skocpol, eds, *Bringing the State Back In* (Cambridge: Cambridge University Press, 1985). For a Canadian application of the independence thesis, see Leslie A. Pal, *State, Class and Bureaucracy: Canadian Unemployment Insurance Policy* (Kingston and Montreal: McGill-Queen's University Press, 1988).

[34]Nicos Poulantzas has been the most vociferous in insisting that the capitalist state is constituted by the structural contradictions of the capitalist mode of production rather than by human agents. See his *Political Power and Social Classes*; 'The Problem of the Capitalist State', *New Left Review* 58 (Nov.-Dec. 1969); 'The Capitalist State: A Reply to Miliband and Laclau', *New Left Review* 95 (Jan.-Feb. 1976), pp. 63-83. For Miliband's views on Poulantzas, see his 'The Capitalist State: Reply to Nicos Poulantzas', *New Left Review* 59 (Jan.-Feb. 1970), pp. 53-60; and 'Poulantzas and the Capitalist State', *New Left Review* 82 (Nov.-Dec. 1973), pp. 83-92.

[35]See, for example, Mary O'Brien, *The Politics of Reproduction* (London: Routledge

and Kegan Paul, 1981); Judith Evans, Jill Hills, Karen Hunt, Elizabeth Meechan, Tessa ten Tusscher, Ursula Vogel, and Georgina Waylen, *Feminism and Political Theory* (London: Sage Publications, 1986); Diana H. Coole, *Women in Political Theory: From Ancient Misogyny to Contemporary Feminism* (Sussex: Wheatsheaf Books, 1988); and Kathleen B. Jones and Anna G. Jonasdottir, eds, *The Political Interests of Gender: Developing Theory and Research with a Feminist Face* (London: Sage Publications, 1988).

[36] Siltanen and Stanworth, 'The Politics of Private Woman and Public Man' (1984), p. 195.

[37] Kathleen Archibald, *Sex and the Public Service* (Ottawa: Queen's Printer, 1970).

[38] See, for example, Sylvia B. Bashevkin, *Toeing the Lines: Women and Party Politics in English Canada* (Toronto: University of Toronto Press, 1985); Janine Brodie, *Women and Politics in Canada* (Toronto: McGraw-Hill Ryerson, 1985); and Joni Lovenduski and Jill Hills, eds, *The Politics of the Second Electorate: Women and Public Participation* (London: Routledge and Kegan Paul, 1981).

[39] For example, see some of the articles in Marion Colby, Shelagh Wilkinson, and Jeanne Maranda, eds, 'Affirmative Action/Action Positive', special issue of *Canadian Woman Studies* 6, no. 4 (Winter 1985).

[40] Judy La Marsh, *Memoirs of a Bird in a Gilded Cage* (Toronto: McClelland and Stewart, 1968); Alvin Armstrong, *Flora MacDonald* (Toronto: J.M. Dent & Sons, 1976); Sheila Copps, *Nobody's Baby: A Survival Guide to Politics* (Toronto: Deneau, 1986).

[41] See Alison M. Jaggar, *Feminist Politics and Human Nature* (Sussex: Harvester Press, 1983), pp. 173-206; and Sandra Burt, 'Women's Issues and the Women's Movement in Canada Since 1970', pp. 111-69 in Alan Cairns and Cynthia Williams, eds, *The Politics of Gender, Ethnicity and Language in Canada*, Collected Research Studies, Royal Commission on the Economic Union and Development Prospects for Canada (Toronto: University of Toronto Press, 1986).

[42] See Catherine A. MacKinnon, 'Feminism, Method, and the State: An Agenda for Theory', *Signs* 7, no. 3 (Spring 1982), pp. 515-44; MacKinnon, 'Feminism, Marxism, Method and the State: Toward Feminist Jurisprudence', *Signs* 8, no. 4 (1983), pp. 635-58.

[43] See Elizabeth Wilson, *Women and the Welfare State* (London: Tavistock Publications, 1977); and Mary McIntosh, 'The State and the Oppression of Women', pp. 254-89 in Annette Kuhn and Ann Marie Wolpe, eds, *Feminism and Materialism* (London: Routledge and Kegan Paul, 1978).

[44] Lois Sweet, 'Is Women's Advisory Group Pandering to Petty Politics?', *Toronto Star* 18 Dec. 1987, p. E1.

[45] See Nicole Laurin-Frenette, 'On the Women's Movement, Anarchism and the State', *Our Generation* 15, no. 2 (Summer 1982), pp. 36-7.

[46] Crittenden, 'Women Against Women' (1988), pp. 27-35; Gray, 'Why Can't Women Get Their Act Together?' (1988), pp. 82-3, 232-40.

[47] For the frustrating experiences of one feminist trying to work through the state, see Sue Findlay, 'Facing the State: The Politics of the Women's Movement Reconsidered', pp. 31-50 in Heather Jon Maroney and Meg Luxton, eds, *Feminism and Political Economy: Women's Work, Women's Struggles* (Toronto: Methuen, 1987).

Appendix B:
Job-Evaluation Factors

Most job evaluations use the four factors of skill, effort, responsibility, and working conditions, which in turn are broken down
into a number of subfactors. Examples of these subfactors are
shown below.

SKILL

Ability to do detailed or
    routine work
Accuracy
Analytical ability
Aptitude required
Communication skills—verbal
Communication skills—written
Communicating in a second
    language
Dexterity
Difficulty of operation/work
Education
Experience
Ingenuity
Initiative
Interpersonal

Judgement
Knowledge
Knowledge of machinery
Knowledge of materials
    and processes
Managerial techniques
Manual quickness
Manual or motor skills
Physical skill (co-ordination)
Problem solving
Resourcefulness
Social skills
Time required to adapt skills
Time required to become 80 per cent
    effective
Versatility

EFFORT

Attention demand
Concentration
Manual effort
Manual effort/demand
Mental fatigue
Monotony and discomfort
Muscular or nerve strain
Physical fatigue
Pressure of work
Stress from dealing with difficult people (e.g, sick, handling complaints)
Visual application
Volume of work

RESPONSIBILITY

Accountability
Accuracy
Adjustability
Cash
Confidential data
Contact with public, and/or customers/clients, etc.
Co-ordination
Cost of error
Consequence of error
Dependability
Details
Determining company policy
Effect on other operations
Equipment and machinery
Goodwill and public relations
Material
Methods
Monetary responsibility
Personnel
Physical property
Plant and services
Protecting confidentiality
Product
Quality
Records
Safety of others
Spoilage of materials
Supervision of others
Volume of work

WORKING CONDITIONS

Attention to details
Cleaning up after others
Constant interruptions
Danger
Dirtiness
Disagreeableness
Exposure to accident hazard
Exposure to health hazard

Intangible conditions
Monotony
Out-of-town travel
Physical environment/
   surroundings
Stress of multiple demands
Time pressure

Source: Ontario Pay Equity Commission, *How to Do Pay Equity Comparisons* (Toronto, March 1989), pp. 27-8.

Index